The Complete Idiot's R

Ten Truths of Bre

These 10 truths will remind you that you are on the right track. Place this list in a strategic place so that you can reach for it when a sudden case of panic erupts.

1. When you are feeling out of control, remember…

   Initiating a breakup can be empowering.

2. When love disappoints you, remember…

   You can learn a lot about yourself and relationships through adversity.

3. When you are rejected by a love interest, remember…

   They weren't the right partner for you.

4. When you fear being alone, remember…

   Breaking up frees you to conduct explorations and make new discoveries.

5. When you feel like getting cozy with an ex, remember…

   Sex can seriously complicate the breakup process.

6. When you think you will never find the right partner, remember…

   Breaking up is a natural part of the dating cycle and the quest to find a permanent love mate.

7. When you aren't suffering any heartaches, remember…

   Someone who has not experienced any breakups isn't thoroughly exploring the possibilities of love.

8. When you think your breakup is absolutely the most devastating, remember…

   Breaking up is never easy.

9. When you worry about tarnishing your reputation, remember…

   One partner usually looks like the bad guy in a breakup.

10. When you think you'll never get over him or her, remember…

    You can and will recover from the most painful parting of ways.

alpha
books

Rebound Reminders

A rebounder's fragile frame of mind can get the dumped or dumpee into trouble. Until you completely shed the rebound mentality, use these reminders to steer clear of adversity:

1. Just because you need to feel desirable…

   Doesn't mean you have to hop into bed to get feedback.

2. Just because you are panic-stricken that you won't ever find anyone to love…

   Doesn't mean that's true.

3. Just because you require reassurance that there is nothing wrong with you…

   Doesn't mean you should jump into a new relationship.

4. Just because you are lonely and miss your ex…

   Doesn't mean you should call him or her up.

5. Just because you miss reaching orgasm…

   Doesn't mean you can't find a temporary sexual substitute.

6. Just because your Cinderella story didn't have a happy ending…

   Doesn't mean that all romantic hookups end unhappily ever after.

7. Just because you currently feel awkward without a partner…

   Doesn't mean you can't function well on your own.

8. Just because your new romantic interest eases the pain of your breakup…

   Doesn't mean you have found true love.

9. Just because your date claims this couldn't possibly be a rebound relationship…

   Doesn't mean you should believe it.

10. Just because your level of self-esteem has plummeted…

    Doesn't mean you aren't responsible for building it back up.

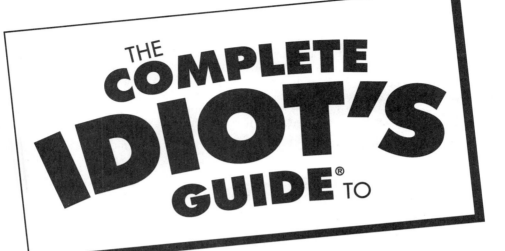

THE COMPLETE IDIOT'S GUIDE® TO

Handling a
Breakup

by Rosanne Rosen

alpha
books

A Division of Macmillan General Reference
A Pearson Education Macmillan Company
1633 Broadway, New York, NY 10019

Macmillan General Reference books may be purchased for business or sales promotional use. For information please write: Special Markets Department, Macmillan Publishing USA, 1633 Broadway, New York, NY 10019.

International Standard Book Number: 0-02862928-0
Library of Congress Catalog Card Number: 99-60668

01 00 99   8 7 6 5 4 3 2 1

Interpretation of the printing code: the rightmost number of the first series of numbers is the year of the book's printing; the rightmost number of the second series of numbers is the number of the book's printing. For example, a printing code of 99-1 shows that the first printing occurred in 1999.

Printed in the United States of America

Note: This publication contains the opinions and ideas of its author. It is intended to provide helpful and informative material on the subject matter covered. It is sold with the understanding that the author and publisher are not engaged in rendering professional services in the book. If the reader requires personal assistance or advice, a competent professional should be consulted.

Contents at a Glance

      The inside story on rebound love and the outside chance of
      finding happiness with a rebounder.

27 Love Is Around the Corner   255
      Knowing which direction to go in to find fun, romance,
      sex, and love.

Appendices

      A Resources   265

      B Are You Primed for Rejection? Quiz   267

      C The Cohabitation Agreement   269

      D Love Lingo Glossary   271

         Index   273

Contents

Foreword

Each year approximately one million couples in this country file for divorce. Marriages that fail typically do so within the first seven to 10 years and frequently contain at least one child. Over time individuals have formed family bonds with in-laws and extended family, therefore with each divorce comes the heartbreak of countless others. As a marriage and family therapist, I am always relieved when a couple comes to me BEFORE they get married to work out problems and issues that inevitably arise when courtship moves toward commitment. With these couples I can work to re-establish negotiation and communication patterns that can result in a mutually satisfying relationship.

All too often, however, couples do not make the decision to enter into therapy until after they are already married and the relationship has progressed to the brink of disaster. Then, with young children involved, I'm faced with the arduous task of bringing disillusioned, angry, bitter people back to a place of cooperation and teamwork. An enviable task it is not! What typically happens with these cases? One partner already has a foot out the door and is looking for therapy to fail so as to jump ship and start again elsewhere. Put simply, nobody wins.

What do I hear from the heartbroken? "I knew before we got married that it wouldn't work." "I should have listened to my instincts!" "I married for all the wrong reasons." Given these groans of frustration, it was refreshing to pick up Rosanne Rosen's book *The Compete Idiot's Guide to Handling a Breakup* and hear a common-sense voice instruct people on how to assess their relationship and get out of poor ones while they can!

If you know you are in a relationship that just isn't right for you, read this book! Rosen provides step-by-step assistance to help you with orchestrating your departure. She begins by encouraging some forethought into what the relationship is all about and explains the differences between inflation, lust, and love. She stresses the importance of knowing why you are breaking up, evaluating your relationship for potential, when to decide a breakup is inevitable, and how to actually do it, including canceling wedding plans. Most importantly, Rosen guides you through the aftermath of the breakup and helps re-establish relationship goals. I've not seen a more complete and thorough approach to ending a relationship.

If you can't decide whether to stay in your current relationship or not, read this book! Rosen does not push anyone out of a relationship that has the potential to be satisfying. In fact, I think this book just might point out how great your relationship might be and yet provide insight into areas that need to be worked on to make the relationship more gratifying. This includes assessing your relationship fairly, learning to read the signals your partner is giving out, and avoiding unintentional breakups.

It's so much easier to get out before you say "I do." Take a moment and honestly evaluate your relationship. There has to be some reason you picked up this book!

—Julianne Serovich, Ph.D.

Julianne M. Serovich, Ph.D., is an Associate Professor and Director of the marriage and family therapy doctoral program at Ohio State University. She earned her Ph.D. at the University of Georgia and has taught marriage and family therapy at Texas Tech University. She has been practicing marriage and family therapy for over 14 years, is a clinical member and approved supervisor of the American Association of Marriage and Family Therapy, and is a member of the National Council on Family Relations. Dr. Serovich has published her research in such journals as *Journal of Marriage and Family Therapy*, *Journal of Divorce and Remarriage*, *The American Journal of Family Therapy*, and *Family Relations*.

Introduction

The pain of love is never so clear as it is during the process of breaking up. I have been privy to the tears and disappointments of so many disillusioned men and women who have shared the intimate details of their dating, marriage, and live-in relationships with me. Their distress has disturbed me. However, the laughter and pleasure many more have found in partners discovered after breakups has maintained my optimism. Each and every individual who wants to overcome love's failings and find a more suitable partner can and will.

The truth is some men and women have a knack for getting through romantic ups and downs better than others. They also have an easier time springing back and jumping into the social arena full of vigor and excitement. No matter if you belong to the teary contingent or the one who laughs in the face of unrequited love, there is much you can learn to do to soothe your hidden emotions or those you wear on your sleeve. There are truths to be uncovered, techniques to master, and suggestions to try in the pages that follow.

This information has been sifted out of hundreds of interviews and the most up-to-date research on love relationships. In turn, this body of knowledge has been applied with sound, objective reasoning to the anguish of breaking up and the joy of emerging enlightened at the end of a dark, solitary tunnel.

I am a pragmatist when it comes to love. The best lasting relationships forged between self-confident men and women reflect the results of forethought, deliberation, and effort. Therefore, it is the object of this book to provide you with insights that will help you determine when breaking up is the right path for you or whether you need to engage in more enlightened forethought. Whether you or your love interest have chosen to stop seeing one another, the contents of the chapters ahead have been carefully constructed to assist you in analyzing what went wrong and why.

Although you may feel that the subject of breaking up ultimately deals with all those nasty, negative elements of love and your personal sense of failure, that is hardly the case. Understanding the dynamics of love will prove to you that breaking up is a natural and important part of ultimately finding your own true love. Putting this piece of the puzzle into perspective will diminish future disappointments and open your eyes to happiness and personal satisfaction.

Yes, after all this critical information has been imparted, you are given a pep talk and rightfully so. Everyone needs a cheerleader now and then to remind them that they are special and deserve someone who will appreciate and support them. There are times when we need encouragement to take new risks that will enable us to find a more meaningful future.

I am convinced that there is much you can gain reading the pages that lie ahead and participating in the quizzes prepared for you. It is my hope that you find comfort, reassurance, advice, insights, and information that will assist you in overcoming sadness and realizing your dreams of love.

How This Book Is Organized

The Complete Idiot's Guide to Handling a Breakup is organized into five parts. It is best if you read them in order. However, on any given page there is a worthwhile tip or consideration that should benefit your exploration.

Part 1, "Contemplating a Breakup," gets right to the heart of the problem. Most men and women don't know how to break up or engage in a budding romance that they won't have to weasel out of later. It should be abundantly clear after the first few chapters why love and forethought should go hand in hand. Granted, that isn't easy with passion and romance tempting one's heart and body parts to take precedence over the mind's rational thought process. Still, it can be done once you become alert to the forces at play.

Part 2, "The Anatomy of Breakups," takes you through the stages, gender differences, signs, and doubts everyone faces when breaking up. It prudently points out in Chapter 11, "Unintentional Precipitators of Breakups," how you might be sabotaging your relationships unknowingly. This is an important new concept to consider with an open mind. Without fully comprehending all of the dynamics involved in a breakup, one cannot break up effectively and wisely incurring the least amount of harm to themselves or someone else.

Part 3, "Complex Breakups Beyond the Dating Game," is dedicated to the special issues confronted by engaged lovers, live-in couples, and married partners. The heartache and complexity of a breakup depends a great deal on the length of the relationship and the nature of the couple's involvement. There is something to be gleaned from these pairings even if you don't fall into one or another of these categories. Take time to read these chapters and apply them to your special needs.

Part 4, "The Breakup," will take you by the hand and lead you through your breakup. You will find assistance in establishing critical goals, selecting wise tactics, and achieving closure. If you follow along conscientiously, you will be better prepared to reap the benefits of Part 5.

Part 5, "Surviving the Breakup," takes you beyond your breakup. The story of breaking up does not conclude when you say good-bye. In reality, it ends when you are ready to appear once more on the social scene. To make this big leap requires handling the anger, rejection, and depression that unrequited love unleashes on the most self-confidant lover. There are quick fixes for the absence of a sexual partner and the lack of companionship. To make sure that future decisions are not made out of pain and loneliness, a discussion of when to forgive and forget offers pertinent help.

The last steps of your searching for answers come in the final chapters. They will equip you to shed your rebounder mindset and enter the singles arena worldly wise. You will be smug with the knowledge of all you have learned and cautiously open to love interests just around the corner.

A list of resources is at your fingertips in the appendices and index at the back of the book. In Appendix A, "Resources," there are suggestions on how to locate a premarital program or counselor or qualified legal representation for divorce, child support, or child custody issues. The names and contact numbers for relationship enhancement groups are also provided. In the event that you require direction in finding help as a victim of domestic violence, several avenues are recommended. Appendix B, "Are You Primed for Rejection? Quiz," gives you a worthwhile quiz to test how rejection-prone you might be. Living together is a tricky business despite the growing numbers of men and women moving in and out with each other. Consider the guidelines presented in Appendix C, "The Cohabitation Agreement." And Appendix D, "Love Lingo Glossary," is an easy reference guide to the many terms introduced throughout the book.

Extras

There is so much to tell you. To help you absorb it all in a friendly and easy fashion, *The Complete Idiot's Guide to Handling a Breakup* includes helpful bits of wisdom in entertaining boxes throughout the book.

Bits and Pieces

Here you'll find extra tidbits of pertinent information to add to your knowledge. These boxes are worthwhile findings to share with your friends.

Heart to Heart

In these boxes, we'll speak right to you. We'll offer you additional pieces of advice and give you something extra to think about.

Blow the Whistle

Here, we'll call your attention to important warnings. Read these boxes thoroughly to avoid additional problems.

Love Lingo

Love Lingo boxes introduce you to love's vocabulary. By no means do you know all the terms.

Acknowledgments

As always, there is one large group of people I must thank for making a book possible. That is the men and women who have so honestly and intimately opened themselves up to me. Not only are they my inspiration but the audience I so wish to benefit by my words.

I am also privileged to have worked with men and women who encouraged, mentored, and helped me in my career. Each step I take is a result of their kindness. To friend and editor T. R. Fitchko I will always be indebted. Her appreciation of my work has made an immeasurable difference. Jeff Herman, my agent, will always be the recipient of my gratitude, as is author Bob Shook. To my new colleagues, Jessica Faust, Matthew X. Kiernan, and Christy Wagner, I offer my thanks.

It is appropriate that I write about love relationships. I am fortunate to be surrounded by them. Thanks will forever be extended to Mark, Halley, Sara Jane, and Brian. A special acknowledgment is necessary to a lifetime support of friends known by the signature, Love from the Six of Us.

Part 1
Contemplating a Breakup

So you want to break up, but you just can't make yourself do it. You've agonized over it and changed your mind a thousand times. If that's the case, you haven't given it enough forethought, tested the reasons, or revealed your innermost feelings. Don't worry. That's just what you are about to do.

A walk through the romance—what attracted you to that Joe or Jane and how you arrived at your present predicament—will put you on solid ground.

In Part 1 you will objectively examine the breadth and depth of your relationship, what's missing, and why you're dissatisfied. The odds of breaking up and coupling will assure you that what you are about to do will not usher in the end of your world. You will learn the value of time, where to find help, and how to develop the courage to move forward.

I think it's time for some thoughtful action..

Chapter 1

Introducing the Need for Thoughtful Action

In This Chapter

➤ When sex gets in the way

➤ Saying "I love you" is dangerous

➤ Bailing out takes courage and forethought

➤ Reducing breakup aftershocks

➤ Taking an IQ test

Whether you are doing the dumping or getting dumped, breaking up is never easy. No one can totally eradicate the inherent sting of rejection, the disappointment of unrealized dreams, or the pain of a bruised heart. Still, breaking up need not be the messy, uncomfortable, no-win situation most women and men say it is.

I doubt that it is out of meanness or a lack of caring that you or others fail to do a better job at calling it quits. You simply haven't been shown how. That is about to change!

As soon as internal rumblings or external signs suggest a breakup may be lurking, stop whatever you are doing. Go no further. Gently unlock that embrace, carefully listen to the mind's whispers, and silently evaluate the evidence around you. If you don't, runaway emotions—and an out-of-control libido—may take charge. The result could be anguish and discomfort that cannot easily be wished away.

Unfortunately, the stop, look, and listen three-step won't solve the problem. Clues are camouflaged by gender and muddied by biology and personality. A preliminary series of questions can get you started on your way. If answered thoughtfully, they will help prevent the occurrence of repeated seismic aftershocks that accompany ill-prepared breakups.

Chances are until you meet that one true love, there are numerous beginnings and endings yet to be experienced. To prepare for the ups and downs, test your current level of breakup proficiency as the dumpee and the dumped. It's never too late to improve your breakup skills.

Don't Break Up Without Forethought

It's relatively simple to use logic in our work, in the purchase of a car, and in the choice of a home. These activities are void of the strong emotional component that characterizes our love relationships.

But take the administrative assistant out of the office, the corporate executive out of the boardroom, the surgeon out of the operating room, or the teacher out of the school. Put these same level-headed individuals face to face with a love interest and what happens? Their logic goes on the fritz.

Fortunately, the short in your reasoning is not permanent. But to react or make decisions when emotions—not reason—do the thinking leaves too much room for error. Wisely waiting for the return of your good sense prevents premature action and subsequent regret.

Practice using control and wait for objectivity to resurface. This is a prudent practice to employ in all aspects of your romantic relationships. The more you use it, the more automatic it becomes.

How Most People Break Up

Unfortunately, if you look at the way most people break up, it isn't hard to see they are caught in the throes of emotion and self-interest. Their power of logic cowers in the shadows. The emotional overload of anger, pain, or fear thrusts them into thoughtless action. Consequently, they either:

➤ Procrastinate, hoping that the problem will resolve itself

➤ Break up hastily, trying to quickly rid themselves of discomfort

➤ Play silly, superficial games, sabotaging the relationship in order to cause a mutual split

➤ Prefer deserting, thereby avoiding a confrontation

That's not the way you want to break up!

Key Factors That Inhibit Sound Decision Making

Sound decision making is at bay with a number of factors that clutter logic's pathway. Before you advance

Heart to Heart

It's time to toss out the ridiculous "unisex" verbiage of the '90s. There are two distinct sexes awaiting the advent of the millennium. Unless you accept that men and women act, think, love, and stop loving in their own unique ways, you will have difficulty when it comes to romance.

and investigate your own unique set of circumstances as they arise in each relationship, pay attention to the most common factors that affect each of us. Contending with these elements first clears the way for your final decision.

Men and Women at Odds

We're at it again. That old argument over the male and female species has reared its ugly head. Only this time it isn't a battle about superiority. Nor is it about equality. It's about differences. And scientists have discovered exactly what they are and why.

Research has proven that the two sexes see the world differently due to distinguishing characteristics in the male and female brain. The hemispheres of a woman's brain are less specialized than that of a man's, enabling women to display greater ability to think cognitively, deal with a number of thoughts simultaneously, fuse ideas, see beyond the periphery, and be generally intuitive. Consequently, women are more prone to describe their feelings and emotions with language than men. The more specialized male spheres of the brain, however, dictate that guys focus on one idea at a time. They rarely combine the elements of language and emotion. Unless women are aware of this scientific explanation, a man's seeming unwillingness to voice his feelings and emotions is often interpreted as a lack of interest, commitment, or caring.

The converse is true with men. The open gesturing and verbal display of female emotion may confound, confuse, and frighten men.

Even without the normal conflicts and fluctuating passions, the sexes stand at odds. Toss sexual and raging emotions into the mix, and no wonder misinterpretation and misunderstanding run rampant when dealing with matters of the heart.

Bits and Pieces

The depth of differences between men and women influences even what they gossip about. Women like to gab about people in their lives and how they look, think, feel, and act. Men prefer to discuss one subject at a time—sports, business, or politics.

Uncontrollable Body Heat

Long before recent studies at Ohio State University revealed that the desire for sex was one of 15 basic human motivators, Freud proclaimed it the number one driving force. Sorry—logical thinking did not make the list.

But despite the pleasures of immediate sexual gratification, practically nothing gets you into hot water quicker. We're not talking diseases. (Hopefully everyone is aware of the deadly penalty of unprotected sex today.) What we are addressing is entrapment.

5

More often than not, women view sexual intercourse as a sign of commitment by the man she frolics with under the sheets. Her expectations of the relationship immediately rise to new heights. But according to the guys, that's not the message they intended to send. They simply can't stop thinking about getting a woman into bed when they start dating her. It doesn't have a thing to do with how they see her fitting into their future.

Love Lingo

You never leave home without your **libido**. Sigmund Freud, the father of psychoanalysis, discovered it. This instinctual drive associated with your need to fulfill sexual desires and seek sexual pleasures influences practically everything you do. According to Dr. Freud, that *is*.

Blow the Whistle

Cool-down time. Men think about sex on an average of three to five times a day. The thought crosses women's minds several times a week and as little as several times a month.

Sex has complicated enough liaisons that you won't have trouble finding men of all ages with healthy *libidos* who now forego the premature pleasures of intercourse rather than create the wrong impression.

Evidently, Freud didn't realize how his libido could result in sticky breakups.

Too Much Romance

Passions rise, lights dim, music flows. You both say, "I love you." The loud thump, thump, thump of your hearts drowns out the whisper of sense that asks, "What does that mean?"

The reality is, it can mean any variety of things. You mustn't take it for granted that the two of you necessarily share the same concept of love. No one has yet come up with a universally accepted, concrete, definitive definition of love.

Love, whatever it is, can be:

➤ Superficial

➤ Of short duration

➤ A state of friendship

➤ An unsuitable foundation for an enduring relationship

➤ An addiction

➤ An expression of sexual attraction

➤ A pledge of undying devotion

➤ An inexpressible connection that makes you feel complete

While it lasts, love makes us feel good enough to say and promise things we ordinarily would not. We imagine all sorts of things we can do together tomorrow, next week, and next year that will be enhanced by one another's presence. The implication is that there is a future together. But love—if it isn't the real thing—is moving you to speak out of turn.

In the throes of passionate love, Ken bought tickets for himself and Kelly to go to Acapulco and gave them to her for safe-keeping. Their departure date, unfortunately, postdated Ken's announcement that he wanted to break up.

Furious that Ken's pronouncements of love turned out to be empty vessels, Kelly was determined to strike back. She never handed over the tickets that rightfully belonged to Ken. Instead, she tricked the airline and used them for herself and a substitute beau. Ken knew he had treated her poorly, so he did nothing. Ken and Kelly both would have been better off saving the "love word" for later. It raised Kelly's expectations and caused a hard fall.

Failing to Exchange Shoes

The sizes of women's and men's shoes are as different as their perspectives. That's why it's so hard to step into them. Still, it is a worthwhile exercise, especially when dealing with the subject of breaking up. Without developing *empathy*—the attempt to emotionally and intellectually share someone else's feelings—you are likely to miscalculate the affect of calling it quits.

Men automatically assume that women will be sad and cry when they try to extricate themselves from her life. Because they can't stand to see those salty tears run down her cheeks, men often forego the truth. If they would wear her slippers, they might realize that women are quite capable of dealing with the facts. There is less potential for havoc and damage to a woman's self-esteem and ego when she is confronted with the problem maturely rather than later realize she was deliberately maneuvered out of love.

Despite women's gift of intuition, rarely are they aware just how fragile men's feelings are. Behind their hearty male exteriors lie emotional scars from previous relationships. Once men have been dumped, they stockpile true and false notions of being misunderstood, unappreciated, and betrayed.

They won't tell you any of this, but in private interviews with me, many men admitted they feel sorry for themselves, suffer diminished self-esteem, and question their worthiness as a potential mate after women send them on their way.

Bits and Pieces

Severing a marriage relationship is more difficult, emotional, and problematic for a longer period of time for men than it is for women. Furthermore, men voice greater confusion over the problems that relate to the breakup than do their spouses.

Before You Bail Out

When you utter the phrase "I think it's better if we stop seeing each other," or whichever version of this you choose to verbalize or act out, a mix of volatile emotions are sure to erupt. Failure, disappointment, sadness, fear, rejection, guilt, resentment, ambivalence, disbelief, and anger head straight to the heart.

Heart to Heart

The "Lost Love Project," a study at California State University, discovered that 10 percent of the population attempts to rekindle the fire with old flames. Under the circumstances, it would be prudent to keep a portion of the wick intact.

While some measure of these emotions is bound to strike, the intensity and the duration can be minimized by thoughtfully answering the following questions. Failure to sufficiently answer them could result in aftershocks down the road.

Ask yourself four basic questions:

1. Have I considered the consequences of breaking up right here and now?
2. Do I have damage controls in place?
3. Do I have a plan of action and a firm conviction?
4. Can I part without burning bridges?

Don't underestimate how critical these questions are to arriving at a healthy breakup. The proof is in the remaining pages.

Potential Aftershocks

Aftershocks are negative repercussions of breakups. Just when you think it's safely all over, something happens that rocks the landscape. Everyone is bound to experience some form of aftershocks; however, they aren't entirely predictable. They may be highly personal, internal shockwaves or directed from the outside. The best way to lessen the impact is to engage in calculated behavior and adequate forethought—both of which you will learn how to do in this book. For the moment, here are some aftershocks that you should be on the lookout for:

1. Suffering through lonely nights, freezing in an empty bed, concluding a good one got away.
2. Acquiring spots on your reputation as an unfair and dishonest romantic player.
3. Damaging relationships with mutual friends or coworkers.
4. Inviting the wrath of your ex.
5. Facing recurrent recriminations and pangs of guilt.
6. Losing the opportunity for a potential future relationship.
7. Experience a change of heart and no way to rekindle the romance.
8. Recklessly lying in bed with the same partner.

What Happened When Roz Failed to Stop, Look, and Listen

There is a lesson to be learned in this mini-saga.

Randy and Roz had been dating for a few months. Things seemed to be going along rather well. A romantic weekend for two seemed like a good idea. But no sooner had they unpacked than things went drastically wrong. Roz was ready for their first night of lovemaking. Evidently Randy was not—at least not at that moment.

Feeling humiliated and rejected, Roz left in a huff, hopped the next plane home, and removed Randy's number from her book. Embarrassed by his performance, guilt-ridden, and ambivalent, Randy never picked up the phone to explain what was on his mind.

Neither Randy nor Roz stopped to consider that something had brought them together months earlier. The time they spent together had been fun. Hastily bidding adieu, however, prevented the opportunity to examine what went wrong and what could they do about it.

What if Roz had been more open-minded? What if Roz didn't interpret Randy's behavior as a rebuff? What if she took his momentary lack of interest less personally? What if she curiously searched out the roots of Randy's behavior?

She might have been the gal who walked down the aisle with him less than a year later.

Heart to Heart

Believe it. Men worry about their sexual performance. And why not? There are a variety of uncontrollable factors that act as libido-reducers for both sexes. A few to look out for include: stress, anger, depression, inadequate sleep, smoking, too much exercise, and some prescription drugs. To revive a temporarily weakened libido, experts say try a bath or a crisp walk.

Your Breakup IQ

Answer each question truthfully with a yes or no.

1. Did you ever simply not call back? ____

2. Did you ever not show up at an appointed time and place? ____

3. Did you ever lie to get out of a relationship? ____

4. Have you continued to tell someone you love him or her when you no longer do? ____

5. Are you unable to refrain from having sex with an ex-partner after the relationship is over? ____

6. Are you addicted to love? ____

7. Are your perception skills weak? _____

8. Do you easily get tired of someone of the opposite sex? _____

9. Do you engage in fantasies? _____

10. Do you stay in relationships long after the interest has declined? _____

11. Do you fail to respect your partner, or even other people in general? _____

12. Do you opt not to take any responsibility when a relationship doesn't work out? _____

13. Do you refrain from knowing others intimately? _____

14. Do you prevent others from knowing you intimately? _____

15. Are you afraid to hurt someone's feelings? _____

16. Are you fearful of making a mistake in a love relationship? _____

17. Have you purposely confused and mislead a boyfriend or girlfriend? _____

18. Do you question your own judgment in matters of the heart? _____

19. Would you rather walk down the aisle than back out? _____

20. Have you taken a vacation with a love interest with whom you planned to break up? _____

21. Do you display little patience getting to know how someone else thinks? _____

22. Do you think the best way to break up is the quickest way? _____

23. Do you dwell on the pain caused by past lovers? _____

24. Are you prone to making promises you cannot keep? _____

25. Do you easily feel rejected? _____

26. Are you quick to form new love attachments? _____

27. Have you canceled an engagement more than once? _____

28. Do you have a pattern of dating old flames? _____

29. Do you frequently act impetuously? _____

30. Are you desperate for love? _____

If you have answered all 30 questions "yes," then you have done the impossible—failed the Breakup IQ Test. A true sign of a high breakup IQ would be in the range of at least 25 "no" responses. Do not expect a perfect score. We all make mistakes in love's wake. The object is to begin making less of them when cupid retracts the arrow. This quiz lets you know how much work is ahead of you.

A high breakup IQ means you have displayed enough correct answers on the quiz to demonstrate at least a moderate level of intuition when it comes to soundly severing relationships. Fortunately, your intuition can be supplemented by solid information and sound insights.

The Least You Need to Know

➤ The art of breaking up wisely does not come naturally.

➤ It is no one's fault if a relationship meets a dead end.

➤ Our natural instincts compound the difficulty of calling it quits.

➤ You can learn how to break it off with less wear and tear.

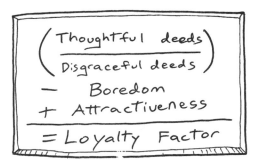

$$\dfrac{\left(\dfrac{\text{Thoughtful deeds}}{\text{Disgraceful deeds}}\right) - \text{Boredom} + \text{Attractiveness}}{= \text{Loyalty Factor}}$$

Chapter 2

The Probabilities for Breaking Up

In This Chapter

➤ The story behind attraction

➤ Why infatuations don't last

➤ How to turn it into love

➤ Reasons we make couples

➤ The natural forces behind breaking up

The chances of a budding intrigue flowering into full bloom are slim. The odds of romantic love lasting are rare. Simply put, not every romance endures. Nor would you want it to!

Before you catch that other person's eye, be aware that forces beyond your control take hold. The journey to a mature, reciprocal love relationship is complicated and mysterious. Nature's tricks confuse and confound us along the way. Without taking time to explore the intrigues of attraction, you may stumble along love's pathway and not know why. Once you accept that relationships—from dating through marriage—are risky business, you will be better prepared to ward off or face the demise of love.

In order to emerge unscathed from the flighty passions of infatuation, approach each new love interest with cautious optimism. Finding love is a process of natural selection. Enjoy it. Breakups are an inevitable part of it. Don't fight them. The need to couple will ultimately help you find your own true love.

The Instant Attraction

That's exactly what you have—the flash of a second to catch someone's eye. Fortunately, other well-documented stages that move an attraction forward involve a slightly larger window of opportunity. Nonetheless, attraction is fleeting and tenuous at best. Here's how it works.

Heart to Heart

Research shows that women start flirtations. Men are reticent to approach without signs of encouragement. Time after time, desirable, eligible men admitted waiting for a woman to signal her interest first. Many would rather go home alone than initiate a flirtation and risk rejection.

At First Glance: What Gets Her Noticed

Don't moan and groan. Facts are facts. This is what catches his eye at first glance and arouses interest.

➤ A youthful, rounded, curvaceous female body

➤ Blue eyes and blonde hair

➤ Figures that emphasize buttocks and breasts (not too large)

➤ A woman self-confident in her appearance who looks like she is enjoying herself

You can't fight it. But you can understand it. And if you wish—get what it takes to catch his eye.

At First Glance: What Gets Him Noticed

Women are equally superficial at the outset. Here's what she picks up on:

➤ A tall, dark man whose height makes him look powerful

➤ Symmetrical facial features

➤ Strong jaw and cheekbones

➤ A muscular frame without extreme bulk

This is just the beginning. Don't fret if your physique doesn't match this description.

The Four Steps to Firm Up the Attraction

These have been tested out in bars, laboratories, and social settings around the world. They are the initial screening tests you use when feeling out a prospective love interest. Each successive step must earn a check mark in order to continue the encounter.

1. Eye-to-eye contact gets the ball rolling. A demure, flirtatious, seductive gaze adds the necessary encouragement.

2. The right smile is imperative. Mona Lisa's won't do. She isn't wearing the "pickup smile" ethnologists have documented that works—wide open lips and fully exposed teeth. Clenched teeth are a turn off.

3. The sound of your voice must be music to his or her ears. Melodious, high-pitched tones get positive responses. Low tones and matter-of-fact sentences are less appealing.

4. The slightest touching of the knee or an innocent rubbing of the shoulder registers pleasure in the brain. You must hit that nerve in order to advance toward phase two—*infatuation*.

Bits and Pieces

Anthropologists who studied women's flirtatious smiles discovered a discrepancy in interpretation. Women who used the "pick-up smile" said it was a signal meant to imply they would like to talk with and get to know the man. Men insist the pick-up smile is a sign of women's willingness to have sex.

Firefly Infatuation

The attraction has taken. You are giddy and euphoric. The fever-pitched interest stirs up those romantic, passionate feelings indicative of infatuation. You are full of idealistic sentimentality and the desire for reciprocated love. Fearful of failing to acquire that, you are at once apprehensive yet uncontrollably carried away by emotion.

The light of the firefly infatuation is fragile. It flickers on and off until the course of romance is decided.

What Keeps the Firefly Aglow?

The answer—mystery, passion, and sex. The intrigue of the unknown, the humming of hormones, and either the hope of sex or the pleasures of it keep interest alive. The problem is the overwhelming number of factors that can cause the light to go out.

What turns out the light? Nearly everything has the potential to extinguish the glow.

➤ *The absence of "feel-good" factors, many of which we have no control over.* We like people who

Love Lingo

Infatuation is an early stage of love void of the mutual understanding, caring, and support that is the hallmark of true love. The infatuated lover is driven by passion, fantasy, and expectations that are often unrealized. It is that heady, irrational feeling that causes one to obsess over a potential love mate, maintain a frenzied level of romantic interest, and be unable to think of anything else.

make us feel good. Since we know that good news and funny movies contribute to that, we can steer clear of the tragic drama or bad news. Hot and humid weather arouse negative feelings, so be aware of the temperature when you accept a Saturday-night date with someone you long to establish as your lover or plan a vacation with your husband to the Caribbean.

➤ *Revealing too much too quickly.* In a moment you can reveal idiosyncrasies and intentions that turn the other person off before he or she has the opportunity to discover all of the things that turn them on. Taboo subjects when first you meet are past relationships, your children, if you have any, or the importance of commitment.

➤ *The conquest and sexual satisfaction.* Now, this is tricky. You're damned if you do and damned if you don't. But based on sexual dossiers, Freud would claim that after sexually frustrated individuals satisfy themselves, they fly off to light someone else's glow. Perhaps that is why the testosterone-rich men in a Massachusetts study frequently had poor relationships.

Blow the Whistle

Are you head-over-heels in love? Did he or she knock you off your feet? If you're smiling and nodding yes, approach with caution. Research shows that love of this fast, furious, and intense nature may be passionate but painful. It's called **infatuation**, and it rarely lasts! Seventy-five percent of infatuations fall by the wayside. Signs of the ailment include a loss of reason and self-consciousness.

➤ *A mismatch with your "love map."* What turns you on and peaks your interest is not serendipitous. Sexologist John Money coined the phrase "love map." It refers to the collection of items on your partner wish list that you gathered over the course of time. In Chapter 3, "Are You Sure You Want to Break Up?" you will have the opportunity to draw your own important map.

Part of the selection process and the purpose of dating once attraction takes hold is getting to know each other and seeing how you fit. More often than not, you find that nothing behind the pleasing exterior matches what you have longed for in a partner. If that other person does not make your heart beat, arouse you sexually, share your values, satisfy you emotionally, provide companionship, or stimulate you intellectually, the relationship's over before it's begun.

Racing Against Love's Timetable

Love has its own timetable tied up with several chemicals in the body. These substances play a prominent part in the outcome of that first glance or an eventual parting kiss. Enough is known about these chemicals to demonstrate a strong cause and effect between body chemistry and emotion. There is insufficient information, however, to brew your own love potion.

The Chemistry of Love

Those who subscribe to the chemical and biological underpinnings of love tie their theory to four million years of evolution and the reproductive cycle. Instead of the undefinable magic of romantic love that requires thoughtful nourishment in order to arrive at mature love and children, these scientists say chemicals are the basis from which adult love is established. The release of ample amounts of chemicals stimulates progress through the following sequence:

1. Attraction
2. Attachment
3. Mating
4. Birthing
5. Early childhood development
6. Detachment

DHEA, or *dehydroepiandrosterone*, is the most prevalent hormone in the male and female bodies. It affects sex drive, sex appeal, and sexual performance. DHEA better be present to get the most out of that first glance!

Not even social scientists deny the importance of sex. If forced to give a definition of love, Ellen Berschied, Ph.D., psychology professor at the University of Minnesota, said she would whisper "It's about 90 percent sexual desire."

PEA, or *phenylethylamine*, the "love hormone," is released when one becomes aroused and causes a pleasurable sensation. This amphetamine-like high is associated with the stages of attraction in animals and infatuation in humans. Should you need to add a little of your own PEA to love's elixir, it is found in chocolates, diet soft drinks, and artificial sweeteners. But no matter how delectable and delightful the pangs of attraction and mating are, for the most part the body does not want to maintain this heightened level of excitement and headiness associated with infatuation and sexplay.

Endorphins and *oxytocins* create a desire to be close to a potential mate and promote attachment. In the very practical realm of mother nature, the comfortable state of attachment lasts long enough to ensure procreation and the survival of offspring.

Love Lingo

Dehydroepiandrosterone, or **DHEA**, is the hormone from which most of our other sex hormones are derived. One of the acute sexual signals it releases in the animal world is scent.

Love Lingo

Phenylethylamine, or **PEA**, is an amphetamine compound in the body that explains the biological and chemical components of love. Released in the presence of passionate, sexual, and romantic feelings, it causes a pleasurable high similar to that induced by amphetamine drugs.

Blow the Whistle

Don't overindulge. There is evidence that individuals become addicted to the pleasurable rush of PEA and develop into "love junkies."

17

When chemicals associated with attachment dissipate and are not replenished by a resurgence of PEA, papa bear enters the detachment phase and trudges off through the forest.

Few Animals Mate for Life

Monogamy is not a fact of nature. Just the opposite. Three percent of mammals are monogamous. Primates, including humans, can boast a slightly higher rate of monogamy, coming in at around 12 percent. Birds tip the scale entirely in the other direction. Ninety percent of this species are monogamous.

Being *monogamous* means having one mate at a time. If a monkey seeks a sexual encounter with someone other than his or her mate, researchers call it an *extra-pair copulation*. You and I refer to it as cheating! (Whether to forgive and forget is discussed in Chapter 24, "When to Forgive or Forget.")

Serial monogamy seems to be the prevalent pattern among humans these days. One mate at a time, true. More than one over a lifetime, yes.

When Time Runs Out on Love Potions

Love potions lose their fizz over time.

Only a quarter of infatuations last. Strongly predicated upon sexual desire, infatuations hardly have a chance—particularly for men in their 20s who are testosterone-driven during this decade. Furthermore, the entire cycle of attraction through detachment has generally been determined to last around three years, no more than four.

Bits and Pieces

Males are more sexually driven than women. Some say the sex drives will never be equal. We know that men are more easily turned on visually than women. They react even to pictures—hence the sexy magazines on the rack. Women connect better to emotional gestures and thus prefer romantic novels.

The question then becomes "What takes the place of a love potion?"

Spinning in Control of Love

"Love is strongest in pursuit, friendship in possession."
—Ralph Waldo Emerson

We know that romantic love is part attraction, part infatuation. We also know that there has to be more to love to make it last.

The technical term for the enduring love you want is *companionate love*. The formulation of this mature love is founded upon desire for companionship and intimacy. Love potions won't do the job here. Still, for lasting love you must buck the biological timetable.

The most helpful model to explain what companionate love is, how it grows, and what keeps it going is the *wheel theory*. Created by sociologist Ira Reiss in 1960, it is still widely adhered to and amended by experts. There are four essential elements that must be developed in sequence and then repeated without end in order to sustain it. This spins the wheel of love and allows you to take charge of the destiny of your relationships.

Love Lingo

Companionate love is the descriptive term psychologists use for love that embodies feelings of affection, intimacy, and attachment to individuals with whom our lives are intricately woven.

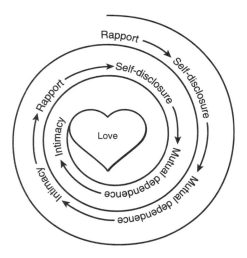

Spinning clockwise will reach love.

1. *Rapport.* Rapport is the development of a harmonious relationship that provides comfort and pleasure. Each individual brings something to the relationship and carries away something of the other person. Rapport is never one-sided. Both the man and the woman must feel they benefited from the connection.

2. *Self-disclosure.* In order to create a feeling of closeness and a bond with another human being, you must begin to exchange information about yourself—feelings, dreams, aspirations, fears, hopes, disappointments, and successes. This abets mutual understanding and appreciation. Without self-revelation, you would be hard-pressed to fulfill the requirements of the next element.

19

3. *Mutual dependence.* If the seeds of lasting love are truly beginning to sprout, both a man and woman begin to enjoy fulfilling the needs of one another. Mutual dependence is not a state of dependence. Rather, mutual dependence is exhibited by engaging in mutually satisfying sex, being each other's cheerleader and coach, and approaching the world as helpmates. Your happiness is enhanced by, and to a degree dependent upon, your partner sharing your life.

4. *Intimacy.* If you are successful in building rapport, revealing your identity, and accepting and giving support, you will have arrived at a wonderful new juncture in a relationship. The secrets you exchange, the knowledge you have of one another, and the experiences you partake in together provide a familiarity that is luxuriously comfortable and pleasurable. A connection between the two of you arises that each wishes to keep because it is so satisfying.

Heart to Heart

If you don't play games, don't count on winning any prizes. A shot of PEA now and then keeps everyone in the ring. Try sex in the bathtub, a surprise weekend getaway, "I love you" packages, or sweets and treats of your own making. These goodies, however, are reserved for someone who is worthy of the key to your heart.

Do You Have to Be Dizzy in Love?

Not necessarily. But let's address what happens if the wheel slows down, stops spinning, or goes in reverse. The slowdown is natural; we can't always give our love relationship the attention it needs. Even stopping now and then is acceptable; the most happily married couples I interviewed for *Marriage Secrets* (Birch Lake Press, 1993) admitted they didn't love their spouse 365 days a year. Of course, a standstill for very long requires a jump-start. The big problem can be going in reverse; crumbling rapport, secrets, total independence, and a demise of intimacy signal serious trouble.

One sure way to get the wheel in motion and very possibly avoid a breakup is by returning to the stage of infatuation. There is no substitute for the playful, frolicking, tingling high you get at this stage to revive interest.

Experiencing Breakups Is Inevitable

It should be clear by now that breakups are a risk to everyone who ventures out into the world of love. There is no formula that will calculate how many you should expect to have.

➤ *Too few breakups.* Some men and women have less difficulty finding lasting love than others. However, if you aren't suffering through any breakups, you probably haven't gone exploring, expanded your horizons, or exhausted every possibility. Get out, seek adventure, and don't be afraid to experiment.

➤ *Too many breakups.* If you have too many breakups notched in your belt, you either aren't select enough, give your heart away too easily, could be a love addict, or are too reliant on sex determining who you partner with. Employ a little more caution before you leap into a relationship!

Statistical Odds of Breaking Up

A few numbers to keep in mind are:

➤ Most romantic relationships die within 18 months to three years.

➤ At least 40 percent of couples who live together break up quickly.

➤ Divorce rates may be edging downward, but your chances of separating are still more than 40 percent.

Bits and Pieces

Romantic love is not confined to the United States. Out of 166 other cultures, 88 percent of them had evidence of romantic love.

Testing Your Odds: Is It Love or Infatuation?

To get a better handle on your odds, check to see where you stand. Are you infatuated, or have you acquired the glue of companionate love? Respond to each question with a numerical answer: 5 = Always, 4 = Most of the time, 3 = Half and half, 2 = Hardly ever, 1 = Never.

1. Does your love interest enhance your self-concept? _____

2. Is life better and are you happier because your love interest reciprocates your feelings? _____

3. Do you like sharing your intimate thoughts with this person? _____

4. Do you reveal your innermost concerns with them? _____

5. Do you enjoy having sex with this person? _____

6. Do you want to spend time with your love interest caressing, kissing, and laughing? _____

7. Are you good friends? _____

8. Can you count on this person in a jam? _____

9. Does this person put your needs above his or her own? _____

10. Do you feel as if your love interest understands you in a mystical, empathetic way? _____

11. Does your love interest help you to be the best you can be? _____

12. Do you hope your relationship with this person will last indefinitely? _____

13. Do you feel secure in this relationship? _____

14. Do you both show a willingness to compromise? _____

15. Do you derive enjoyment giving your love interest gifts? _____

16. Does he or she reciprocate? _____

17. Do you feel comfortable and happy when you are together? _____

18. Do you sexually crave each other? _____

19. Are you good at making allowances for his or her faults that are not detrimental to your well-being? _____

20. Can you be more honest with this person than any other previous lover? _____

To find out if it is love or infatuation, add up your score.

100–90 points = A definite love match

89–70 points = On your way to love

69–50 points = It could go either way

49 or below = An infatuation for sure

In Your Favor, a Need for Coupling

Don't let the clouds of breaking up discourage you. It is natural to couple. Just take a look at what is in your favor:

1. Pair-bonding is said to be part of our four-million-year evolution and the core of family life in humans.

2. Physically, we are made to bond.

3. Bonding is healthy. Marriage increases men's lives three to four years.

4. The affect of marriage on the mental and emotional health of both men and women is measurably positive.

5. Society is committed to the idea of love and procreation by twos.

These are optimistic thoughts that ought to drive out some of the pain and fear of breaking up without another love interest in the wings.

Bits and Pieces

Marriage is good for you. That ought to prevent a few breakups. Try this info on for size: Married individuals in 18 countries including the United States are happier than their unmarried peers.

The Least You Need to Know

➤ Breaking up is an inevitable part of the process when you are looking for that one true love.

➤ Infatuation is not a lasting form of love.

➤ Love can and should be nurtured.

➤ It is wise to regularly assess your relationship either to avoid breakups or prepare for them.

➤ Breakups should not discourage you from finding love.

Are You Sure You Want to Break Up?

In This Chapter

➤ Learning to be objective

➤ Drawing and using your "love map"

➤ Uncovering the reasons for breaking up

➤ Establishing your breakup criteria

➤ Making your decision

Breaking up is hard enough. But deciding whether or not to hand someone their walking papers may be tougher. Complicated by ambivalent emotions, opposing motives, wishful thinking, and blurred vision, one remains at an indecisive standstill. Uncertainty keeps men and women in unwise, unhealthy, and unsatisfying relationships way too long.

How many times have you threatened to break up? How many times have you been lulled back into the arms of your lover by romantic gestures, an artful arbitrator, or a dateless Saturday night?

Your decision is too important to be based upon a large bouquet of roses, a near-perfect night of sex, or a moderately pleasing partner.

Fortunately, you can make a near air-tight case for breaking up or staying together. This chapter is your mini-workbook. It assists your exploration into the facts and uncovers pertinent evidence designed to erase ambivalence and indecision. For maximum results, proceed step by step.

Developing the Necessary Objectivity

Developing the necessary objectivity for your investigation is absolutely imperative, but it's a tall order. You must be detached and free of bias. Without taking this first step, there is no need to continue. You will be just as confounded and confused after the necessary extensive soul-searching.

Blow the Whistle

Stop and think! Don't allow your decision to be a crime of passion. You could get a life sentence.

Play a game to get started. Pretend the relationship you are examining is a friend's. She has come to you for advice. Rid yourself of prejudice and personal feelings, but maintain granules of sensitivity. Position yourself on the outside looking in. You may be amazed at what you see.

Three Requirements for Romantic Objectivity

Turn on a Neutral Mindset. There are abundant studies to convince you of the importance of a neutral mindset when making a romantic decision.

To get yourself into neutral territory, clear your head of thoughts that could color your perception. Sit yourself down in a seat of judgment that won't be tainted by a bad mood. Otherwise even the best of times together could take on an unfair dinginess in this dimmed light.

Heart to Heart

When evaluating a love relationship and making the determination whether or not it is worth continuing, dispense with fictionalizing the future. Ask yourself instead, if what you are looking for in a relationship and a partner is a real possibility with this individual. If the facts indicate the answer is no, it may be time to let them go.

If you have to blow steam before your can begin fair and square, go to the gym or eat that piece of cake. But find your mental balance.

Stop Listening to Your Heart and Body. Stow the passions of the heart and the heat of the body. Previous chapters have provided ample evidence that ought to persuade you that neither are reliable or objective decision makers.

That means put a lid on the anger. Toss the disappointment. Stow the longing for love. Squelch the hurt feelings. Can the plot full of revenge. And dump the denial.

If you want to maintain this thoughtful balance when making a romantic decision, don't sit in a darkened theater watching a romantic movie. Don't visit a cozy, intimate restaurant full of loving couples. Don't listen to ballads of love.

Rely on the Facts. If you have been able to fulfill the requirements of the first two steps, the facts should surface clearly. How you interpret them might be another story. There have been enough celebrated court cases to remind us that even substantial evidence can be twisted inside out.

But if you rely on the cold hard facts, you will be less likely to be led astray by wishful thinking, disappointment, or perceived rejection. If your love interest didn't call when he said he would, don't guess why not. Ask why! If your date doesn't show up to take you to an important engagement, don't make excuses for her. Get to the truth. Ask where she was. Accept only the plausible answers.

To illustrate these points, let's examine "Sally" and see how she does with objectivity.

A Case of Missing Objectivity

Sally's case is classic. It has all the elements akin to missing objectivity. She had been involved with Sam for more than a year when she began telling me about their relationship. At first she made it sound ideal. Sam was in law school. They would most likely marry when he finished.

When I saw Sally several months later, they were living together. She was working hard to pay their bills. Sam was regularly skipping classes but told Sally not to worry. She still believed he would graduate and that they would marry. She complained he wasn't doing his share in the house and that the relationship was troubled. Nonetheless, she had no intention of calling it quits. She had high hopes things would improve.

As you have probably guessed, the last time I saw Sally, Sam had dropped out of school completely. But he had not gotten a job. Rather, he was "sorting things out." Evidently he had ample time to strike up an extra relationship that Sally discovered. She was crafty enough to find the phone number and contact his undercover girlfriend who then bid Sam farewell.

Sally took consolation in successfully severing Sam's extracurricular activities. However, steeped in longing for her relationship to work out, she rejected the unbiased perceptions of bystanders and refused to view the plentiful evidence objectively. She allowed Sam to stay, extracted promises that proved empty, and set deadlines for reform that went unmet.

Bits and Pieces

If you believe that mutual trust is imperative for a good relationship, you stand shoulder to shoulder with 90 percent of your peers in a national survey. Unfortunately, we don't often practice what we preach. Sixty-nine percent of those in the same survey said mutual trust was not part and parcel of their current love relationship.

Plotting Your Destination on a "Love Map"

Every time you meet someone who strikes you as a potential date or partner, unknowingly or not you superimpose your "love map" on top of his identity. If the physical characteristics sufficiently match what turns you on, you automatically advance the comparison to the next level.

Because your love map secretly follows you everywhere, it is a worthwhile exercise to get it down in black and white. Your map explicitly reflects the sum of your experiences as they add up to form the ideal picture of a mate. The purpose of employing your love map in the discussion of breaking up is to locate your destination and check if your compass is pointing you in the right direction.

Filling in the blanks from head to toe is your next assignment.

Bits and Pieces

Men and women in 33 countries said they most wanted a mate who was kind and intelligent. Close behind on women's lists were men who would make a good partner, provider, and parent. To ascertain if he has what it takes, women look at men's status, ambition, and earning potential.

Use Caution Following Your Map

Remember that your map represents your ideal partner. Don't let it trip you up. Research has unearthed enough people who, in pursuit of Prince or Princess Charming, continuously discard love interests and end up alone.

Your map is a wish list, not a must-have list. No one fits into all these lines of longitude and latitude perfectly. Sorry, mates are not made to order.

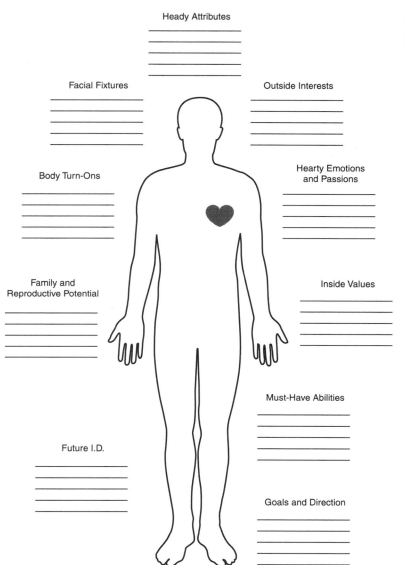

Heady Attributes

Facial Fixtures

Outside Interests

Fill in the blanks to make your own love map.

Body Turn-Ons

Hearty Emotions and Passions

Family and Reproductive Potential

Inside Values

Must-Have Abilities

Future I.D.

Goals and Direction

Create a Realistic Picture

Use your love map to your advantage. List each of the qualities you have noted on your map in order of importance. Next, assign each quality a percentage point that represents the minimum amount of this trait that is acceptable to you. Keep in mind that you are after a reasonable combination of traits and characteristics. Demanding 100 percent fulfillment of your love map is folly.

Blow the Whistle

Open your eyes! One of the most serious errors women tend to make in love relationships is thinking that a man can change into a horse of a different color. No one can. All of us have the ability to temper and tone down behavior, learn to compromise, or become more flexible. Whether our basic personality will accommodate the change is the real issue.

Try to be realistic. Say that the number one attribute your love interest must demonstrate is intelligence. You have an ideal level of intelligence in mind. Now ask yourself what percent of that ideal would be acceptable. Then assess what percent of the ideal your love interest actually possesses. This is how you record your findings:

Quality	Acceptable Percent	Actual Percent
Intelligence	80%	75%

Comparing your love map expectations in this manner ought to tell you something! Falling short in too many categories is either an indication that this person just doesn't have what you are looking for or what you are looking for may be hard to find.

Quality	Acceptable Percent	Actual Percent
1. _____	_____	_____
2. _____	_____	_____
3. _____	_____	_____
4. _____	_____	_____
5. _____	_____	_____
6. _____	_____	_____
7. _____	_____	_____
8. _____	_____	_____
9. _____	_____	_____
10. _____	_____	_____
11. _____	_____	_____
12. _____	_____	_____
13. _____	_____	_____
14. _____	_____	_____
15. _____	_____	_____
16. _____	_____	_____
17. _____	_____	_____
18. _____	_____	_____
19. _____	_____	_____
20. _____	_____	_____
21. _____	_____	_____

Quality	Acceptable Percent	Actual Percent
22. _____	_____	_____
23. _____	_____	_____
24. _____	_____	_____
25. _____	_____	_____

What Do You Want Out of This Relationship?

You can't apply critical standards of measurement to a relationship unless you determine what it is you want out of it. Complete, unadulterated honesty is called for. There is no purpose in fooling yourself. If you are looking for a husband, admit it to yourself. If you are looking for a romantic traveling companion, that's okay too. But make a determination. After you do, here are my recommendations:

➤ If it's marriage you are after, apply the strictest, most reasonable standards of your love map.

➤ If live-in love will do, no less than spousal requirements are permissible.

➤ If you are uncertain but think this person has possibilities, then proceed slowly. No one is forcing you into a decision.

➤ If it's a romantic fling you want, make sure neither of you will be damaged by a breakup.

➤ If a sexual companion is what you seek, be prudent. Make sure he or she is free of deadly organisms, is a fabulous lover, and that both of you are on the same page.

Heart to Heart

Want to test if it's love? According to 100 people, evidence of love is found in such acts as gift giving, contributing financial assistance, sexual fidelity, a proposal of marriage, and sex. Sounds pretty reliable to me!

What's Your Reason for Wanting to Break Up?

If you can't put your finger on it, maybe one of the reasons listed below will do. When you choose one you like pay particular attention to the warning labels. Some things are easier to fix than others.

Boredom. Boredom is the number one reason couples report breaking up and applies to both men and women. Whether accurately perceived or unduly exaggerated, if one person feels she has fallen into a rut and is trapped by routine, she is likely to try to escape.

However, setting every scene with mystery and choreographing each act with new steps is going too far. The boredom is most likely evolving out of a mismatch—personality, interests, needs, and passion simply don't create enough excitement. The world outside the confines of the relationship looks more appealing and stimulating than what's happening inside the supposed love nest.

If your eye keeps wandering because you think your partner is too predictable, reverts to the same conversation, is unwilling to try new things, or doesn't raise your thermostat, you're probably struck with boredom.

Standing Still. Your relationship is at a standstill, you are stranded at critical intersections, and no one is making a move in any direction. In other words, this relationship isn't going anywhere, or at least not in the direction you want it to. For women that direction is usually marriage. For men it is usually sex or living together—then marriage. However, if there aren't any real signs of love, you could be stalled for years.

The impetus for men to marry or commit is nearly always romantic love. They were romantics long before women agreed that love was the best reason to give their heart away. A study of college men showed that 80 percent said they would not marry someone unless they were in love.

One the other hand, don't forget the model in Chapter 2, "The Probabilities for Breaking Up." Real love takes time to develop.

A Change of Heart. You just realized you have been fooling yourself. Your relationship is based on nothing more than familiarity and comfort. You were content to have a partner who fit your immediate but not your long-term needs. Then you took a job in another city, made new friends, or went through a life-altering experience. Something happened to shake off your complacency. Suddenly you are critical of your partner and unhappy with your relationship.

Be careful, however, that your change of heart is permanent and not a temporary detour.

No Chemistry. Okay, you just aren't getting turned on. Your love interest is a great person, has all the attributes you are looking for, but doesn't float your boat. The fact of the matter is, you can't talk yourself into attraction.

A 30-year-old medical resident confessed he had found the perfect woman. She was bright; they were great friends and had a wonderful time together; her family was terrific; she could be a real asset to his career. Nonetheless, there wasn't any passion in his lovemaking. He tried to talk himself into a romantic relationship that would lead to marriage, but he couldn't do anything to improve the chemistry in the lab. Eventually, he broke it off. There was no surprise on the other end.

Love Lingo

Psychologists who delve into the innermost recesses of love acknowledge that men and women make a distinction between **loving** and being **in love**. To be in love means to be under the spell of romantic love—the kind that burns with desire, need, and commitment. To simply love someone suggests something more platonic and less passionate.

Bits and Pieces

A bright, handsome young law student once told me "If a woman turns you on, it doesn't matter if she's robbed a bank." Evidently some things are more important than others.

Five Reasons to Stay

Before you say good-bye, consider whether or not you are ignoring some good reasons to stay.

Your love interest:

1. Makes your day better purely because she is a part of your life
2. Makes you feel wonderful about yourself
3. Is fun to be with, and you want to learn more about him
4. Is someone with whom you share affection, values, and goals
5. Stimulates you and contributes to your growth

Ten Reasons to Leave

Too many reasons to leave overrule reasons to stay. Each of those posed below are serious indications of an unhealthy relationship. You can do better!

1. The relationship is lopsided and lacks equality.
2. You caught this person repeatedly lying. (Lying is a reflection of character. For a full discussion see Chapter 10, "Is There Room for Honesty?")
3. He or she cheated on you more than once.
4. Your love interest shows little consideration by frequently breaking dates, canceling plans, or showing up late.
5. This individual is emotionally, verbally, or physically abusive.
6. He is not paying his fair share for your live-in abode.

Blow the Whistle

Jealously can be flattering, but both men and women agree it is problematic and hard to deal with in a relationship. Countries in which more people admit to showing jealously are the United Kingdom, Spain, Germany, Portugal, and Turkey.

7. She lowers your self-esteem, stunts your growth, or prevents you from obtaining your personal goals.

8. Your partner lacks tolerance and is dangerously jealous.

9. You don't make each other laugh.

10. He was just a meal ticket, and you're going on a diet.

The Least You Need to Know

➤ To evaluate a love relationship requires objectivity and an unbiased mindset.

➤ Your "love map" holds the secret of your destiny.

➤ Using your love map is of no avail unless you are realistic.

➤ Pinpointing the reason you want to break up will motivate you to take action.

Chapter 4

Still Suffering from Uncertainty?

In This Chapter

➤ Where to find fresh advice

➤ Learning how to conduct a love talk

➤ Checking your relationship for quality

➤ Unforeseen dead ends

Don't panic if you are stuck in romantic limbo. Evidently, your love interest warrants a second look. That's okay. You wouldn't want to pass up someone of merit or stick with a Joe or Jane undeserving of your affection. Nor would you want to dump a perfectly fine mate just because you've hit a bump in the road of love. You are wise being cautious, especially if this relationship started to sound serious.

Try digging a little bit deeper to unearth your answer. Yours is not a hopeless case you have to solve on your own. There are still unused tools and tricks at your disposal.

Getting to the hard-core identity of your love interest and assessing the realistic potential of your future together is time well spent. It sharpens your perceptions and improves your odds of finding lasting love either now or later.

Feedback in Your Own Backyard

There are people out there just dying to give you their opinions. Some are worth listening to. Open your mind, hear what they say, digest it in private, and apply what seems appropriate. But never, absolutely never, turn the decision making over to someone else!

How Reliable Is a Friend's Input?

A good friend who has your interest at heart and knows you well is a groundswell of help. She sees things you don't. For instance, Hannah warned Jane that Josh was the kind who would forever disappoint her. She had seen the type before. He was strong on courtship but weak on commitment.

Waving the red flag in front of Jane was just the cautionary signal she needed to improve her vision. Although she didn't break up with Josh right away, Hannah helped Jane see Josh's actions in a new light. Thereafter, she kept him at arm's length.

"It's Your Mother, Dear"

Hopefully your mom doesn't shower you with unsolicited advice. However, you might be wise to ask her opinion. In all probabilities she is your greatest support and your most biased onlooker. She above all has her protective guard up and isn't about to let anyone take advantage of you or treat you as less than a "royal."

Of course, you have to weigh her words. Nonetheless, she is, in most cases, the best person to give you added insight. Her intuitive powers can determine what your love interest is adding or subtracting from your life.

Bits and Pieces

According to a national survey, a majority of single women view their mothers as the person who supports, appreciates, and loves them the most. Until she marries, mom is her number-one confidante.

Straight from the Horse's Mouth

Don't play a guessing game. It may be time to approach your love interest for the proverbial *love talk*. He alone may hold the key to your decision.

Generally guys aren't the ones to initiate a conference on a romantic relationship. They are unlikely to reveal themselves and hazard a show of weakness that could diminish their status. Even if a woman starts the infamous talk, men find this exercise uncomfortable and normally aren't prepared to answer questions.

Plow ahead anyway, whether you are Deborah or Dan. There is much to be gained. To get the most out of your talk, obey the following dos and don'ts:

➤ Don't put the other person on the defensive or make her uncomfortable with your questioning. You are having a conversation, not conducting an interrogation.

➤ Don't insist that every question be answered right there and then. A love talk is valuable if it gets both of you thinking.

➤ Don't make any final decisions or pronouncements during the talk.

➤ Don't try to talk anyone into loving you. Maintain your self-confidence, self-esteem, and composure.

➤ Don't attack, accuse, or blame.

➤ Don't lose track of what it is you wanted to accomplish.

➤ Don't be afraid to express your concerns and feelings. However, be careful not to divulge or reveal something you might regret later.

➤ Don't lie. It is better to take the fifth amendment than give an untrue answer you feel comfortable with at the moment.

➤ Do listen carefully. Don't interrupt, and don't monopolize the conversation.

➤ Do take time alone to think about what was said. Then act.

Love Lingo

When you try to pin one another down, decipher where your relationship might be headed, and get a grip on each other's level of commitment, you're having a **love talk**.

Deborah and Dan's Love Talk

Let's pretend Deborah had something on her mind. She approached Dan in just the right way and was savvy enough to get him to respond in an ideal fashion. Pay attention to how she did it. Don't think she was being too syrupy and sweet; Deborah was merely candy-coating her message.

Deborah: "Dan, I have something on my mind that I would like to share with you. Don't jump to any conclusions. I know guys hate 'the talk.' I don't want to put you or myself in a tough spot. Both cities are appealing to me. Each has different pluses. I am trying to weigh all considerations before I make my choice. We have been seeing each other for nearly nine months. I have been having a great time and up until now didn't feel any urgency to know how you see things between us. But I think if I understood more about how you felt about me, I would know whether I might like to be out on the coast or closer to the D.C. area where you are."

Dan: "Deborah, I can't make that decision for you. I mean, heck, that's putting a lot on my shoulders. You have to do what you want."

Deborah: "Of course, you're right. I didn't mean it to come off that way. I wouldn't expect, nor would I want, you to make that decision for me. I guess I am just asking you to be honest about whether or not we may have a future together. Hey, don't feel uncomfortable letting me know it has been all fun and games. I've had a ball. I haven't taken sleeping together as a sign of an indefinite commitment. I think you have really been up front and never said anything you didn't mean. I appreciate that. I think you're great, and I truthfully don't want to nip something in the bud that could grow into something more later. All I am asking is how do you see our relationship?"

Dan: "I haven't given it much thought."

Deborah: "Do you want to think about it?"

Dan: "I don't know if there is anything to think about."

Deborah: "Well, let's put it this way. I am asking if you see us getting married some day. I couldn't answer that one myself. But say, if I moved to New York or San Francisco, would it influence how often or how little we would see each other? Excuse me. I'll be right back. I'm going to the ladies room."

Deborah: "Listen Dan. If I thought you were a real jerk, I wouldn't take time to have this conversation with you. I don't want you to feel any pressure. I am not asking you to commit to anything. If you want to talk about it later, I understand. I just kind of wanted to start to get my ducks in a row."

Heart to Heart

Your love talk will fail dismally if you fill in the blanks. When your inquiry is met with an awkward silence, sit patiently and wait for a response. If you must, excuse yourself, go to the restroom, take a bite of your sandwich, or order a drink. Do anything. But don't start answering the question you just asked. Stay in control. Get what you came after!

Dan: "You really are understanding. I am a little confused about what to say. I mean you have been so available and all. Yeah. I think I would miss you if you moved away. I can't say how often I would be up in New York. It seems reasonable to think I'd get there more often than San Francisco. I think it kind of has to sink in that you won't be just around the corner. Are you mad at me?"

Deborah: "No. I'm not going to say I wouldn't have been flattered if you had gotten down on your knees and pleaded I not leave you, but I'm not mad, not at all. I have some time before I have to turn in my final decision. I do think you owe it to me to think about it. Can we talk about it later?"

Dan: "Yea. That might be best."

The Objective Professional

Consider seeking the advice of an objective third party. Relationship counselors and premarital counseling centers are popping up all over the place. With divorce costing billions of public dollars, Maryland and Michigan have proposed laws to delay licenses for those couples who have not taken a marriage class. Alaska and Kansas have considered reducing fees for those who have.

Florida has a program in play that works like this: The state's Marriage Preparation and Preservation Act calls for a three-day cooling-off period for couples who do not elect to take a one-hour premarital counseling class. The act hopes to reduce quickie marriages that end in divorce. A further incentive to sit down and listen to some words of wisdom is a $32.50 reduction in the $88.50 marriage license. Check to see what offers your state is making.

Most people who enter premarital counseling programs take the stroll down the aisle together. There are others, however, who don't have the right stuff for a lifetime together and bow out gracefully before the wedding march begins.

A worthwhile premarital counseling program:

➤ Identifies a couple's strengths and weaknesses

➤ Locates potential trouble spots

➤ Enhances communication skills

➤ Teaches conflict resolution

➤ Encourages intimacy

If you are interested in premarital counseling, check Appendix A, "Resources," at the back of the book for more information.

Blow the Whistle

Do your homework! When selecting a relationship professional, inquire about his training and certification. Be aware that he comes to the table with his own bias. If selecting a premarital counseling program, get the facts. Check out the philosophy and success rate. You don't want to be a guinea pig.

Dispel Doubt with a Change of Scenery

Coasting through the routine of daily life rarely opens the way for new explorations into your love interest's identity. We become complacent seeing each other in the same settings. Responses become habitual and even anticipated. The subtle expression of attitudes or behavior is overlooked. With a little bit of effort, however, you can encourage or forge new discoveries that are worth every bit of the effort.

Be creative. Get out and visit new vistas that provide the opportunity of seeing your questionable love interest in a fresh light.

Try New Horizons

To help you along, here are five ways to set the scene for making new discoveries:

➤ Make plans with friends you don't often see.

➤ Throw a dinner party together.

➤ Visit your folks.

➤ Baby-sit for a friend's kid.

➤ Drive to an overnight destination that takes hours to get to.

Come up with five novel ideals of your own and test them out:

1. _____

2. _____

3. _____

4. _____

5. _____

Roadside Warnings

Don't take everything you discover at face value. Some situations are more stressful and call for putting on one's best behavior. The first home visit is outwardly awkward and formal. Reaching a level of comfort tells you a lot. Look carefully and you will get a glimpse of something you haven't seen before. It might turn you in one direction or another.

Be discerning in your judgments along the path of discovery. Kimberly was concerned when Robert would become annoyed with crying babies in restaurants and was only lukewarm to the newborn babies of their friends. She questioned whether he had the patience to be a good parent. However, seeing him in action with his own niece and viewing the collection of pictures he had of them together changed her mind.

Unforeseen Dead Ends

Have you ever considered that you may be spinning your wheels trying to decide whether or not to break up when in reality the relationship has its own dead end?

You may be doing precisely that if your relationship reads like "the old divorce story" or "the serial saga of the romantically addicted" or "the tale of waiting for love to strike like lightning."

Blow the Whistle

Watch out! According to a university study, addiction to falling into romantic love is more prevalent than addictions to alcohol, caffeine, and nicotine. One in 12 are love addicts. Two-thirds of those are males.

The Old Divorce Story

"I am absolutely never getting married again. I refuse to face the possibility of another divorce." Ever heard that one? If you have, don't disregard the message—especially if you have your eye on the golden ring.

Howard admitted that after his second divorce he was a "male slut." His self-image was damaged. It took a while for this hard-driving businessman to repair the damage.

He fell deeply in love with a woman near his age but wouldn't even consider the idea of marriage. She bid him adieu. When he finally found a compatible partner, he settled into a live-in relationship. Howard was to be taken at his word!

The Serial Saga of the Romantically Addicted

Repeat users keep looking for that high. They discard the empty bottles and butts.

Roy is just that kind of guy. You would have to fall in love with him. He makes you feel fabulous, showers you with gifts, whispers sweet nothings in your ear, and responds to your every whim. In the last 10 years he has had more than five serious relationships. Each ended with a less than happy female who thought she was and would be forever the love of Roy's life. The best way to detect an addict is to read his case history and have him spell out the future.

The Tale of Waiting for Love to Strike Like Lightning

This is a dead end if there ever was one. Claire was madly in love with Clark. Clark was not madly in love with Claire. Claire wanted to become Clark's bride. Clark did not share her desire. The one and only thing that could make Clark commit to marriage after a previous love affair left him deserted was, he said, the magic and passion of being swept off his feet. He was always looking over his shoulder in case the woman of his dreams was nearby.

The problem with guys like Clark is that they don't trust love that takes time to grow and wrap strings around their heart. Frightened off by the pain of unrequited love, they whittle away the rest of their lifetime waiting for that storybook entrance and strike of lightning that signals their perfect partner has just waltzed in the door.

> **Love Lingo**
>
> A **pragmatic lover**, according to John Alan Lee, professor of sociology at the University of Toronto, is an individual who consciously seeks a **compatible** partner based on similarities in background and interests.

A Quality Check

There are specific qualities no relationship ought to be without. If they aren't present in yours, it's time to bail out. No equitable and satisfying relationship is minus a single one of them. The absence of even one of the following should sound your quality control alarm.

➤ *Compatibility.* You don't need it for a one-night stand or a brief, passionate fling. But without something in common, something to share, something to bring you together besides sex, you can count on a short relationship.

➤ *Comfort.* Not only must you be comfortable in the presence of one another, but you must be able to bring comfort to your partner. If he or she can't help heal

41

your pain, dry your tears, appease your loneliness, support your decisions, or be a sincere helpmate, what you have is a playmate.

➤ *Caring.* A caring partner is kind, protective, and concerned about your well-being. She will go out of her way to make life easier, not harder, for you.

Heart to Heart

Facing adversity is one of the best tests of a compatible relationship. How you respond to and fair through ups and downs in finances, a bout of bad health, a family death, or a beleaguered battle should influence your breakup outlook.

➤ *Respect.* The kind of respect you should be looking for has little to do with putting the toilet seat down or squeezing a tube of toothpaste from the bottom up. A man or woman worth keeping around is one who respects your feelings, opinions, needs, desires, and privacy.

➤ *Responsibility.* Two people must take responsibility for the relationship to make it work. It doesn't have to be 50-50 every day or every week, but it should average out over the year. A good indication if someone accepts his fair share of responsibility is whether or not he can admit he was wrong and say "I'm sorry."

Bits and Pieces

The top three preferred sexual practices among American men and women include intercourse, oral sex, and observing a sex partner taking off his or her clothes.

The Feel-Good Scale

Whether you agree that love is 90 or 50 percent sex, your score on the "Feel-Good Scale" is important. (If you think that love is less than 50 percent sex, you may need to rethink your percentages.)

Rate your partner on a scale of 1 to 10 (10 being the best).

My partner:

1. Is romantic   _____

2. Gets me in the mood for sex   _____

3. Is not a selfish lover   _____

4. Tries to find new ways to satisfy me   _____

5. And I take turns initiating sex   _____

6. Respects me when I don't want to do something I find
   distasteful sexually or am not ready for   _____

7. Makes me feel sexy and special   _____

8. Doesn't make me feel guilty if I beg off sex, even though
   I am normally a willing partner   _____

9. Says "I love you" during sex   _____

10. Tells me what a wonderful lover I am   _____

Total points scored: _____

0	Forget It!	*The Feel-Good Scale*
10	Slam the Door	
20	Don't Answer the Phone	
30	Break the Next Date	
40	Wave Good-Bye	
50	Not Worth the Effort	
60	Seek Improvement	
70	Worth Hanging Around	
80	A Feel-Good Contender	
90	A Real Heavy Weight	
100	Highly Unlikely	

43

The Least You Need to Know

➤ There is no need to agonize over a decision alone.

➤ A "love talk" is a valuable resource if you know how to listen.

➤ Don't be afraid to look for new ways to reveal your love interest's hidden identity.

➤ Never fool yourself about a person's potential if she fails the quality control check.

Chapter 5

Time, a Double-Edged Sword

In This Chapter

➤ The sights and sounds of a stonewalled romance

➤ Regrets of a hurried breakup

➤ What to do while you wait for clarity

➤ When to sound the final bell

Time can either be your friend or foe in the breakup process. If you aren't in control of the hour hand, someone else will be setting the alarm or pressing the snooze button.

The topic demands your attention and requires precision tuning. It might be the most critical issue that influences a good or bad decision when it comes to ending a love relationship. You must, therefore, decipher if time is working for you, learn how to wind the clock to your advantage, and be certain it isn't ticking to your disadvantage.

The signs are clear in either direction. They need only to be pointed out to remain illuminated on the dial.

> ### Bits and Pieces
>
> Up-to-the-minute research by York College social psychologist Perri B. Druen, Ph.D. provides insight into individual attitudes and the length of love relationships. Men and women who believe that love alone is the foundation of a strong relationship tend to have short romances. Longer romances are evident among those who focus less on their choice of a partner and more on their willingness to work on the relationship.

Time as the Enemy

In a world that is spinning by in the midst of your own hectic schedule, the passage of time is sometimes overlooked. Decisions that are purposely delayed or long overdue are less apparent. The timing is perfect for someone who wants to stonewall a decision.

Stonewalling is a defensive measure to gain time, to put off commitment, or to make a decision regarding the direction of a relationship. The act of stonewalling is fraught with uncertainty and is a sign of one party's ambivalence toward the other. It can be prompted by an inadequate amount of love to advance the relationship.

Generally, men are the ones who take advantage of stonewalling—particularly those who aren't ready to relinquish their cherished freedom for a more committed relationship or a walk down the aisle. As soon as they feel pressure from a female with a different agenda, they either flee the scene or move into stonewalling mode.

Heart to Heart

Men, especially young men, have a difficult time giving up their freedom for a committed love affair. Let your guy work his way out of it slowly. Don't ask him to give up all his nights with his buddies and take all his fishing trips with you. Little by little you will become the main event. Don't press too hard to be the only one in the ring.

The Sounds of Stonewalling

Sentences that may signal you are dealing with someone engaged in stonewalling may read like the following:

> "I love you, but I can't think about marriage until I get a promotion."

> "I am not ready to take on the financial responsibility of a partnership until *we* pay off the credit card bills for the trip to Hawaii, the TV, and the new car."

> "We need more counseling. Two years hasn't taken care of all our differences."

"I don't want to have kids, so let's just keep living together."

"I don't know where this relationships is going. If you had told me you loved me a year ago when I told you, then I wouldn't be so confused. I have gotten used to holding back with you now."

"I take you to all the nice places. I don't sleep with anyone else. I buy you all kinds of presents. How can you complain about our relationship?"

"I just spent several years in a serious relationship. I only want to be with you, but I am not ready to set any kind of timeline here. Maybe you could move in instead. It would make our relationship more convenient."

"I love you madly, but I'm afraid to get engaged."

"I have to get to know you all over again."

The spoken sounds of stonewalling should make you sit up and listen. You may not want to hang around if there is nothing positive coming next.

Suspicious Scenarios

Stonewalling is not always expressed in words. Sometimes it is acted out. Take a look at these common stonewall scenarios:

➤ *The Stonewall Engagement.* The absence of a sound wedding date or the engagement that lasts for more than a year is suspect. Someone is probably stonewalling. Even more of a red flag is that the word "engagement" appears to have taken on a different meaning of late. A guy proud to be betrothed to Karen told everyone of the pending marriage. One step behind him Karen was whispering, "I have no intention to wed."

➤ *The Financial Stonewall.* This is the most prevalent stonewall scenario utilized by men or women whether sharing the same abode or living apart. They use financial obligations—car loans, accumulated credit card debt, or school loans—as a reason for not approaching the altar. Curiously some buy the validity of the stonewall excuse even though they are living together and already sharing living expenses.

➤ *The Living Together Stonewall.* The lower marriage rate is attributed in part to the large numbers of individuals who are cohabiting instead of becoming Mr. and Mrs. This stonewall is easy to slip into. The object is to perpetuate a state of limbo. Howard and Becky have been living together for five years. She wants to wed. Behind closed doors Howard admitted, "I am not 100 percent sure if I am in love with Becky. I hesitate over the finality of marriage and can't picture myself married."

Blow the Whistle

Pack the bags! Live-in couples have undefined futures and show less of a commitment toward the institution of marriage. Among those who do wed, the incidence of divorce is higher than it is for couples who did not cohabitate before exchanging nuptials.

➤ *The Rebound Stonewall.* "I haven't completely gotten over my previous relationship." Ever hear that one before? Sometimes it's true. Sometimes it's not. Interviews with persons (primarily males) interpreted that sentence for me. Collectively, they agreed the trouble was they were looking for fireworks—a more passionate, movie-like attraction and love connection to a woman. The women currently in their lives didn't have it. If and when they came across someone who did, they were planning to jump ship.

Don't be fooled and caught behind a stonewall, even if you have a ring on your finger. The best and biggest sign of stonewalling is that your love interest isn't budging or moving quickly enough in the desired direction.

More Signs of the Stonewall Mode

You think you are on your way to a committed love affair. Think again if any of the following statements apply to you:

➤ You haven't been taken home to meet the folks.

➤ You are rarely included in family events.

➤ You don't know how much he or she earns.

➤ You weren't asked to help pick out the couch.

➤ You don't spend holidays together.

➤ You haven't met the boss.

➤ You weren't invited to the company picnic.

➤ You don't have an engagement ring.

➤ You aren't treated like a permanent fixture by his or her folks or kids.

➤ You aren't talked about as an integral part of his or her future plans.

What these signs indicate is the absence of a partner mentality. Until your love interest sees and treats you as an essential buddy, your relationship is at a standstill.

> ### Bits and Pieces
>
> People who spend long periods of time between relationships may be expending their energy looking for the ideal partner. Research shows that these guys and gals carefully focus on the qualities of the other person. They believe that a lasting relationship hinges more on the stuff the other person *is* made of than themselves.

Tipper Ran into a Stonewall Before She Saw It

Tipper had been living with Tom for nearly a year. Still, when Thanksgiving and Christmas rolled around, she trudged off to her parents' home, and Tom ate turkey at a table with his mom and dad. When an invitation arrived in February to Tom's cousin's wedding, Tipper's name wasn't on it. She told Tom she was furious and that he needed to call up his cousin and ask that she be invited.

"After all, I am your significant other. Aren't I?" she asked.

Actually, she may not have been significant enough. He refused.

Several months later when he cancelled a trip the two of them had been planning for ages so that he could go camping with his immediate family, she realized their relationship had hit a stonewall. She wasn't included. The reason? It was family members only. Evidently she was considered a little more than an insignificant and, most likely, temporary live-in lover. Once she recovered from the head-on collision, she packed her bags. The scene of the accident was littered with signs of a stonewall mode.

Patience Can Be a Virtue

It takes time for the rain to end, the wind to subside, and the blue skies to return. Nature has a way of working things out. Time is on its side. It can be on yours as well if you stop being so impetuous and impatient.

As long as you aren't in jeopardy, allow indecision to slowly melt away. You might need more information that only time can provide in order to make a comfortable decision.

Why rush love? It is one of the worst mistakes you can make.

Pushing things along too quickly and demanding untimely answers adds premature stresses and strains to a budding relationship. For a more complete look at what happens when you rush love, see Chapter 11, "Unintentional Precipitators of Breakups."

> ### Bits and Pieces
>
> Over the last 30 years, the proportion of never-married women in their late 20s has risen from 11 to 33 percent. The median age at which men marry hovers around $36\frac{1}{2}$. For women it is $24\frac{1}{2}$.

A Case of Lingering Doubt

Penny agreed to share her story. She met and started dating Paul when she graduated college. They had a great, relatively short-term relationship that was characterized by mutual respect, kindness, affection, and genuine caring. The potential for a committed and enduring love match was apparent to both Penny and Paul. However, Penny did not let the relationship continue long enough to test the outcome or learn everything she needed to know about Paul.

A job took her to a different city. She wanted to begin her professional and social life unencumbered by any ties. During the last several years, she has advanced in her career, picked up a graduate degree, and dated all kinds of men.

What she keeps wondering is, was Paul the right guy after all? There really isn't any way to tell at this point. Any answer would be purely supposition. Is what she remembers fact or fantasy?

If you met Penny, you would probably tell her to give Paul a call. He's still single. But Penny can't. She already broke his heart once. Without knowing exactly what would happen if she stoked up the fires, she doesn't think it would be fair to reopen the wounds.

She wants to advise you not to act in haste, lest you end up with a case of lingering doubt as she has. In retrospect she wishes she had continued to date Paul long-distance. "It was a foolish decision, and one I regret today. If we had dated just a little longer, I might not be feeling this way."

While-You-Wait Strategies

Uncertainty should not be accompanied by inaction! Select from this recommended list of strategies until you decide whether or not breaking up is in the game plan.

1. Date around.
2. Work on yourself—inside and out.

3. Don't obsess over the relationship. Talk about something else.

4. Spend time with your friends.

5. Distance yourself from the relationship and take a vacation—alone.

6. Take up a new hobby.

7. Do things you have put off finding time for.

8. Make an effort to meet new people.

9. Get out of the house. Don't sit home.

10. Exercise daily. It relieves tension and gives the extra surge of energy you'll need for all of the above.

If Absence Makes the Heart Grow Fonder, Is This a Good While-You-Wait Strategy?

That depends on whether or not you want to chance letting your partner get the jump on breaking it off first. Before you take a long-distance hiatus from Ralph or Rose, consider these possibilities. Otherwise this strategy could backfire.

➤ Unless there is already sufficient breadth, depth, and length to your relationship, along with a history of working out trials and tribulations, merely being absent from your love interest's daily life could cause it to fizzle. There are individuals who require readily available intimacy to maintain even a modest love relationship. Without a relatively close proximity, they may be tempted to begin a new attraction with someone conveniently close at hand.

➤ On the flip side, there is evidence that your questionable love interest is likely to sit by the fire and wait out the winter alone if he is the kind who likes developing lasting relationships. Then chances are he will miss you, yearn for your return, and think about the good times you've shared.

However, counting on absence to make the heart grow fonder is risky business. I wouldn't advise it.

Blow the Whistle

Stay put. If you are pondering breaking up but are even slightly insecure, don't test whether absence will make your heart grow fonder. You will probably be miserable out of watchful sight of your love interest. Your mind will play tricks on you and invent all kinds of scenarios just because he or she doesn't answer their phone.

Heart to Heart

Do your friend a favor. Tap him on the shoulder and hand him a calendar. Mark a big, wide, bright red X on all the years he has spent in a dead-end relationship. He probably needs someone to remind him how much time has elapsed.

When Patience Loses Its Virtue

How long is too long to wait for something to transpire in your love relationship before calling it quits? This is a complicated question.

We've all met men and women who have spent five, six, even seven years with a romantic partner, then poof! it's all over. Generally a stalemate endures this long because:

➤ Each person has a different agenda and thinks they can convince the other to adopt theirs.

➤ You have a "marrying kind" involved with a "singularly satisfied" prototype.

➤ The romantic partners are not equally "in love" with each other.

A Critical Set of Variables

The correct amount of time to linger on each and every relationship should be evaluated in light of the following circumstances.

➤ *Age.* Obviously if you are in your early 20s there is plenty of time to look around and explore relationships. But one thing remains constant for everyone; if you spend a prolonged period of time involved in a relationship that fails to meet the desired end, regret becomes pervasive when you part. Anger, admonitions, and a diminished self-image accompany the breakup.

➤ *Satisfaction.* Time flies when you are snuggled into a cozy, comfortable, pleasing, romantic relationship. Granted, it isn't easy to give away something that feels good at the moment. However, if you are trading long-term satisfaction for immediate comforts, patience may not be a virtue.

➤ *Previous marital status.* Dating a divorced man or woman in any decade of your romantic life is a distinct possibility. It is reasonable to give them time to adjust to a failed marriage, catch up with their financial obligations, and learn how to parent part-time. If, however, you don't see progress in these areas, time may not be the only factor you are bucking.

➤ *Goals.* You can't fault anyone for wanting to finish law school or get their MBA before they assume the responsibility and partnership of a marriage relationship. You could, however, chastise yourself for putting your life on hold, following them around the country, and ending up on graduation day without knowing what your future holds. Without some concrete plans, patience is no longer a virtue in this waiting game.

➤ *Reproductive desires.* Men and women both feel the pinch of reproductive possibilities around age 30. Benny admitted that he planned to wed close to his 30th birthday because that was the time frame he had in mind for fathering kids. Women justifiably express concern about their biological clock and start to panic after 30. So when it comes to blowing out all those candles on the cake, don't suddenly become breathless realizing you have been too patient waiting for Joe or Jane to commit.

Bits and Pieces

According to American Demographics, not only are women having children later in life than the previous generation of mothers, but they are averaging fewer children. In 1965 women bore, on average, three children. By the 1990s, the percentage fell down to less than two children.

Take a good look at these variables and set your watch on the correct time. Never jeopardize your goals and desires indefinitely for someone else's timetable.

Love Has No Substitute

Tracy was young, pretty, vibrant, fun, divorced, and the mother of two. She had been going out with Tommy for nearly four years. He divorced when his kids were in high school and had been in at least two other relationships that lasted anywhere from three to four years. He was the perfect companion, helped with the kids, ran errands, took trips, made love, and filled Tracy's lonely hours. What he was terrible at was what Tracy wanted most—making commitments that had to be signed on paper, filed with the courts, and officiated by clergy. It took Tracy 48 months to accept this love affair would never end the way she dreamed it would. It took another six months to make herself break it off.

What puzzled her the most was a concurrent relationship an acquaintance was having that appeared nearly identical on the outside but must have been different on the inside.

Tracy watched the other pair walk down the aisle. So did Tracy's ex-lover, who was seated in the second pew with his new romantic interest. She had easily stepped into Tracy's shoes.

The critical element that gave Tracy's acquaintance the Cinderella ending was love. The groom had fallen "in love" with his bride. It was the magic that distinguished her from his former long-term, satisfying string of lovers and playmates.

Love is what raced this second-hand forward. The absence of love can put a stop to the clock. It happened to Tracy.

The Least You Need to Know

➤ Time can be your friend or foe.

➤ It is safe to bet that if your love interest is stonewalling, you need to push for a resolution or leave the premises.

➤ Don't let any grass grow under your feet while you wait.

➤ Patience loses its virtue under the right conditions.

Chapter 6

Get Ready, Get Set, Break Up

In This Chapter

➤ What's holding you back?

➤ A four-step lesson plan to get you going

➤ What happens when you don't say "good-bye"

➤ Unacceptable excuses

➤ How to construct a daily exit planner

Are you having trouble getting out of the starting gate? Perhaps you are feeling a bit lethargic. What you need is one more little shove to break up.

It's time to collect the evidence, call in a verdict, and make a plan for action. After you have accomplished this enormous feat, the remainder of the book will provide the insight and tools required to get you to the finish line.

Why Some People Won't Leave

Here is what others have to say. Unfortunately, not one answer is a legitimate excuse for staying in a relationship. You can be sure that these men and women are merely prolonging the agony, wasting time, and preventing advancement to a brighter future.

➤ They are afraid they won't find anyone else.

➤ They are dependent upon the relationship for an identity.

➤ They are financially insecure.

➤ They are blind with love.

➤ They are users and like the comforts of home and convenient sex.

What's holding you back? Examine your own motives and record them honestly. Ask yourself if they resemble the excuses above.

1. _____
2. _____
3. _____
4. _____
5. _____

Blow the Whistle

Jump! Remember the wheel of love can go in reverse for a few days, maybe even a few weeks, without shutting down completely. But if it gets stuck moving backward and doesn't start spinning forward, this love affair is O-V-E-R.

Blow the Whistle

Run! Couples who roll their eyes at each other's comments, act defensively, are critical, or try to stonewall during individual counseling sessions have approximately a 90 percent chance of splitting up. Does this apply to you?

A Remedial Lesson Plan

This is a four-part lesson plan designed to provide additional insights and information that should make your decision conclusive and absolute. It brings together everything we have been discussing in the previous chapters, gives you one more opportunity to test his or her love, evaluate your love interest's character, and state your own case.

Lesson One: Loves Me, Loves Me Not

Don't pick one daisy petal at a time reciting the verse you learned in childhood. There is a better way to use this flower to forecast love. Pluck a petal for each of the following loving actions your beau displays toward you. If all of your petals are plucked, there is no question you are loved. What you must decide is if you can love this person back. If the daisy looks fresh and untouched, however, sorry, but there are no signs of true love.

"Loves me, loves me not" is only the first test of his or her love. Try the next one to see if it adds up to love.

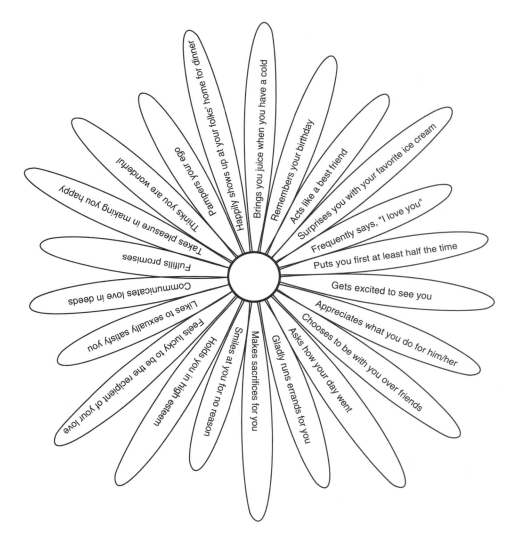

Loves me, loves me not…

Lesson Two: How to Add and Subtract

Love must be plentiful in a relationship that is enduring and satisfying. It is not, however, the only ingredient. Character is a close second. Use the tables below to put the stamp of approval on your breakup. Circle words in each table that seem to describe your Ms. or Mr. Caution: Click in the neutral mindset described in Chapter 3, "Are You Sure You Want to Break Up?"

Table A		
Tolerant	Patient	Passionate
Fun	Sexy	Generous
Romantic	Honorable	Truthful
Respectful	Caring	Confident
Giving	Supportive	Responsible
Mature	Compassionate	Interesting
Flexible	Communicative	Stable
Smart	Motivated	Kind
Thoughtful	Loyal	Listens
Understanding	Nurturing	Independent

Table B		
Dishonest	Roaming eyes	Juvenile
Stubborn	Dependent	Self-centered
Undependable	Lazy	Selfish
Insecure	Humorless	Close-minded
Bossy	Uncompromising	Abusive
Disrespectful	Jealous	A taker
Unkempt	Stingy	Intolerant
Impatient	Moody	Irresponsible
Mean	Inflexible	Helpless
Demanding	Complainer	Egotistical

Heart to Heart

Carol told me that after her divorce—before she found an exciting job as a firefighter and entered college—few men came calling. Now that she is busy and happy, they are attracted to her. That's because men are turned on to women who are self-sufficient rather than needy. There is no way to hide which category you fall into.

Now add up all the circles from Table A: _____

Add up all the circles from Table B: _____

Subtract Table B from Table A: _____

Evaluate your score:

+30 = You cheated

+25 = Try again with a more objective mindset

+20 = Admirable

+15 = Less admirable

+10 = Improvement required

0 = What's there to like?

−10 = Why have you waited around this long?

Numbers don't lie. If it doesn't add up to love, what are you going to do about it? Start by using forethought.

Lesson Three: Practice Using Forethought

Engage your logical mind here. Set it down on paper so you can refer back to see why your present relationship is not a good one.

List five reasons why this is not a good relationship for you.

1. _____
2. _____
3. _____
4. _____
5. _____

If you failed the daisy test, you scored less than 10 points on lesson two, and you don't have a good relationship, why are you still hanging around?

Lesson Four: Combine Intuition and Intellect

What you need to do is quietly tell yourself why your intuition and intellect are screaming to call it quits.

List five reasons why you should leave. The five answers above won't fit here.

1. _____
2. _____
3. _____
4. _____
5. _____

These four exercises were designed to get you thinking and acting. Pay close attention to what the results indicate. It is spelled out in front of you. You don't want to get stuck in the mud, afraid to initiate that necessary breakup.

Bits and Pieces

Therapists report that a lack of sexual desire is the most frequent complaint made by committed couples in regard to the intimate component of their relationship.

You Can't Afford to Get Stuck in the Mud

Donny and Donna had been stuck in the mud for four years when I first interviewed them. "I love her, but I'm not in love with her," Donny admitted. "She isn't my ideal of a sexual woman. Getting into the mood to have sex is slow. I want that passion to be there for us."

Consequently, Donny told Donna he could not commit to a marriage relationship although that's what she wanted—to be a wife and mom. Still, she agreed to remain in their exclusive relationship and was patient until she discovered Donny was close to an affair with another woman. Then she insisted they go to a therapist for help.

Heart to Heart

Here is a good place to ask yourself, "What happens if I don't break up now?" Go through all of the scenarios. Do any one of them offer you adequate satisfaction? You might very well find greater happiness in a new relationship. The unknown sounds scary, but it could be better than the certainty facing you if you stay.

The crux of the matter is you can't be talked into falling in love. You know from Chapter 2, "The Probabilities for Breaking Up," that's not how it works.

After more than a year of weekly visits to a therapist's office, Donny and Donna were still at the same place in their relationship, although they understood their personal emotions better. Even if Donny never wanted to marry or have children, Donna admitted, "It is hard to put a time limit on it. I don't know if I will be able to walk away from him."

She hasn't. Six years later Donna and Donny are living together, but there is no ring and no kids.

Quit Making Unacceptable Excuses

Quit making excuses for a poor relationship and his or her lack of commitment. They've all been heard before and are empty phrases composed of misguided judgment and wishful thinking. If you are spouting one of them, stop!

Refrain from repeating any of the following until you are firmly convinced your assessment of this stalled relationship is justified.

"He is going through a bad time."

"When he gets over feeling guilty, he'll leave his wife."

"She loves me so much. She just doesn't know it."

"He said we'll get married. He just doesn't know when."

"I'll never find anyone better."

"She hasn't healed from her other relationship."

"He doesn't want to make a mistake. We're getting close. Maybe he needs another month or two."

"I know I can make it work. I just have to try harder."

"He's such a sweet guy. He'll change."

"If she loses weight, then maybe she'll turn me on."

Looking for excuses? Don't. Get ready and break up.

Putting Your Plan into Black and White

The object of your plan should be to make breaking up easier for you, and if your previous love interest deserves it, kinder for him or her.

1. Repeat after me the "Breakup Pledge":

    "I will be better off.
    My courage will be rewarded.
    I have made a thoughtful decision.
    I won't be swayed.
    I will stay on course."

2. Do the following: Select one person as confidante and supporter.

3. Use your artistic abilities. Make a sign with the Breakup Pledge on it and hang it up. Don't take it down until you have reached your goal.

4. Make a daily planner. Find a date that is good for you to break up. Begin your preparation in advance. Plan events to divert your attention after the breakup. Work hard at getting into the right frame of mind. How to break up will be covered in the remaining chapters.

Review the following sample planner then make one for yourself.

You have come a long way since first opening this book, admitting your indecision, acknowledging a twinge of heartbreak, and floundering over a breakup. You even have a plan right in front of you if you have been doing your homework.

You are properly primed to begin making confident decisions that will enable you to handle a breakup. After all, you understand the importance of thoughtful action in romantic endeavors, you recognize the complexities in building meaningful attachments, and you are able to detect signs of true love.

Before you think you have all the answers and make a critical error in judgment, better take time out to dissect the intricacies of the breakup anatomy.

Love Lingo

To **hug** is to comfort, affectionately embrace, squeeze, or cherish. Therapists advise four hugs a day to satisfy one's needs. However, 98 percent of a large population sampled by Northwestern University Medical School wanted to be hugged more often. Hugging and touching are good medicine for support during breakups.

A Sample Daily Planner

	Sunday	Monday	Tuesday	Wednesday	Thursday	Friday	Saturday
Week 1	Find a confidante Hang up sign	Recite the Breakup Pledge	His exams start Recite the Pledge	Recite the Pledge Your annual work evaluation	Recite the Pledge Call confidante	Recite the Pledge End of his exams His weekend away	Recite the Pledge Begin new activity
Week 2	Recite the Pledge Make dinner plans for Wednesday	Recite the Pledge Don't listen to romantic music	Meet confidante Recite the Pledge	Recite the Pledge Dress up Dinner Break news	Recite the Pledge Don't call Talk to confidant	Take your one-week vacation Recite the Pledge	Recite the Pledge Don't call Do something out of character
Week 3	Concentrate on self	Flirt but do not begin a new romance	Pamper yourself Don't read a romantic novel	Go for a second adventure	Recite the Pledge Do not call Get ready to go home	Recite the Pledge Have confidante pick you up at airport Don't stay home	Recite the Pledge Stand firm Go out with the girls
Week 4	Keep your eye on the sign if he calls Talk on phone only	Recite the Pledge Renew efforts on the job Have dinner with a new friend	Recite the Pledge Get fixed up Call your confidante	Recite the Pledge Pamper yourself after work	Recite the Pledge Go to a new dance place	Recite the Pledge Visit Mom, Dad, or sister for the weekend Get hugs!	Bask in home cooking and lots of family lovin'
Week 5	Return to apartment excited about starting over	Take down sign					

The Least You Need to Know

➤ You must use your objective mindset to evaluate your relationship and to determine the time to break up.

➤ Your heart can and will play tricks on you.

➤ You cannot change the basic character of an individual.

➤ If he or she loves you, there will be plenty of evidence to prove it.

➤ Thorough preparation before breaking up will make the task less traumatic.

Part 2
The Anatomy of Breakups

Get ready to look at breaking up from all angles. There is no deciding how, why, or where to initiate your own split without recognizing the complexities of a breakup.

Men and women do it differently. That's why it is so hard to see it coming sometimes. It is advisable, therefore, to recognize his or her maneuvers, understand each other's mindset, re-evaluate your own actions, and learn to proceed in a manner that is empowering.

Being defeated by love's game leaves lasting affects. Ward them off at the breakup.

Chapter 7

☆ Breaking up
☆ Considering it
☆ Should, but won't
☆ Co-Dependent
☆ Addicted

Dissecting the Beast

In This Chapter

➤ Sexual mind shapers

➤ Breakup stages

➤ From ridiculous to sublime breakups

➤ Unfair practices

We are going to put the pieces of breaking up under the microscope. Understanding the nature of the beast will enhance the effectiveness and ease the pain of your breakup. It helps to know what issues will trip you up, the feelings you cannot avoid, and the choices you must make. Knowing the steps each breakup takes makes the climb less cumbersome for everybody.

True, each breakup is unique. Personality, intensity of the relationship, length of togetherness, and sexual involvement put their own marks on the event and complicate the process. However, the thorough preparation in Part 1, "Contemplating a Breakup," has equipped you to objectively sort out these issues.

A Set of Absolutes

Breaking up has its own set of natural properties. They are part and parcel of the beast. It is worthwhile to keep them in mind.

➤ *Breaking up is no one's fault.* It is a natural course of the dating process and a hazard to be anticipated.

➤ *Breaking up is never easy.* To break up is to admit that you've made a mistake. Changing romantic courses is bound to be uncomfortable.

➤ *Someone is going to feel bad when it's all over.* If you've been fair, you needn't blame yourself.

➤ *The duration of attraction and infatuation is not always equal among two parties.* If it doesn't turn into true love, it eventually fizzles. When this happens is out of your control.

➤ *Someone will feel or look like the bad guy.* Whoever takes responsibility for the breakup assumes the guilt and posture of the outlaw even if it is not warranted.

➤ *Breaking up is a no-win situation.* No matter how carefully you try to sever ties, someone is going to feel hurt, rejected, and unhappy.

➤ *Rarely is severing romantic ties accomplished with complete honesty.* Instead, individuals skirt the truth, tell large and small lies, and make up stories to avoid saying "I just don't care enough for you to continue our relationship as companions or lovers."

➤ *Nearly everyone prefers to avoid conflicts in calling it quits.* It only increases the discomfort.

➤ *Feelings of ambivalence haunt at least one of the romantic partners.* No matter how right it feels to sever ties, someone worries they are taking the wrong course of action—if only for a moment.

➤ *You can recover from even the most painful parting of the ways.* Breaking up is not a fatal condition. Surviving the breakup and rising above it will be covered in full in Part 5, "Surviving the Breakup."

Love Lingo

The "Great Debate" of 1998 will be recorded in history as what constitutes **sex**. The truth is, to most people having sex in the formal sense means engaging in intercourse. Informally—and perhaps more accurately—sex means engaging in intentional, intimate bodily contact that is normally pleasurable and gratifying.

Heart to Heart

Males—psychologists and participants—say women beware; what a man has on his mind is getting a woman into bed. Men lie more in the beginning of a relationship to accomplish this goal. However, if they tell you that a daily orgasm lessens their risk of prostate cancer or wards off impotence, they're spouting the truth.

As if breaking up wasn't hard enough with this list of absolutes! But add in the element of sex, and things get really complicated.

Sex: A Complicating Factor

From the initial eye-catching attraction to the last shred of romantic involvement, sex complicates a relationship. Fear of contracting fatal diseases may have put the brakes on purely recreational sex, but it hasn't done anything to stall the libido over time. Normally, some degree of sexual intimacy has been established before the stage of romantic atrophy sets in. Supposedly, there are 2,800 ways to satisfy a lover without having intercourse.

It shouldn't take adherents of the National Chastity Organization to convince you that sex confuses love and lust, may interfere with developing the strong fundamentals in a relationship, opens the door for recrimination, or makes breaking up a whole lot harder. By now that should be obvious.

Hot and Heavy Sex

Casual sex is short-term, based primarily on lust, founded on need, and gratified by a physical release. Sex in romantic relationships is generally long-term and performed with affection, trust, and desire specifically for one another.

The woman who engages in intercourse under the latter circumstances views it as the ultimate act of sexual intimacy (giving part of herself away) and interprets it as a meaningful sign of commitment. She expects this guy to stick around for a while and he knows it.

In short, she is more emotional about sex than a man. Twenty-seven-year-old Cynthia made the point when she said, "If you ask a man what he is thinking after sex and he says 'nothing,' he means it. He has nothing going on in his head. The woman is lying there thinking, 'This is wonderful. We are so close. All of the problems we were having in our relationship must be resolved now.' And she's thinking that he is thinking the same thing."

Each of you need to be aware of the opposite gender's take on sex. That's the only way to avoid significant misinterpretations that stir up romantic complications later.

Bits and Pieces

Fifty-five percent of women surveyed said that sex without love was not pleasurable. But it's healthy. Sex reduces stress, assists fertility, helps migraine sufferers, induces better sleep, and raises estrogen levels.

Unwise Clinches

There is no getting away from the fact that both parties enjoy sex. Equally true is that women love the affection. Few men or women are eager to give up sex with a partner that is pleasing and with whom they feel secure and free of health risks. Nonetheless, these encounters border on unwise clinches.

No wonder sex is commonly the last thing to go in a relationship. It sometimes becomes a tool used by women to try and hold onto the relationship. The ridiculous thing is, as Chegal admits, "Every woman has the same parts. So what the hell is the point? If the man really loves her, the sexual thing isn't going to sway him."

Nonetheless, even when love starts spinning backward, sometimes sex keeps moving forward. Some guys say it's no great shakes to keep having sex with one woman while looking for another. "I have liked her and cared about her, so what's the difference? It's not like I don't care about her."

But sex is the big fooler, and we know what she's thinking!

More precarious yet is when old lovers get together for sex because they haven't found other suitable partners. Although they enter into the romp fully cognizant of their intentions, it isn't difficult to stir old emotions, forget why they broke up in the first place, begin a second round of the relationship founded on sex, and go through the entire breaking up process again.

Stages of Breaking Up

From start to finish, breakups are comprised of at least five stages—unless the romance ends in an unexpected explosion of emotion.

1. *The Awakening.* The period of awakening is characterized by the end of the infatuation, a drop in attraction, a loss of excitement being together, and the onset of reality. The problems, deficiencies, or differences that did not seem to matter in the beginning take on greater importance. With a change of heart, a love interest is seen more clearly, understood better, and carefully scrutinized.

2. *Lingering Doubt.* In this stage, men and women aren't sure exactly what they are feeling. They question whether their disinterest is momentary or permanent.

3. *The Lull of Inaction.* At this point it seems more comfortable to coast. It takes time to get used to the idea that you are no longer attracted to your previous love interest, that you are ready to move on, and that your future is uncertain. Doing nothing is safe and only mildly uncomfortable.

4. *Making Clumsy, Half-Hearted Attempts.* One day you refuse to see him or her, make up an excuse to break a date, and in a round-about way that no one could possibly decipher say that you want out. Then two days later you want a play-mate to go to the movies with and call your nearly ex love interest. You put off your plan of breaking up for the present.

5. *Responding to the Final Straw.* You just can't play the charade any longer. You've had it. You want to move on. You experience panic at the thought of not breaking the ties and determination to set yourself free. Now and then, urgency is based on someone else who looks too attractive to pass up. You do it! How you do it and whether or not your breakup is damage controlled depends on the amount of forethought.

Bits and Pieces

According to therapist Dr. Gilda Carle, men and women remain in relationships out of fear of not finding anyone to love them. But the change can be beneficial and make you happier and more likely to discover a meaningful, supportive lover.

A Tale of the Five-Stage Breakup

John and Janet had grown up together and became romantically involved for a few years in their mid-20s. John's *awakening* occurred after he moved to a new city away from Janet. He was surprised at how little he missed her and how his passion had cooled. He *doubted*, though, that what he was feeling was a good thing. It seemed so right to love Janet, to marry Janet.

For months John did nothing. He ignored all the signs. Taking no action was the safest thing to do. He was having great difficulty imagining the turmoil his breakup would cause everyone. The *lull of inaction* wasn't hurting anyone, he thought.

Eventually he made a *half-hearted attempt* and broke it off. But because his determination was limp and his courage faulty, he found himself back in Janet's arms. The prospect of her coming to join him and moving in loomed large. One can only wonder how much longer the limbo would have gone on if Janet had not posed her ultimatum.

"Put up or shut up. I want a ring before I pack my bags," was Janet's message. John took it as the *final straw*.

Love Lingo

Dory Hollander, Ph.D., author of *101 Lies Men Tell Women* (HarperPerennial,1997), believes that at the core of one's ambivalence over breaking up is a conflict between the need to be free and the need to connect. Her colleagues have named this the **porcupine dilemma**. Animals are drawn together for warmth, but in the case of the porcupine, pushed away because of the sharp quills.

Sizes and Shapes of Breakup Styles

What style did John use to break it off? Select your answer from among the most common examples.

➤ *The Classic Breakup*. It sounds like this: "I care about you, but let's be friends. I think you are wonderful. We haven't had a bad relationship, but something major is missing." It is as plain and forthright as some Susies and Sams can get. Normally women get huffy over this size and shape breakup. Men take it better.

➤ *The Cowardly Cop-Out.* Philip did not want to get talked into marriage. If he went away with Paula for the weekend, he was afraid he might come back engaged. "It really spooked me," he said. "You never break up with anyone in bed. Sex is the perfect way to get talked into something." Philip took the coward's way out. He simply did not show up for the trip at the appointed day and time. "I felt badly dumping her that way. I just hoped I would never see her again."

➤ *The Night-Crawler Maneuver.* He or she slowly wiggles their way out of a relationship. They disguise their primary concern for themselves by voicing concern over the other person. "I don't want to hurt them. I don't want to upset anybody. I don't want anyone to cry. Conflict is the worst."

➤ *The Peace Accord.* When two people come to a simultaneous agreement that their exploration into a more committed relationship doesn't seem likely to work out, they part peacefully. Evidence of the Peace Accord style of breakup is a show of honesty, forthrightness, and concern for others. Only valiant, honorable warriors are capable of engaging in a peaceful resolution.

Not all breakup styles are equally healthy or fair. The Cowardly Cop-Out and the Night-Crawler Maneuver are by far the least commendable of all. The Peace Accord, on the other hand, may be one of the most difficult to carry off, but it is certainly the most admirable. The Classic Breakup is, however, the most popular.

Blow the Whistle

Don't listen! Men admit they tell women exactly what they want to hear. They know exactly what it is women have been programmed to believe, experts say.

Warranted Non-Breakups

The warranted non-breakup is perhaps the most disturbing situation of all. It is a breakup that should occur but doesn't. From the hundreds of individuals I have interviewed about their love relationships, I have to conclude that women are most prone to this mishap. There are two reasons women generally fail to act when a breakup is warranted.

The Desperate Woman Syndrome

These women absolutely, positively do not allow themselves to see the truth. They are blind to bright red obvious rebuffs and oblivious to verbal baloney. Instead of breaking up, they keep trying to set things right and become experts at making excuses for their lover's behavior. Although this is a definite pattern among healthy and unhealthy women, it is pronounced and exaggerated among females who look like, sound like, and smell like desperate women who indiscriminately grab a mate.

Are you a desperate woman? Want to know the answer? Take the following quiz.

Question	Yes	No	Sometimes
1. Will you latch onto anything in pants?	❏	❏	❏
2. Do you have a set agenda when you meet a guy?	❏	❏	❏
3. Are you fearful that you will never meet a decent man?	❏	❏	❏
4. Are you concerned you won't have the opportunity to marry?	❏	❏	❏
5. Do you fall in love with every guy who demonstrates interest in you?	❏	❏	❏
6. Do you chase after guys?	❏	❏	❏
7. Are you dying to be loved?	❏	❏	❏
8. Do you constantly require the company of a man?	❏	❏	❏
9. Do you feel incomplete without a man in your life?	❏	❏	❏
10. Do you go out searching for guys?	❏	❏	❏
Totals	___	___	___

Ten "yes" answers mean you are desperate and obsessed. Any number greater than three is suspect.

Ten "no" answers mean you are too laid back. Try being a little more aggressive.

Ten "sometimes" answers mean you are basically honest. Nonetheless, a little more show of independence would be a step away from becoming a desperate woman.

"Yes" and "no" answers mixed equally together means you may be somewhat desperate, but the evidence may be hidden well enough to allude your love interest.

The Pleasure Takeover Syndrome

There are women who know they are involved in a relationship that is headed for disaster. Despite the inevitable unhappiness the relationship will eventually cause them, they refuse to give up the pleasures, love, fun, and good sex the relationship is providing. They pack their common sense in the closet.

Emily failed to see her second warranted non-breakup. She thought she had a clear picture of what was going on. She was having an affair with a married coworker at the same time she was Edward's betrothed. She was starting to go crazy cheating on her boyfriend. Nonetheless, for several months she was unable to halt the affair because her lover provided her with things her fiancé couldn't. He shared her intellectual interests and was more supportive and understanding of her hopes and

Blow the Whistle

Hold it right there! If you have any of the signs or symptoms of being a desperate woman, don't lose a second of time. Start changing your ways now. Not only is this an indication of an unhealthy you, but it scares away any potential love interest. Desperate women turn men off and are easily picked up by male radar.

dreams. Eventually, however, Emily managed to summon her common sense and break off all communication with her lover.

She understood that she was adrift in the Pleasure Takeover Syndrome and that a breakup with her married lover was warranted and immediately called for.

A breakup with her fiancé may have been warranted as well, and certainly not on the grounds of her sexual indiscretion only. Due consideration should have been given to splitting based on Emily's perceptions of what her fiancé was missing. There was evidence he lacked prominent qualities on her love map, could not hold her undivided attention, nor keep her under his sheets. It sounds like there was too much room for dissatisfaction, too little fertilizer for the seeds of happiness to grow, and too little commitment to prevent a dismal marriage forecast.

Unfortunately, Emily failed to recognize that it isn't always a glaring mistake or the Pleasure Takeover Syndrome that indicates a breakup is advisable.

Unfair Breakup Tactics

Sorry, but all is not fair in love and war. There are some tactics that are way out of bounds when breaking up:

➤ Don't flaunt a new love interest in front of an old one.

➤ Don't keep anyone dangling over the cliff.

➤ Don't lie about loving.

➤ Don't treat anyone as if they are a throw-away lover.

➤ Don't break up when someone is boarding an airplane or has no chance for a rebuttal.

➤ Don't break up by leaving an e-mail or voice mail message.

Breaking up always leaves a tad of a sour taste, but that doesn't mean you have the right to do it distastefully. In a world of love, what goes around comes around. Forego the unfair breakup tactics. You will be taught enough of the good ones to do just fine.

The Least You Need to Know

➤ Ambivalence should be expected in forming and breaking attachments.

➤ Sex is a mega-complication when it comes to breaking up. Careful evaluation of sexual conduct in a waning relationship is key to a successful breakup.

➤ Few people decide in an instant that they want to break up.

➤ Desperate women frequently fail to act when a breakup is warranted.

➤ You deserve a sullied reputation if you break up using unfair tactics.

Gender Differences

The contrast between men and women's mode of breaking up and responding to a split is startling. If ever you were looking for divergence in gender behavior, you've found it here!

A great deal of the confusion surrounding breaking up can be dispelled with exposing the unique mindsets and maneuvers of both men and women. It is time for everyone to go on the alert, get the inside scoop, and understand the games people play when severing relationships. Doing so will avert harm to yourself, to others, and to future romantic hookups.

Who Has a Harder Time Breaking Up?

Women find the decision-making process of whether or not to break up excruciating. Once they make up their minds, however, they move forward with less game-playing than men. And more often than not women are the ones who call it quits on a bad relationship.

Nonetheless, if a women in her 20s or 30s gets dumped, she has a harder time getting through a breakup than men. Guys simply tell themselves "Okay it's over. She's dumped me." Women, however, sit and analyze the relationship to death—its demise and her role in it.

Heart to Heart

Ladies, a smart guy thinks a smart gal is one who knows how to handle a dying relationship and isn't afraid to deal with the truth. She wants to be treated ethically and honestly and is mature enough to accept that the attraction simply didn't last.

Men's Breakup Inadequacy

Harry, a 30-year-old ivy-league grad working in Washington, D.C., accurately assessed his peers and admits "Breaking up is not something most men do particularly well. The very nature of it brings out the worst in us. The bottom line is, women are sometimes treated abominably by men when they break up. I know guys who treat people awfully in this situation. It is simply a fact."

Harry is not a guy without blame or a conscience. At least he added "I felt crappy when I was trying to break up with someone and wasn't being completely honest."

Bits and Pieces

Gender differences run the gamut in the story of love and sex. Three-quarters of the women in a study of 19 countries said that kissing was more intimate than having sex. Only half the men agreed.

Inside Men's Minds

When a guy decides to break up either because he is no longer is interested in the woman or he simply wants to regain his highly prized freedom, why can't he just say it?

The problem is, men are captive to four preconceived notions. Each influences and plays a part in how he decides to get out of the relationship. Consider the following:

1. *In the Name of Chivalry.* The need to gain social acceptance is plugged into men's breakup scenarios, say psychotherapists. They are programmed from youth to be good little boys who should lie rather than hurt someone's feelings.

   Therefore, men go to unbelievable lengths to protect their self-image and spare women's tears. If they had their druthers, they would prefer to be thought of as a partner in a lousy relationship rather than be exposed as a louse who dumped a woman after leading her on.

2. *Guilty in Quicksand.* Men jump into relationships, spout "I love you," make love, and then realize "Oops, I changed my mind. I don't want to be with this woman."

   He knows he's going to look like a jerk; he knows the woman is going to be madder than hell to find out he doesn't like her as much as he thought he did. He feels guilty as can be.

3. *Confrontations Are Ominous and Should Be Avoided.* Confrontation makes men extremely uncomfortable. They can't stand to see a woman cry. They can't stand to be the object of her wrath. They don't want to deal directly with a woman's accusations, particularly if they are true. Confrontations may be more difficult for men because they lack the ability to verbalize emotions and feelings as well as women.

Bits and Pieces

Women want to discuss problematic issues in their relationship. Most men, however, prefer avoiding talks they believe will result in a fight. If a disagreement occurs under these circumstances, which it usually does, men are more apt to withdraw and become silent. Women believe men view them as irrational beings during arguments and that the issues at hand are hers not his. Only a small number of men say "I'm sorry" after a confrontation.

4. *Words Won't Work.* Men don't trust straight talk. It is a lesson they think they learned out of experience. The best way to explain this is to use 30-year-old Josh as an example:

   "Women just won't believe you," Josh said. "If I break a date, come down with a three-day illness, or act bored, the woman will complain that I don't treat her right. She'll say she isn't happy with me, that I am selfish. I am not selfish. I don't want to be with her. I will tell her that this is who I am. I can't say I don't like you because she will argue that of course I do, I am just tired and should take a nap. They don't want to believe you. You can't tell them in words. Actions speak louder."

Male Maneuvers

The male mindset sheds a bright spotlight on his breakup maneuvering. Here's how he goes about accommodating these preconceived ideas.

➤ *Complete Honesty and Forthright Explanation of Feelings.* This is by far the least called upon maneuver. Most men admit they don't have the courage to do it. Granted, the less involved you are with a woman the easier it is to be honest and forthright. Some men, however, pull it off admirably.

Kyle had just gotten out of a long-term relationship. He met Kathy shortly thereafter and was attracted to her in a romantic way. He thought he was prepared to go forward with a fresh romance but realized he was not yet himself. He began to worry that he might be projecting a poor side of himself to Kathy and told her the truth. She admitted that she was pretty much in the same boat. They opted to keep seeing each other, not as lovers, but for now as friends.

➤ *Total Avoidance.* Plenty of guys use this, but it is not number one on their list. Avoidance is harsh and cowardly. Men either never call back, skip out the back door, or disappear without a trace. This hardly appeases the need to be chivalrous, but it certainly takes care of avoiding any discussion or witnessing any tears.

➤ *Playing the Precipitous Trump Card.* This is the preferred plan of action. Guys of all ages use it, acknowledge it, and perfect it. The object is to create a situation or atmosphere that causes the woman to do the breaking up. That way he can alleviate his guilt, think he is protecting her feelings, and make himself look better.

Love Lingo

According to *Webster's*, Susie or Dick **jilted** Sam or Jane when, unprovoked, they recklessly tricked and indiscriminately rejected them to satisfy their own whims.

Love Lingo

Dory Hollander, Ph.D., author of *101 Lies Men Tell Women*, defines the **set up** as the period in which a deliberate exit plan is implemented in order to facilitate a mutual breakup.

How Men Cause Women to Break Up

If a man deliberately makes a woman dissatisfied enough with a relationship that she does the leaving, he thinks he has chivalrously spared her feelings. It may take weeks or months. It doesn't matter. He is willing to wait. To accomplish his goal he suddenly:

➤ Picks fights

➤ Makes himself less available

➤ Becomes more distant sexually

➤ Purposely does annoying things

➤ Does not exhibit respect

➤ Revokes his emotional support

➤ Shows up late

➤ Breaks dates

➤ Calls less

➤ Acts moody

➤ Is not cooperative

➤ Ignore her needs

Heart to Heart

You aren't alone when you suffer the pain of heartbreak. The whole world is singing about it, research points out. The experience and emotions of being dumped have been put to words. If you listen to the lyrics of almost any song, you'll hear words describing the humiliation, betrayal, and anger felt by the jilted, dumped, and misled. Turn on the radio for company.

More Than Meets the Eye

Aside from escaping a woman's wrath or acting under the pretense of chivalry, setting a woman up to go for the break:

➤ Keeps men in control

➤ Relieves them of responsibility

➤ Eliminates need for uncomfortable truthfulness

➤ Enables them to stay in fairly good graces and hold their place if they wish to return

A Tale of Two Male-Style Breakups

Lee's Outrageous Antics. Lee, an attorney in his mid-50s, said he always does something precipitous to end his love relationships. Here's one story for the books.

Despite his younger girlfriend's protest that she did not care about having children, he knew she did. It was something he definitely was not interested in repeating. He already had two grown children. So, at a charity auction for the Society for the Prevention of Suicide that she took him to, he bid on and won a vasectomy.

At the end of the evening when his girlfriend asked if he bought anything, Lee replied, "A vasectomy." She became infuriated and asked how could he have done such a thing. He said "Why are you so angry? You saved a life. If you became pregnant, I would have to kill myself."

That was their last date!

Michael's Conventional Turn-About. Michael is typical of his friends in their mid- to late 20s. He's into body building and looks great and is having fun being single, but he falls in love quickly and stays with one woman nearly a year. He took approximately a month to extricate himself from the clutches of his previous love until she finally said, "I don't think this is working out anymore."

"In my mind I knew I should be honest," Michael said, "but then I felt she wouldn't like me. I was hoping she would drop me. It would be a relief. I had tried so hard to get her to like me and then she became possessive. It was a long-distance relationship. Sometimes I didn't return her calls and then every time she wanted me to drive up and see her I said I was busy and came up with an excuse."

Blow the Whistle

Attention men! According to people in the know, women would rather hear the truth. Your lying and scheming is condescending, experts say.

"She kept saying that I had made time for her before and wanted to know why I couldn't then. She started saying she wanted to finish off the relationship. I told her I wasn't sure if I wanted to but if that's what she wanted, well I guess that was it."

Michael and Lee's breakups demonstrate two typical male-style moves. The details will change from couple to couple, but the underlying elements are likely to remain the same.

Bits and Pieces

Paradoxically, men say that the more they like a woman, the harder it is to break up with her. Therefore, they may lie more to protect her feelings before they would admit they don't love her.

Are Men Pulling the Wool Over Women's Eyes?

Yes and no.

Yes. Frequently, women are left in the lurch with unclear answers. They are confounded and confused by their love interest's inexplicable and sudden change in behavior. Mistakenly, they intensify their efforts to correct what they think is wrong. Therapists found that women will go to extreme lengths to protect a relationship. Having to guess what is going on puts any gal at an unfair disadvantage. Women grope in the dark for answers that aren't there. If and when they find out they have been maneuvered into a break by a man who was no longer interested in them, it makes matters worse. They feel rejected and humiliated.

Yes. Then there are those women who refuse to see the truth. Either they aren't perceptive enough or they are blinded by excess passion of the heart.

No. "I see guys breaking up by not approaching the subject and not wanting to deal with it. They are breaking up with a passive-aggressive approach," says 26-year-old Tish. "They stop calling or go away instead of talking about the issues. There is no clear, defining line when the relationship ends. It is very ambiguous."

No. "Most men just try to avoid the responsibility of confronting the woman," thinks a 26-year-old woman now in a serious relationship. "I have a friend who changes women like shirts, but he always has one around. The women usually break up with him when they see someone else is moving in. Men get easily bored, but they don't say they are bored. They just avoid you."

No. "Guys get really despondent and withdrawn when they want to breakup," said Sally, age 27. "They just show you they are not interested, and they don't ask questions. They call less and less. It is like they are almost forcing you to do the break up."

In all probability, you guys aren't fooling anyone, least of all the women involved. Sounds like they are on to your tricks. Are you on to theirs?

Women's Maneuvers and Mindsets

Women display a different breakup mindset than men. They have their own gender-related attitudes and maneuvers. Here are some of the basic viewpoints widely expressed by females:

➤ Women are confused and look for answers to problems in their relationships. Breaking up provides the clarity they are searching for.

➤ Women don't go in for elaborate schemes like men do.

➤ Women more often rely on honest and direct verbal exchanges to express their desire to break up.

➤ Women feel guilty and express concern over men's feelings.

➤ Women will use avoidance tactics to break up but not as often as men do.

➤ Women prefer to get the breakup over with quickly.

➤ Women opt most often to do it face to face.

Heart to Heart

Be guided by your self-worth. There is no substitute for self-esteem. In Maya Angelou's poem, "Phenomenal Woman," she wrote "The fellows stand or fall down on their knees...Men themselves have wondered what they see in me... When you see me passing, It ought to make you proud...'Cause I'm, a woman Phenomenally. Phenomenal woman, That's me."

➤ Women are generally more emotional than men when they break up.

➤ Women require closure.

➤ Women report that after they initiate a breakup they feel sad but are relieved and empowered.

What's Empowering About Breaking Up?

Everything.

If you look at breakups from all angles, you will appreciate the side that shows you how severing a relationship can actually be empowering. In a seemingly out-of-control situation that pulls the rug out from underneath both men and women, it is wise to seek out this viewpoint.

This is what breaking up can do for you:

➤ It gives you back control over your life.

➤ It demonstrates that you will not allow yourself to be treated poorly or unfairly.

➤ It shows you aren't afraid to say you've made a mistake.

➤ It shows you have the courage to move on.

➤ It proves you have confidence in your ability to fly solo.

➤ It shows you haven't found what you want and deserve and are not willing to settle for less.

➤ It demonstrates a fundamental belief in yourself.

➤ It shows you aren't afraid to make things happen.

Now, that ought to make you feel better and far more empowered. There is a very bright side to your breakup. Just go toward the light.

Women's Files

These cases demonstrate how women who felt empowered afterward broke up.

Case File: 30-year-old Marie. "The last guy I broke up with I did it in person, at his office, in front of others. I told him he should never call again and asked him for the money he owed me. He wrote me a check and I walked out completely satisfied."

Case File: 26-year-old Betty. "I didn't have a guy waiting for me. I just wanted to be alone. It took me weeks to tell this guy I dated for two years that I wanted to break up. Finally at a bar I told him that we had a problem. I was the one doing the breaking up, and I was the one crying. He was understanding and told me not to worry. I woke up the next morning and felt great. I never thought about him again. It took a burden off my shoulders and I felt relieved. Four months later he started pursuing me again, but I told him we could not get together."

Case File: 29-year-old Anita. "I told my last boyfriend that I wanted to get on with my life. I am usually pretty honest. I told him we were on different paths and that I had met someone else I thought was more like me."

Case File: 26-year-old Debra. "I had several wonderful, fun summer months with a guy who told me he loved me. If that was love, I can do without it. He was a great playmate but too self-centered to be a good mate. It took a while to see it. I kept hoping I was missing something that would change my mind. After he came to visit me for a weekend, I knew I was fooling myself. My intuition had to be right. I called him up, told him I had a great time, but that he just wasn't good for me. I asked him not to call me ever again. I didn't want to be talked into anything. I thought I would cry all night. Instead I felt fabulous and full of energy, so I went out to a bar with some friends. It feels great to have it over with even though I felt disappointed for a while."

Just in case you didn't believe that breaking up could be empowering, these testimonies were put here to prove the case.

Is Someone Trying to Break Up with You?

If you aren't sure, ask yourself:

1. Have you heard any infamous break up lines lately? (See the frequently quoted list in Chapter 9, "SOS: Reading Signs or Signals.")

2. Is he or she suddenly a different person?

3. Are you constantly being disappointed by this person?

4. Does this person fail to care when he or she doesn't meet your expectations?

5. Does he or she appear less interested?

If you answered "yes" to all five questions, that's not a good sign. For more information on the subject, go on to Chapter 9. It will provide you with additional warning signals from the bedroom, ways to develop extrasensory perception, as well as ways to identify the men and women who are most likely to break up with you.

Blow the Whistle

Give it to him straight! If he is setting you up, tell him, "Adios. You aren't fooling anyone." Chances are he'll be shocked. Guys said they haven't met many women who had enough guts to remark, "I know you want to break up with me but can't, so I'm doing it for you."

The Least You Need to Know

➤ Men and women do not approach breaking up with the same mindset or goals.

➤ Women should be on the alert if her lover starts acting strangely. He may be setting her up for a turn-about breakup.

➤ Women experience positive feelings along with sadness when they break up.

➤ Men and women both could stand to improve their breakup maneuvers.

Chapter 9

SOS: Reading Signs or Signals

In This Chapter

➤ What aren't you seeing?

➤ Learning to read bedroom signals

➤ Developing extrasensory perception

➤ Identifying men and women who are most likely to break up

➤ A trick for avoiding needless breakups

Love's endings should not be as mysterious as love's beginnings. Breakups don't occur out of the blue. We have already assessed the odds of relationships surviving (Chapter 2, "The Probabilities for Breaking Up") and covered the stages of breaking up (Chapter 7, "Dissecting the Beast"). By the time you or your partner enter into the Stage of Awakening and the Lull of Inaction, whoever is considering the breakup is sending out signals. The receiver ought to become alert to them. Even if it doesn't change the outcome, it can make recovery less difficult, damaging, and devastating. Removing the surprise lessens the depth of the wound.

There are a multitude of ways to prepare. Don't be so cynical, however, that you enter every relationship waiting to break up. But understanding the complete dynamics of breaking up as thoroughly as you do the dynamics of falling in love will help you seek better lovers and protect you from heartbreak. Keeping this information in your back pocket gives you greater control over your romantic destiny.

"I Didn't See It Coming!"

All too often a bewildered, disillusioned lover or spouse comments, "I was shocked when Paul/Pauline said it was over. I had no idea he/she felt that way. There weren't any indications our relationship was in trouble."

Blow the Whistle

Get real! People who refuse to see their relationships realistically are prone to distort perceptions of their love interest's words and deeds.

Impossible. Research shows that although attraction, satisfaction, or love begins to wane and doubt sets in, a romantic or spousal partner will remain in the relationship until they are sure what they want to do. True, their wavering feelings are kept secret, but emotions are hard to conceal. During this time period, the unsuspecting partner usually gets mixed signals.

Women are more prone to disbelieve the danger signs than men. They take any small love signal as reassurance that conflicts, arguments, or suspicious irregularities are nothing to be concerned about. Consequently, they are stunned by their romantic or spousal partner's declaration of lost love and abrupt departure.

The Picture Is Clear in Hindsight

Hannah called Hank all night but never got an answer. Over the year and a half they had dated and the six months they were engaged, he had never stayed out all night. Not that she knew of anyway. She figured Hank must be misbehaving and in the morning went to his house to wait for him to return home. When he did, he was full of unreasonable excuses.

Finally Hannah screamed, "Just tell me the truth!" Hank came clean with a confession. He had recently started seeing someone else with whom he had spent the night, and he was no longer interested in maintaining his relationship with Hannah.

Although initially shocked, Hannah admitted that looking back there were signs she missed. When she delayed setting a wedding date, Hank did not put up a fuss. He let it drop and never brought it up again. She also thinks his recent burst of jealousy, checking her phone and e-mail messages, may have been evidence of his own guilt. The more she thought about it, the more clues she saw sprinkled over the last several months.

Blow the Whistle

When he says "I'm not ready for a love relationship," drop him on his ear! Remember what he's really saying is "DUMP ME PLEASE."

An Outsider's 20/20 Vision

Hannah may have missed the signs and signals in her own relationship, but as the objective observer she had no problem pinpointing some for Pamela.

Pamela and Pete had been on and off for four years. Blinded by love, romance, and passion, Pamela interpreted Pete's behavior differently than her friend Hannah did.

Here's Pamela's version of the romance: "I met Pete, and we instantly fell in love. Within 30 days we moved in together. Then whammy, he found out his old girlfriend was pregnant with his child. He wanted to be there when his son was born, so he moved out. We dated but were on and off for two years. We started living together again a year and a half ago. It was important before for him to be around his son."

Evidently, Hannah saw things that Pamela did not want to. Resolute and confident, Hannah said, "Pamela doesn't see it. What he was doing was trying to decide if he wanted her or his old girlfriend. He wasn't spending that much time just changing diapers! The child was an excuse for his inability to choose between the two women."

Coded Messages

If you aren't proficient at deciphering codes, this section will do it for you. The most common signs, signals, and bedroom alarms will be decoded for your future reference. Don't, however, jump the gun and decide your love interest is trying to end the relationship without sufficient evidence.

Take questionable conduct, look at it in the context of the entire relationship, and watch for corroborating signs.

Infamous Breakup Lines

The first coded message you might hear is one of the more common breakup lines. If he or she recites one of the following, sit up and listen carefully. He or she may be setting you up.

> "I love you, but something is missing."

> "Let's be friends."

> "I love you, but I am not in love with you."

> "You deserve someone better."

> "I'm not good enough for you."

> "I can't make you happy."

> "I'm not trustworthy."

> "I can't give you what you want."

> "I need time to be alone."

Once these words have been spoken, don't be afraid to react. In fact, respond in a sweet, open-minded way. Ask what's missing, why he or she can't possibly make you happy. This way you'll get more insight into the situation and won't have to sit and ponder whether or not what he or she was saying was meant to be an infamous breakup line.

Distress Signals

Fortunately, you never have to rely on just the breakup lines to make your determination whether or not someone is trying to dump you. There's plenty of proof in his or her actions. That's why you should carefully review the distress signals provided for you.

➤ Takes pleasure trips with someone of the opposite sex other than you

➤ Shows no curiosity, concern, or tad of jealousy when a past love calls you or makes an overture

➤ Suddenly changes behavior or expression of affection

➤ Frequently cancels plans

➤ Deliberately attempts to start fights

➤ Exhibits continuous annoying behavior

➤ Shows a preoccupation with everything but you

➤ Makes new references to old loves

➤ Hints at a need for other people in his or her romantic life as well as yours

These are glaring signs that love is waning. The loss of comfort, happiness, and trust caused by these actions are justifiably felt by you. Take them at face value and begin to seriously consider taking action that benefits you!

Bits and Pieces

Although it may not feel like it at the moment, research suggests that women more often than men do not return love's advances. Some experts believe that mutual love is in part dependent upon finding a partner similar in beauty or attractiveness to one's self.

Bedroom Alarms

Want more proof that alarms are sounding? Look in the bedroom next. The following are hardly signs that love is part of these sexual romps.

➤ Rushes out after sex and can't spend the night

➤ Suddenly too tired for sex

➤ The absence of tender moments

➤ Personal insults before, after, or during sex

➤ Lack of responsiveness

➤ Derogatory remarks about sexual performance or participation

➤ Turning over without a kiss or saying good-night

➤ Dismissing you as a nonperson after sex

➤ Interest in their own sexual satisfaction only

➤ A lack of responsiveness to your sexual overtures

By now, if too many of these clues are adding up, your suspicions may be right on target. He or she is either losing interest or maybe has someone else in mind when they look into your eyes.

Signs of Extra-Bedroom Activities

If you think that your guy or gal may be fooling around with someone else, see if any of these extra-bedroom activities have popped up lately.

➤ Keeps coming home late

➤ Doesn't make reasonable excuses about his/her questionable whereabouts

➤ Exhibits a diminished sexual appetite

➤ Shows an overnight improvement or concern with appearance

➤ Buys fancy new underwear you never see him or her wearing

➤ Doesn't look you in the eye

➤ Stops making those private, affectionate gestures you're used to

➤ Makes secret phone calls you discover

➤ Leaves receipts around for gifts you don't receive

➤ Disappears at parties with another man or woman

The signs and signals you have been given thus far should be obvious to the naked eye. As long as you have it wide open, that is. However, not all signs are obvious. That's why you need your radar.

Heart to Heart

Professor Roy Baumeister, in his book *Breaking Hearts* (Guilford Press, 1992), asserts that unsuccessful love relationships result in emotional trauma, personal disappointment, a sense of failure in a critical arena of life, and a blow to self-worth. Although it is difficult to counter this normal aftermath of unrealized love, vow not to get trapped in misery. Don't let others dictate the state of your emotional well-being or damper your self-esteem. Until you do that, you won't attract your true love.

Heart to Heart

The best way to a man's heart is through his ego. Give him a compliment, and he is likely to perk up his ears and wag his tail. Sufficient petting keeps him in one bed only. Men who cheat on their wives or girlfriends aren't getting their egos fed sufficiently, social scientists say. Ego is also tied up in ability to attract and hold onto a woman.

89

Developing Radar

This is imperative in the world of love and romance whether you are tuning into your partner's needs, pinpointing his or her failures, or detecting a breakup. You must be a wise, take-charge person to steer the course of your love life. It can't be done without developing radar. Once you have that skill, it is yours forever.

Here is how to plug in the radar that lets you know what is likely to lie ahead:

1. Watch how he/she interacts with other women/men.
2. Discern their pattern of love relationships.
3. Learn about him/her from friends.
4. Read between the lines.
5. Determine if what he/she is saying is reflected in action.
6. Get verbal validation of your perceptions.
7. Assess his/her normal degree of honesty.
8. Put trust in your instincts.
9. Be a good listener.
10. Become proficient in typecasting (typecasting lessons to follow).

Are You a Good Listener and Skilled Talker?

The following quickie quiz will reveal how good you really are. If you're doing all the talking you won't hear the SOS. If you aren't doing enough talking your partner may not give out the signals you are looking for. Rate your answers on a scale of 1 (the least) to 5 (the most).

Quickie Quiz: How Good Is Your Conversation Know-How?	
1. How much do you learn in your conversations with your love interest about his/her childhood, dreams, inspirations, fears, likes, and dislikes?	———
2. Are your conversations balanced? Is there an equal exchange of information?	———
3. Do you hold off responding or making comments until he/she is finished speaking?	———
4. Can you prevent your partner from getting away with not answering your questions?	———
5. Can you keep the conversation on the track you want if you are looking for answers?	———
Total score	———

A score of less than 20 indicates you are hampering your radar abilities. Improve your conversational give and take.

Typecasting, a Code Buster

Okay, we are taught from grade school not to make sweeping generalizations. Sorry, but sometimes it helps. Typecasting is a handy tool that saves you time. Plugging your love interest into one of the types below gives you the jump on anticipating his/her moves and can avert heartbreak and agonizing breakups.

A note of caution: Summon all your senses and try to be as accurate as possible when you typecast. Not everyone fits neatly into one compartment or another; sometimes they cross lines. Don't cast your initial assessment in stone or hesitate to re-assign a label. Just ask yourself if there is sufficient evidence to warrant a change in typecasting. This is a tool to be used wisely and honestly.

Blow the Whistle

Move on! Men who experience serious breakups or painful divorces express pessimism over finding true love. The sentiments of many men are echoed in the words of a man who confided in me and said, "The mere possibility that a wonderful woman might come along is in itself a fantasy."

A Cast of Male Leads

The basic typecasts for males are provided here in full detail for you. So is a warning label. Read carefully and decide where your guy fits.

Hunters. These men come in different suits, but their role is the same. They love women, the chase, and the satisfaction that comes from catching them. Identifying characteristics include: a history of a large number of sexual partners, boredom after winning the chase, prize their freedom, give up very little of themselves, loads of fun, can be quite romantic, and good for a limited but highly charged period of time.

Warning label: Watch for signs of interest in other women.

Emotionally Unavailable. These men are not adverse to love and commitment, but they aren't in the mood for it right now. How long until they are depends on the depth of their injuries or bumping into a woman that knocks them off their feet. Identifying characteristics include: a love affair that left them wounded, remnants of a broken heart, an unwillingness to expose their emotions, quick to save face, a desire and need for love, searching within themselves for answers, and the determination to date around. The EU won't be rushed or talked into love. A timetable for readiness is completely out of your hands.

Warning label: If there are indications of emotional withdrawal or you tally less time with him than any other woman he is dating, you're sliding out of the picture.

Singularly Satisfied. He should be easy to spot despite the tender side of himself that he reluctantly shows now and then. Identifying characteristics include: likes to do as he pleases, puts himself first, steers clear of commitments, isn't eager to share his re-sources or space, can go anywhere unaccompanied, has stringent qualifications for the women he dates, likes to have a female travel companion, might partake in a live-in relationship, and isn't likely to be monogamous or faithful. The quintessential SS man is not a good prospect for a permanent, loving mate.

Warning label: Generally the SS guy isn't the one to initiate the breakup unless he finds someone who is more attractive and who satisfies him better in bed than you do. Watch for him to become distracted from you and attracted elsewhere.

Limited Companions. These men are usually honest and up-front about their intentions. You have to take them on their terms or not at all. Identifying characteristics include: a history of long-term monogamous serial relationships, easily hookup with new companions/lovers, will not take on extra financial responsibility, rarely lives with a woman, likes a woman close by, and will bolt if you say the "m" word.

Love Lingo

Women can be mistresses of **seduction**. To seduce is to purposely entice, tempt, or lure someone into sexual intercourse. The word connotes being mislead into a slightly wicked set of circumstances or engaging in usury.

Warning label: They will hang on forever if you let them. Make demands and they hit the road. They don't have any trouble saying good-bye.

Awkward Players. They may not be sure of themselves, but they may have a terrific potential to be loving partners. You cannot identify them from external features. There are plenty of good-looking, successful men you would never dream were awkward players. Identifying characteristics include: a scant history of romantic relationships, newly divorced, lack confidence in dating, and are tentative to ask for a date. You might consider grabbing one of these guys before someone else does.

Warning label: A quick boost of confidence could turn him into a Hunter, Singularly Satisfied, or Limited Companion. Watch for signs of a crossover.

Bits and Pieces

Men who tend to remarry after a divorce do so within two and a half to five years after becoming single. Any longer than that and they might not be looking for another Mrs.

Marriage Seekers. These gents are on a practical, focused mission. Their checklist is more important than love. Identifying characteristics include: frequently widowed or divorced men who may have had more than one try at marriage, businesslike behavior in the assessment of romantic or emotional situations, demonstrate a desire for a partner, require care, need company, and test for sexual compatibility. Be careful or you could be turned into a caretaking spouse.

Warning label: If you don't fit the requirements, you'll be passed over. He won't call back.

Did you recognize your love interest? Were you able to typecast him? Remember, it's okay to see him in several of the roles. If this is the case, be astute and pay attention to all the applicable warning labels.

A Cast of Female Leads

Guys aren't the only gender that can be identified by a cast of characters. What is good for the goose is okay for the gander. Men can benefit in the introductory stages of a relationship from seeing where his love interest fits. No one should have an unfair advantage; hence, these female typecasts are also complete with a warning label.

The Seductress. To some extent the seductress is a version of the old-fashioned tease who is now programmed for sex and romance. Identifying characteristics: sexually aggressive and experienced, in pursuit of erotic pleasures, gets high on overpowering men, and has her womanly wiles down pat. You won't end up on top if you hop into bed with this female temptress.

Warning label: After a night of unbelievable passion on Friday, she could easily keep her date on Saturday night with another guy.

Players. These gals are having fun. They gain gratification and pleasure in your interest, will date you temporarily, allow you to fulfill their immediate need for companionship, but aren't attracted enough to get involved with you. Identifying characteristics: has a guy in every port, her romantic history has too many chapters, she doesn't look into your eyes, and she holds out on sex. She's fun if you don't fall too hard for her.

Warning label: Signs of boredom, less playful, an absence of laughter, and a pull back on the flirtation style that hooked you.

Companionately Satisfied. Usually these are women in their 40s. They make good companions and lovers. That and fidelity is want they want from a guy. Love isn't mandatory but makes the whole thing more fun. Sufficient attraction will do just fine, however. Identifying characteristics: financially secure, probably married once before, values her independence, likes her space, doesn't get completely wrapped up in the man she's with, and doesn't talk about marriage. CS women are careful in their selection of a male companion. You may have been hand picked, but if you complicate her life, you will be stamped "no return."

Warning label: Begins to include you less and less in her plans. Moves noticeably toward independence.

Emotionally Defensive. An ED woman is kin to an Emotionally Unavailable man. She's had a tough time with love, is suspicious of men, and isn't going to readily let you in to toy with her emotions. Identifying characteristics: likely to hold out on sex, watches you carefully, puts you through tests, won't take any bull from you, and doesn't reveal herself carelessly or quickly. Like her male counterpart, she will eventually return to love. If you don't cheat or disappoint her, you stand a chance.

Warning label: Subtly enters a protective mode, goes from warm to cold, begins to steadily distance herself from you.

Romantic Idealists. RIs flit from one man to another pursuing love and fulfilling their romantic fantasies often at other people's expense. Identifying characteristics: full of romantic surprises, thrive on romantic pleasures, form strong physical attractions, and may refrain from sexual intercourse. Unless you like fairy tales, having a liaison with a Romantic Idealist could prove risky.

Warning label: Something's up when the candles are blown out and the lights go up.

Clumsy Novices. These women are the identical counterparts to Awkward Players but with less of a propensity to turn into a seductress or male-type player. Once these ladies get their feet wet, however, they become a little more selective in who they spend their affections on. (See Awkward Players under male types for details.)

Warning label: A drop in the number of smiling responses, endearing pats, or affectionate quick kisses.

Scouts. Scouts are looking for their lifetime mates and have their love maps out. Scouting styles vary from coy and undercover to aggressive and up-front. Identifying characteristics: make verbal expressions in favor of marriage, sex is not their number one bag, have an agenda, and don't waste time on frivolous romantic hookups.

Warning label: Refuse future date, don't make time for you, fail to give further encouragement.

In conclusion, a note of caution to all men and women who attempt to use typecasts: There is room for error. Remain open-minded, use all clues or signals, and above all, try to be honest and extract the same from each and every love interest.

The Least You Need to Know

➤ If you didn't see it coming, you didn't have your eyes open and your radar on.

➤ In love's beginning and ending, reading between the lines is a required course.

➤ The bedroom offers a multitude of clues about the well-being of your relationship.

➤ Get a handle on your love's romantic personality first and you won't find yourself heading down a blind alley second.

Chapter 10

Is There Room for Honesty?

In This Chapter

➤ Discovering if he/she is lying to you

➤ Does everyone lie in romantic relationships?

➤ Can you break up without lying?

➤ Learning how to detect lies and assess your love interest's potential for honesty

---

Lying is part of our everyday lives. According to surveys, 93 percent of Americans lie on a regular basis. All of us are tempted now and then to use the little white lie, even the lie that conveniently gets us off the hook in a tight situation. Just put someone under duress, offer the proper incentive, and they'll cave into lies, studies show.

We have already provided ample evidence in Chapter 8, "Gender Differences," that both sexes lie when breaking up with a romantic partner. What we now have to address is whether or not there is room for honesty when severing a relationship. Fortunately there is in-depth research that will help shed light on the issue.

Can honesty and breaking up be compatible partners? Yes and no!

Lies Are Part and Parcel of Relationships

There is a pattern of lying that apparently pops up in most new relationships. A study conducted among college students revealed that 85 percent lied in a romantic relationship about past loves or recent indiscretions.

The so-called "big lies" we spout are directed toward a partner in an intimate relationship, researchers say. These lies pertain to a violation of deep trust.

In marriage relationships, studies show that husbands and wives lie to each other in approximately 10 percent of their major discussions. And a large sampling of individuals from a nationwide survey revealed that one-third of the spouses who have sex outside of marriage lie about it.

Bits and Pieces

Psychotherapist Vesta Callender asserts that women plot their lies more carefully than men. They look at a lie and determine the course it will take from beginning to end as well as what might result from it. Men, Callender asserts, are more likely to lie without forethought to escape a momentary problem.

Stop Lying to Yourself

Before anyone is going to lay off lying in their personal relationships, and certainly before anyone can detect the lies being whispered to them, they must stop lying to themselves.

A Man's Directive. Gentlemen, the act of lying to save someone's feelings is not the selfless act you think it is. You lie, in part, because you don't want to face the consequences, it keeps you in control, and circumvents an honest verbal exchange that may put you at a disadvantage. But whether you realize it or not, you are creating more stress and using more energy to cover up than tell the truth. Look toward Washington, D.C. if you need a vivid example.

Researcher Dory Hollander believes that men don't like admitting uncertainty and have more difficulty dealing with shades of gray than do women. Consequently, they are more apt to lie about their feelings and less apt to say things like "I don't know if I love you. I don't know what I am feeling."

A Woman's Directive. Ladies, stop the charade. Stop believing men's untruths when deep down you know they are lies. You are just fibbing to yourself. There is

Blow the Whistle

Ladies, be on alert. The research is in. Men will lie to attract you in the beginning of a relationship. They may fudge on their income or occupational level and add untrue superlatives about your appearance. These same guys will also lie their way out of your arms.

supposition that your subconscious is pointing you in that direction. Why? Because even though you are a competent, liberated female, you operate under the out-dated notion that your value as a woman is dependent upon being in a relationship.

Who Makes the Most Honest Partner?

Whether or not an individual lies is a reflection of his basic character. However, it is possible for those who are basically honest to wall off a section of their conscience and lie in romantic situations.

Harry has earned the reputation as an honorable young man among his peers and business colleagues. Nonetheless, he admits that although telling lies is out of character, he has used them to wiggle out of relationship hot spots. These were, more or less, pragmatic lies that dealt specifically with the situation at hand.

Still, the man or woman who is basically honest in all other aspects of his or her life will more often than not be truthful with a person of the opposite sex.

Love Lingo

A **lie** is a statement made with the sole intention to deceive and in most instances reflects only the feelings and consequences important to the liar. A lie, therefore, is a self-centered defense mechanism that fails to demonstrate empathy for the receiver.

Bits and Pieces

Those individuals who score high on a scale of social responsibility and have close friend-ships with members of the same sex are least likely to lie.

There are a number of clues to spot the least honest partners:

1. If a man or woman has a pattern of lying, he or she will most likely lie when interacting with a romantic partner.

2. Age may also provide some insight. There are indications that men under 30 are more apt than older men to be cocky game-players who brag about lying in order to end a relationship. Middle-aged men, however, lie more to prevent themselves from getting trapped into a relationship. They view lying as preemptive stroke of self-defense.

3. It has been documented that individuals who are basically manipulative, concerned with personal impressions, or socially extroverted resort more often to lying.

Bits and Pieces

Professionals who study individuals' responses claim it is hard to distinguish when someone is telling a lie, particularly if one is comfortable with the fib. It is possible under these conditions to fool the lie detector, invented around 1921.

Lie Detecting

The guy you have been sleeping with for a month suddenly rolls over and tells you he has a headache. Your fiancé says he forgot to pick up your engagement ring. Your romantic partner doesn't show up for dinner at your folk's house. She claims she got lost. How are you supposed to know if these are legitimate excuses or if your relationship is on the downslide and your friend is engineering a split?

Indications that someone may be lying to you include:

➤ Scratching, fidgeting, blinking eyes, or signs of other nervous habits

➤ Infrequent employment of the word "I" in discussions

➤ Failure to use words like "hurt," "angry," "understand," "realize," "but," and "without"

➤ Noticeably long pauses between expression of thoughts

➤ Does not look you straight in the eyes

➤ Inconsistencies in the repetition of a story

➤ Discrepancies between what he/she says and does

➤ Introduction of evasive lines that redirect an inquiry: "It depends on how you look at it." "Well, it's not so simple as yes or no." "Where is this coming from?" "Why would you ask me something like that?" "What is your point exactly?" "Where did you hear that?" From *Never Be Lied to Again*, David J. Lieberman, Ph.D. (St. Martin's Press, 1998).

Heart to Heart

There is a consensus among relationship experts that women encourage men's lies and make it easy for them to utter untruths. Here's how: Men rationalize that because women don't want to hear or acknowledge the truth, it is okay to lie to them.

Keep these tips in the back of your mind. Take them out and apply them to a situation or conversation in which you think someone may be lying.

Frequent Lies Men Tell Women

Test out what you have learned thus far. When you hear a line like those that follow, note the gentleman's delivery. You'll have a much better indication if he's just using one of those frequent lies guys tell gals or if he's spouting the truth.

➤ "I'll call you."

➤ "I love you."

➤ "I've never felt this way about anyone else."

➤ "My wife and I haven't had sex in years."

➤ "We'll get married *as soon as I...*"

➤ "No, I don't think your thighs (stomach, breasts, hips...) are too big."

➤ "Believe me, my wife and I live very separate lives."

➤ "You just have to believe me when I tell you nothing's wrong."

From *101 Lies Men Tell Women and Why Women Believe Them*, Dory Hollander, Ph.D. (HarperPerennial, 1997).

Why are these considered frequent lies that men tell women? Because all too many guys use them and mean something very different than the words alone would indicate.

An Exercise in Lie Detection

Okay, so what do you do with all this info? Why, use it, of course! This exercise in lie detection is one to keep handy. The questions have been designed to reveal a great deal about one's character and whether or not they are *likely* to lie in matters of the heart. Do keep in mind that love relationships can push the most honest guy or gal into a lie.

Heart to Heart

The consensus of opinion among relationship counselors is that a good relationship is founded upon honesty.

Part 1

Evaluate His/Her Character	Answers 1 (least) to 5 (most)
1. Have you caught him/her lying to family members or friends?	_____
2. Is he/she respected by their coworkers?	_____
3. Does he/she fulfill their promises?	_____
4. Does he/she cheat at games they play?	_____

continues

continued

Evaluate His/Her Character	Answers 1 (least) to 5 (most)
5. Do they make false excuses to a host or hostess about why they have to leave the party early?	_____
6. Is this person a good Samaritan?	_____
7. Does this person exhibit social concern and responsibility?	_____
8. Is this person attentive to older members of their family?	_____
9. Does he/she pay off friendly bets?	_____
10. Does he/she pay back borrowed money in a timely, agreeable fashion?	_____
11. Is he/she concerned with paying bills on time?	_____
12. If he/she runs into another car in a parking lot and causes damage, would he/she notify the other car owner?	_____
Total	_____

Character scale:

60 points = A person of impeccable character who is unlikely to lie

50 points = A person of high character who normally does not lie but may in a jam, then feel guilty about it

40 points = A person of moderate character who probably won't have any problem lying in a love relationship

30 points = Either you've made a mistake, or this person has a defective character and can lie without batting an eye

Part 2

Record suspicious behavior you think indicates lying:

_____

_____

_____

_____

Record possible lies:

_____

_____

_____

_____

Look for and list evidence to corroborate possible lies:

_____

_____

_____

_____

Lies with corroborating evidence:

_____

_____

_____

_____

Evaluate the seriousness of any lies listed above:

_____

_____

_____

_____

The handwriting is on the page! Review it with complete honesty.

Words That May Turn You into a Liar

Premature usage of the following words in a romantic relationship could make a liar out of you later:

Forever	Future	Always
Promise	Never	Love
Eternity	Vow	Marriage

Now that you are aware of the potency of these words, there is no excuse to use them out of turn.

Degrees of Breakup Honesty

Although we have pulled the plug on lying and thrown darts at your love interest's character, the question remains: Can honesty and breaking up be compatible partners?

The answer is, to a degree, yes. Lies are unacceptable; omission of hurtful truths are not. Examine the suggestions below:

Unacceptable Breakup Lines	Acceptable Breakup Lines
You are terrible in bed.	We aren't sexually compatible.
You don't physically appeal to me.	There just isn't that chemistry.
I find so much body hair disgusting.	We don't share the same intellectual interests.
You aren't pretty.	
You aren't smart enough for me.	I don't think we have what it takes together to be good lifetime partners.
You aren't the kind of person I would marry.	
Yes, I said I loved you, but then I realized you weren't that cute, fun, honorable, or trustworthy person I thought you were.	I love you but I am not in love with you. There are too many differences in the way we look at things to make this work.
I need time to think.	
	I really feel this relationship is not going to evolve into anything serious, and I want time to meet other people.

Get the drift?

Lies or radical honesty that wound someone deeply serve no one. Nor does dishonest altruism. I prefer "gentle honesty." So should you. This stroke of honesty will lessen your guilt if you bow out, bode well on your character, and possibly ease disappointment on the other side.

The Least You Need to Know

➤ The inability to deal with delicate love problems often encourages men and women to seek the cover of lies.

➤ Acknowledging that lying is apparent in many romantic relationships does not give one license to avoid honesty.

➤ Honesty is to be expected from oneself and others.

➤ It is best to come clean and ask your love interest to do the same.

➤ Never, absolutely never, allow yourself to be blinded by lies. Prepare yourself to look for and deal with the truth.

➤ Men lie more easily, more often, and with more devastating consequences than do women in a romantic situation.

Chapter 11

Unintentional Precipitators of Breakups

In This Chapter

➤ Who's rejecting whom

➤ Did you scare him/her away?

➤ How to avoid unintentional breakups

➤ Why Johnny and Jane keep missing the boat

Johnny broke up with Jane. Jane thought they were enjoying getting to know one another. She thought there was some real potential for romance. She thought she was playing it smart. Jane wasn't aware that something *she* did caused Johnny to split prematurely.

Get ready to familiarize yourself with the most common accidental causes of breakups. If there is any future breaking up to do, you want to be the one to do it deliberately and with forethought.

Careful reading of this chapter followed by honest soul-searching will put you more in charge of your romantic destiny.

A Self-Fulfilling Prophecy

If you think a love interest will dump you, he/she might very well fulfill your prophecy. Don't think this happens because you have great insight and, therefore, have accurately predicted Johnny or Jane's behavior. Research proves that in numerous instances, an individual actually sets up the conditions for a breakup. If you expect another person to reject rather than accept you, evidence shows your behavior will encourage that very outcome.

This well may be you they are talking about, especially if you happen to be one of those people who:

➤ Overreact to rejection

➤ Are anxious about the possibility of being rejected

➤ Have high rejection expectations

➤ Are ready to accept rejection

Heart to Heart

If you are sensitive to rejection, the problem could stem all the way back to infancy. Babies sense whether or not they are loved. Those who are not develop less self-worth and feel rejection even when it is not present. It may, therefore, be beneficial to find someone to help you discover the roots of your rejection sensitivity and work to become a self-confident individual.

The stats prove that if you have a high sensitivity to rejection, expect to break up more often than those who don't—particularly if you are a women. Social scientists conjecture that men who are rejection-sensitive may not allow themselves to be put in a questionable position and, consequently, won't begin a flirtation.

The quiz in Appendix B, "Are You Primed for Rejection? Quiz," will help to establish if you set yourself for rejection. Be sure to test yourself. For more information on the subject, Chapter 20, "The Emotional Aftermath of Breaking Up," deals with rejection's aftermath and Chapter 23, "Blossom from Victim to Victor," with improving your self-worth.

Individuals with low self-esteem very often think they will automatically be rejected.

According to those who have scrutinized the self-fulfilling prophecy, here's how it could work.

Bits and Pieces

A 1996 study of college students revealed that those individuals who entered a new romantic relationship and expected rejection felt their partner's ambiguous behavior was an intentional maneuver to be cold and distant.

Johnny and Jane have a small argument. Let's say, rejection-sensitive Jane was late getting ready for their date. The movie Johnny wanted to see was sold out by the time they got to the theater. Jane misinterprets his quiet disappointment as a sign that he is rejecting her. Like many people who think that rejection is inevitable, Jane becomes frustrated, angry, and hostile. Her behavior adds a sour note to Johnny's disappointment and reduces the pleasure either of them gets out of the evening. If the scene is repeated too many times, the relationship isn't likely to be satisfying to Johnny who then tells himself "I want outa' here!"

Too Much Need, Too Little Caring

This discovery by researchers may hit home. In the infatuation and passionate stages of love's beginning, it is natural to be concerned with one's own needs. How you feel, what makes you happy, if your attraction is reciprocated, if your hopes or fears will be realized, and whether you achieve sexual satisfaction is first and foremost in your mind. Your partner's needs at this early stage of romance are secondary. If this preoccupation with oneself continues, however, the relationship will not grow the way you hoped it might.

Unless partners switch focus from themselves and their personal needs to caring for and fulfilling the other person's needs, *intimacy* surely won't develop. Without this necessary ingredient, love will die on the vine.

Johnny met Jane, who awakened his libido and raced his heart. He set about to sell himself to her and spoke endlessly about his achievements. He forgot to ask about Jane's. He took her to all his favorite places but had no idea what she liked. He was so preoccupied with himself he failed to stop and focus on Jane. Although there was enough chemistry to land them both in bed and make Johnny blissfully happy, Jane broke it off shortly thereafter. Without the opportunity to tell her story, reveal a thing about herself, have her needs even slightly met, or feel close with Johnny, the relationship was flat and unsatisfying.

Forcing the Issue

You may not think you are pressing for too much too soon but your partner may. People who force the issue prematurely bring up words like "commitment," "relationship," or "marriage." They ask, "Where is this relationship going?" before love has had ample time to take hold. Then they employ psychobabble to explain away their love interest's indecision or unwillingness to commit.

This time Jane fell for Johnny, who had been divorced and subsequently engaged. They dated for several months, took two or three vacations together, and then one night in bed, Jane told Johnny she was looking for a relationship that would evolve into marriage.

Love Lingo

According to psychologists, **intimacy** is the core of a love relationship. To be intimate means interacting in a way that enables two people to get to know each other and reveal things about themselves they normally would not disclose to others. The result is a closeness that perpetuates and deepens love. Without intimacy, there can be no mutual love.

Love Lingo

The pattern to hesitate and avoid telling someone you are not romantically interested or cannot reciprocate their love was dubbed the **mum affect** by psychologists in 1975. It reflects an individual's wish to remain silent and avoid inflicting pain while struggling to give someone bad news.

The mere mention of marriage scared him away. Within days, Johnny, who was far from ready to make a pledge of undying love, started using breakup lines like "There is something missing in our relationship. I can't put my finger on it. But something is definitely missing."

His inability to explain himself more fully exasperated Jane. She responded by escalating the situation and issuing an ultimatum just the way Johnnys know Janes will once they have used the "C," "R," or "M" words: "Decide where this is going. If it's nowhere, I don't want to see you anymore," she said.

The words were spoken, and when Johnny would not come up with a definitive answer, Jane had no option but to see her threat through. Her take on the whole thing was, "Johnny has problems with relationships. Unless he gets help and finds the basis of his hang-up, he'll never be healthy enough to have a relationship."

Playing Your Sexual Cards Poorly

No one wants to know your complete sexual history unless it pertains to your present state of health. Spill too much and your relationship may be in jeopardy. If your partner feels like he/she is one among a hundred lovers, there won't be any reason to feel flattered by your pursuit. Men and women want to think they are your one and only—even when they are fully aware that isn't a possibility.

Heart to Heart

No one is moralizing here or promoting chastity until the right partner comes along. Having sex is and will remain your personal choice. The point is, don't flaunt your past lovers or parade them in full view of a new love interest. Use your experience to make sex pleasurable, not to scare anyone away by publicizing your practiced expertise.

Men especially interpret a woman's sexual aggressiveness either as a sign that she has done this too many times before or that she is trying to trap him into an intimate relationship.

Johnny and Jane were fixed up by friends who said complimentary things about both of them. They went out a few times and at the end of the third evening together, Johnny was certain Jane wanted to spend the night. She made herself right at home, slipped provocatively out of her jeans, and went for his zipper.

The next morning he called his friend and whispered into the phone, "Thanks a lot. It was a hoot having a dominant sexual female for a change, but I don't see anything else happening here. If I started to care about her, it would bother me thinking that she had slept around quite a bit. I know I am not her first, but I sure hope I wasn't her 31st either."

Lying to Your Man

A man's reaction to a woman's lie is the opposite of hers. (Chapter 10, "Is There Room for Honesty?" discusses women's response to lying.) According to Dr. Dory Hollander's observations, men will either challenge the female liar, find her antics amusing and even sexy, or end the relationship. If a lie threatens or damages his power and dominance, he may slough off the untruth by leaving the relationship. In his mind this gives him control over the situation and restores his dominance.

While visiting her parents in her home town, Jane bumped into her old boyfriend. They met up with some mutual friends and spent a night reminiscing at a popular, crowded bar.

The next night they went to a movie together. The third night he held her hand in a movie, and the fourth night she found herself in his arms.

When Johnny picked her up at the airport he asked her how her week went. She said fine. When he inquired whether she had gone out with friends, she mentioned her girlfriends by name and said they were the only old friends she saw. Not long after, Johnny overheard Jane giving someone a more accurate description of her social life at home. He shrunk under the weight of the discovery. The fact that she lied to him was of more serious consequence than her innocent indiscretion. Within a week, he confronted Jane and told her he wasn't interested in a woman who lied to him. No matter how she protested that it was an insignificant leap into the past, Johnny was not about to give her a second chance. No one lies to Johnny and gets away with it!

Dressing Up in Desperate Clothing

A significant number of men will assume that women are desperate for a partner and run the other way after a few dates if you:

➤ Give any sign of needing someone to rescue you from financial uncertainty

➤ Are over 30 and never married

➤ Aren't holding down a lucrative job

➤ Have children but don't get sizable childcare payments

➤ Never offer to pay for a vacation or buy him a gift

➤ Complain about your living expenses

Johnny met Jane at a church mixer for singles. They had an interesting conversation, discovered several mutual interests, and found one another attractive. Without revealing anything more about themselves, they made a date for later in the week. Jane was uncomfortable exposing her two children to her dates and cautiously suggested she meet Johnny at the restaurant he chose for dinner. It wasn't until they had gone out for nearly a month that Jane felt she knew Johnny well enough to allow him to pick her up at home. He was eager to meet the kids Jane had casually mentioned, but, wisely until this point, did not discuss in detail.

Once she decided she could trust Johnny, she not only gave him access to her home but to her troubles. That's where she went wrong.

She saw no reason not to fill him full of her woes, her ex-husband's noncompliance of child support, and the fact that she looked forward to the time when a man would want to share her childrearing responsibilities.

"Hit the road Jack," Johnny told himself. He had the distinct impression that any man could pitch hit as Jane's knight in shining armor. He, however, wanted a woman who proved she loved him and only him. Anyone in her dire circumstances would have had a tough time convincing him they were capable of such pure love.

Bits and Pieces

A survey of 3,407 men between the ages of 18 and 55 showed that second to a woman's beauty, men were interested in her income. Men these days aren't looking for someone who will add pressure to their lives or can't pull their own weight.

Mate Smothering

Love is a human need. Studies show that the most independent among us seek it, thrive on it, and find happiness in it. On the other hand, dependent individuals have been shown to need it to survive. Inadequacies in their personality promote an unhealthy journey into love. They form excessive, fixated attachments that suffocate their lovers. They depend upon these individuals to protect them against the pain and distress their inadequacies cause them. Unfortunately, these liabilities turn off prospective long-term love interests.

Love Lingo

The actor John Barrymore put it this way: "Love is the delightful interval between meeting a beautiful girl and discovering that she looks like a haddock."

Put Johnny and Jane into whichever role suits your fancy. The story works either way.

Johnny was a great-looking, shy, underachiever, devoid of self-confidence who, nonetheless, caught every woman's eye. Jane was the most recent woman to give him a nod. He was flattered by the attention of this self-sufficient, successful business-woman. When he was with her, his chest inflated with pride. He wanted her constantly by his side. Her presence and reassurance was essential to his well-being.

Jane, however, had a busy schedule and found Johnny's needs cumbersome and tiring. He was leaning on her too much, pressing her into verifying her attraction too often and expressed too much anxiety when they were apart. In order to breathe in sufficient fresh air she saw no other option than to separate herself from him.

> ## The Least You Need to Know
>
> ➤ Rejection can be a self-fulfilling prophecy.
>
> ➤ Your needs can turn on and turn off potential love partners. It's best to get them in check.
>
> ➤ Your sexual behavior reveals volumes of information to your love interest. Be careful what you write.

Part 3
Complex Breakups Beyond the Dating Game

All breakups have much in common. A disappointing love affair and a broken heart are painful for everyone. However, there are unique circumstances that the individual who is engaged, living together, or married should consider when anticipating the end of their relationship.

These are spelled out succinctly for you in the next four chapters. Make no mistake, however. The entire book applies to you. Each and every discussion will benefit you in some way—before, after, and during your breakup.

Chapter 12

Stopping Short of the Aisle

In This Chapter

➤ Breaking an engagement is more common than you think

➤ What prevents couples from saying "I do"

➤ When to hang up the wedding dress

➤ Canceled wedding etiquette

Susie and Sam just called off the wedding. Everyone is wondering what could have possibly gone wrong. There are conjectures and whispers galore behind Susie's and Sam's backs. Undoubtedly, they are both embarrassed about cutting out days before they were to exchange vows. Their families give them those pained, consoling looks and pats on the hand. The mother of the bride is rattled to the core. She has no idea what to do and keeps asking Susie if it isn't just a case of the normal premarital jitters.

If you are a Susie or a Sam, are close to becoming one, or have a friend in their predicament, you can benefit from a guiding light. This chapter gives it to you.

Nearly 100,000 wedding plans land in the dumpster each year. And why not get cold feet? Marriage is serious, challenging business. Anthropologist Margaret Mead claimed that modern marriages based on love and attaining happiness are the most difficult form of relationships humans have tried yet. There are bound to be some mistakes in the selection of a mate. Better to break up the wedding now than employ a divorce lawyer later!

Wedding Busters

We can pinpoint some of the surprises, preplanning stresses, and engagement fall-outs that wreak havoc on love. Those to watch out for are sticky prenuptial agreements, reality's magnifying glass, and villainous turncoats.

Bits and Pieces

The real purpose of a prenuptial agreement is to protect one partner's wealth and prevent an expensive law suit in the event the marriage doesn't work. Lawyers charge anywhere from $1,000 to $15,000 for drawing up the contract. Some individuals think this is a practical, offensive maneuver with the divorce rate in the United States hovering around 50 percent. Others think the prenup demonstrates a lack of confidence in the union. Some of these agreements are designed to become null and void after a specified period of matrimony.

Prenup Disasters

Prenuptial agreements are hardly a new concept. The *ketuba*, a Hebrew wedding agreement that stated terms of marital responsibility in the event of a death or divorce, dates back to the first century. Instead of spelling out protective provisions for the bride, the complicated prenup in vogue these days has the potential to create doubt, disillusionment, disappointment, and disruption in wedding plans.

Heart to Heart

The 2,000-year-old tradition of lifting the bridal veil off the woman's face symbolically represents moving into a new stage of life. If you aren't up to the adventure, keep the curtain closed and hightail it out of there.

Until recently, prenup contracts were primarily an instrument used by older couples or those entering into a second marriage. Younger brides and grooms had usually not acquired enough wealth to make a formal agreement worthwhile. However, where family fortunes and businesses are involved, age does not seem to be a factor.

Prenups appear to cause disaster when:

➤ They are unexpectedly sprung on a partner.

➤ They try to control a partner through legal arrangements.

➤ They are lop-sided in favor of either the bride or groom.

➤ They are long, complicated, and cold-hearted.

➤ They destroy trust and the integrity of the union.

I interviewed a couple in their early 30s and witnessed first-hand the mutual excitement over their upcoming marriage. A new house was in the works, loving words were exchanged, and elaborate wedding plans were in place. The scene was idyllic until Fred handed Karen a stack of papers.

Karen was expecting the prenup and said she had no problem signing one because of Fred's interest in the lucrative family business. But what Fred handed over to her was more than she bargained for. After reading the contract that stipulated she could not make any claim on the family business, would have to move out of her home, and relinquish residential custody of any children in the event of a divorce, she was horrified and insulted. The agreement didn't sound anything like Fred but a lot like his family and their legal counsel.

Fred said he would have another draft drawn up. The second version was hardly an improvement. Karen realized Fred's family, not Fred, was calling the shots. She issued an ultimatum: If he couldn't stand up for her and treat her with the respect and consideration she deserved, even if that meant giving up the family fortune, the wedding was off.

Mom and Pop's money proved too much of a temptation. Fred and Karen never made the walk down the aisle. She hasn't spoken to him since.

Heart to Heart

Be careful how you word your prenup. Problems arise long term if either partner feels they are living on the edge of a gang plank, harbor resentment, or lose trust in one another. Whoever has less money feels at a disadvantage, and if personal self-worth doesn't match his or her money, the marriage will probably self-destruct.

Engagement Blues

The period of engagement can serve a worthwhile purpose, although its importance may be usurped by those couples who have been living together. Engagements allow for time to plan the wedding, save to pay for it, develop a marital mindset, and to make adjustments to each other's family. Lengthy engagements may also forestall the wedding date indefinitely. Nonetheless, the average duration of engagements has lengthened since 1990 from 11 months to 13 months.

During those 13 months, premarital bliss may fizzle because of:

➤ Issues that were previously swept under the rug that must now be addressed

➤ Discrepancies in the desire for children

➤ Differences in religion that come to the forefront because of the wedding ceremony or the discussion of childrearing

115

➤ A problematic division of financial and household responsibilities

➤ Impasses with the in-laws

➤ Problems with previous spouses and children

Bits and Pieces

Today, approximately one quarter of all weddings are paid for by the bride and groom as opposed to the traditional financing by the bride's family.

If any of these premarital blues cause the bliss to fizzle, take time out to settle each and every one of these problems that could cause critical problems within the marriage relationship later. And if any of these critical problems seems irreconcilable, now is the time to make a preemptive strike. Break up and call it quits! Just because you are engaged doesn't mean you have to take that final walk down the aisle. You can turn back anytime and feel confident you are making the right decision—as long as you have used all of the forethought due a serious relationship.

Take a look at Tina and Todd:

Todd and Tina were mature adults with very different backgrounds and outlooks who, nonetheless, fell in love. Tina was sociable; Todd was a loner. Tina was serious but fun-loving; Todd was somber. Tina practiced Judaism; Todd was anti-organized religion. Nonetheless, the five years they had spent together as serious and committed partners were satisfying. Neither had any compunction against maintaining independent social lives and lifestyles. When they decided to wed, began combining resources, making future plans, and trying to act like a Mr. and Mrs., inevitable disagreements erupted. The final gauntlet was thrown over pork tenderloin—to be or not to be served at the wedding dinner. Todd and Tina stopped short of the aisle when neither would compromise their position.

Tina made the right decision. She knew the distance between she and Todd was too great to provide everlasting happiness and love. Her positive mindset and enthusiasm for life directed her right into the path of Timothy, who she married a few months later after a brief dating relationship. This time Tina could walk down the aisle without any reservations.

Villains in Princely Fashion

In our highly mobile society, we don't always fall in love with someone we grew up with and whose family has known our family for generations. Anyone who falls blindly in love these days is subject to a very unfairy-tale-like ending.

You may not know anyone who got engaged to a villain or villainess camouflaged in fancy clothing, but it happens all the time. The plots thicken although the details vary. Fortuitous men and women break off the engagement before they incur too much damage. The less fortunate may be on their way to the cleaners.

That's why hiring a private eye or running a police check isn't all that bad of an idea. It's done repeatedly in business and employment circles. And you aren't only sitting across the desk from the gal or guy you meet, fall in love with, and propose to marry.

You may already be sharing the same bed and bath before you have any inkling that he/she is hiding out from an ex-spouse, avoiding child support payments, has a pattern of loving and leaving, is adept at conning you out of your savings, has wives in three other states, or falls back on abusive habits.

A situation that could make anyone's hair curl was reported in the press. A 59-year-old woman became engaged to a wealthy, well-educated, three-time divorced man who needed a kidney transplant within months. The kidney was provided by her brother, no less. Before he had a chance to recuperate outside the hospital, he postponed the wedding and soon thereafter broke it off altogether to marry someone younger.

It wouldn't have taken an experienced private eye to tell this gal that his string of wives ought to tell her something about his character.

Bits and Pieces

In the nineteenth century, law suits against disappointed lovers who were seduced and talked into sex by men were plentiful. However, by the 1930s these breach-of-promise and seduction suits were waning. Sixteen states forbade such suits by 1945, and others revised laws so that only a small amount of claims were filed. Today there is a small group of female legal professionals who think it is time to re-institute some sort of interventionist law that would protect women in these circumstances.

The Critical Temperature of Cold Feet

A more practical exercise is to determine what naturally constitutes cold feet and is of little consequence as opposed to what establishes unnatural causes and indicates a wise, preemptive breakup.

Natural causes of cold feet:

➤ Concerns about assuming the role of a couple

➤ Trepidation over loss of freedom and independence

➤ Flashes of doubt about marital readiness

➤ Worry over financial responsibilities

➤ Fear of marking an entry into adulthood with the promise of a spouse and the potential burdens of mortgage and kids

Unnatural causes of cold feet:

➤ A doubt of feelings of love for one's prospective mate

➤ A loss of trust

➤ Thoughts about the cost of an eventual divorce

➤ Fear over spending a lifetime with this person

➤ Suspicion of deceit

➤ Excessive family control

➤ Unexpected, last-minute, and troubling revelations about one's past life, love, or debts

➤ A loss of excitement and vision of future happiness together

The Graceful Way Out

It is never too late to call off an engagement. One woman remembers with regret her father saying that up to the last minute she could and should cancel the wedding. What seemed like an insurmountable, awkward task at the time resulted in several unhappy years that cost her more in time, money, and pain later.

Two reports, one about a mother of the bride and another about the bride herself, demonstrate how graceful a way out can be. A quick-thinking and very understanding mom took what could have been a financial and family fiasco and turned it around. There was no way to retrieve costly deposits on the caterer, band, or florist, so she sent out a note to her guests that the wedding was canceled but the party was still on.

The publicity surrounding a young woman left waiting at the altar while her groom went flying back home could have been full of pity. Instead it focused on the bride's incredible show of fortitude. In typical show-biz fashion "the reception went on," and this gal danced and partied at what was to be her posh wedding celebration.

Maintain an Enviable Decorum

Avoid public displays of self-pity, and don't give your audience more negative fodder for later gossip. Disappointment alongside a show of courage and grace is equivalent to a royal's behavior.

A trick to appear poised, charmed, and enviably in control is to concentrate on your groomsmen, bridesmaids, and anyone else who has been inconvenienced or incurred costs because of your change of plans. This exercise will momentarily take your mind off of your broken heart and help to maintain your composure until you are able to escape into the private corners of your home to grieve.

Bits and Pieces

One week before their wedding ceremony, socialite and fashion designer Carolina Herrera refused to sign the prenup proposed by her fiancé, wealthy hotel owner Ian Schraeger. The standoff continued; the groom did not make sufficient changes, and the bride, dressed in her gown, refused to sign. Sources say she gracefully traded in her wedding dress for a party ensemble and ate lunch with guests who had come to witness her walk down the aisle.

Wedding Breakup Planner

To help you undo all of the detailed plans you so carefully and meticulously made, follow this wedding breakup planner.

Wedding Breakup Planner

Task	Date Completed
1. Notify bridesmaids; offer to pay for dresses.	_____
2. Notify groomsmen; offer to pay deposit on tux.	_____
3. Cancel clergy; write thank-you note for holding the date.	_____
4. Cancel florist; negotiate cancellation policy; try to get credit for future event.	_____
5. Cancel reception hall.	_____
6. Cancel hotel for out-of-town guests.	_____
7. Cancel all other items ordered.	_____
8. Make ledger for credits due.	_____

continues

Wedding Breakup Planner (continued)

Task	Date Completed
9. Notify guests; you do not owe them a full explanation as to why the wedding is off.	_____
10. Return gifts without a personal inscription or monogram; include a thank-you note.	_____
11. Cancel honeymoon plans, unless you want to take a friend.	_____
12. Write thank-you notes for monogrammed or personalized gifts.	_____
13. Return family heirlooms; the ring is not included in this if it was purchased for you. In this case the bride decides what to do. (My suggestion if you keep it is to reset it in a less-sentimental bracelet or necklace.)	_____

Completing the tasks on your wedding breakup planner will keep you busy. Once those chores are checked off, here are a few tips on how to maintain the faith in future romance:

➤ If you can't return the dress, tuck it away for future use.

➤ Develop a sense of humor.

➤ Remember coupling is natural.

➤ Learn from experience.

➤ Chuck the embarrassment.

➤ Give love another chance.

Now move forward. You have averted a major disaster. Marvel at your own ability to break up and begin the survival process.

The Least You Need to Know

➤ Broken engagements are more common than you think.

➤ Calling off the wedding is nothing to be ashamed of.

➤ It is better to stop short of the aisle and face temporary discomfort than a lifetime of regret.

➤ In the light of disappointment, behave in a manner you won't show remorse for in the dark.

Chapter 13

When Live-in Lovers Quit Loving

> ### In This Chapter
>
> ➤ Why living together is a poor foundation for a lasting relationship
>
> ➤ The perils of breaking off a live-in relationship
>
> ➤ When all the evidence points to breaking up
>
> ➤ How to get out with the least amount of pain and damage

The number of unmarried, heterosexual couples who are living together has increased seven-fold since 1970. The larger number does not mean that living together has become an unproblematic panacea. In fact, far too many couples are not finding the happiness they expected. It is common for men and women of all ages who were full of love and hope to experience a breakup shortly after moving in together.

Why? All too often live-in lovers have not given enough thought to moving in or the consequences of wanting to move out.

Unfortunately, the unique set of circumstances surrounding living together make it one of the most difficult relationships to break off. There are ways, however, to minimize the trauma and the damage.

The Nature of Live-in Love

The reasons couples generally move in together provide a poor foundation for a lasting relationship. Jimmy and Jane most often decide to share a home because:

> ➤ He/she sleeps over most nights anyway.
>
> ➤ Splitting rent and household expenses is more economical and raises the potential for a better standard of living.

➤ Sex is more convenient.

➤ He/she likes the companionship.

➤ She thinks it will lead to marriage.

➤ He thinks he can put off getting married.

➤ They want to test their compatibility.

➤ He wants the benefit of a wife but not the legal commitment.

These certainly aren't good enough reasons to commit oneself to an exclusive live-in partner. Unfortunately and all too often, couples don't realize this until they have already set up housekeeping.

Bits and Pieces

The best of live-in love is among those men and women who have already established a committed relationship, share the same agenda, are engaged with a wedding date set, are divorced and equally financially well off, or are independent and do not believe in the institution of marriage.

The Reality of Live-in Love

It may take time, months, and for some even years, but eventually reality sets in. A vast number of live-in lovers realize that moving in together did not meet their original goals or expectations. Here's what they found instead:

➤ Living together does not turn out to be the road to matrimony women think it will be. At least 40 percent of partners never walk down the aisle together.

➤ Couples who live together may outwardly resemble other families but lack equal commitment and security.

➤ Extended family members and friends do not view live-in couples in the same category as married couples.

➤ Live-in couples appear to be equitable in superficial things like housekeeping but do not equally divide childrearing responsibilities. Women bear the brunt of this task.

➤ Live-in lovers do not have the same expectations of one another that they would of a spouse.

➤ Women do not find a live-in relationship as satisfying as men and express a loss of self-esteem and regret when it is unsuccessful. A majority say they would never live with someone again.

➤ Living together is not a compatibility tester. Those who live together have a higher divorce rate than couples who have not cohabited.

➤ Rarely is living together the monogamous sexual arrangement it was thought to be.

➤ Living together does not provide the legal protection of a marriage relationship.

➤ Significant numbers of individuals who have experienced both divorce and separation from a live-in lover say it is more difficult to break off the latter.

Love Lingo

What's the new up-to-the-minute name for live-in lover, cohabitor, and significant other? According to the U.S. Census Bureau, it is **spouse equivalent.**

At the end of this tarnished rainbow is often a blackened pot of gold. Separations can be bitter, angry, and lead to serious disputes. The problems become more pronounced without protective legal measures already in place.

Breaking Up Without Legal Benefits

Unlike Sweden, where living together has been recognized as a legitimate social institution that requires regulation by law to protect participants, men and women in the United States and a number of other countries are not afforded this legal consideration. And when couples move in together, romance, love, and passion are on the upswing; imagining a bitter end is way out of sight. What they don't realize is that the generosity and kindness shown in the early stages of a romance do not accompany the breakup phase. Consequently, the notion of implementing a legal contract that might serve them later is not uppermost in their minds.

Dangerous Liaisons

If you have ever met a couple like Henry and Sandra, you know how important it is to at least give a living together contract a thought. These two moved in with all the optimism that lovers do. Sandra even accompanied Henry to a new city and happily set up housekeeping in his home until she came to the realization that Henry wasn't the marrying kind.

Sandra was angry, bitter, and frustrated. She had contributed to the household finances, spent money on wall-coverings, and handed over her tax refund. When Henry was out of town, she hired a moving truck and took everything she thought was rightfully hers.

The problem was Henry didn't see it that way. He thought what Sandra took was his. He wasn't buying her idea that a number of the expensive household items were gifts he had purchased for her. They both adopted a mode of revenge and filed lawsuits and counter-suits. It was impossible for them to be civil to one another. The breakup brought out the worst in both of them. Sandra, it is thought, sabotaged Henry's relationship with his employer and before long he was out money from legal fees and lost his job.

Blow the Whistle

Go to a lawyer! Go directly to a lawyer! Do not move in without a cohabitation agreement. Make sure you each have your own lawyer. One cannot adequately represent you both fairly. Forget the protection of common-law marriages and palimony. Both are nearly extinct. Less than 13 states recognize common-law marriages.

More Legal Bombshells

Can you imagine how hard it would be to deal with serious issues if Henry nearly sent Sandra to the slammer over taking what he argued was his expensive, antique grandfather clock? Try these on for size without a legal contract:

1. What happens to a joint lease or loan on a home, car, or appliance?
2. What recourse would you have without written proof you loaned your lover a thousand dollars?
3. How do you divide the joint savings account that you contributed well over half of?
4. How do you get child support when paternity was never formally established?
5. How can you get repaid for the five years you took off work to further his/her career and be the homemaker?

How to Gauge If It's Over

Don't let the prospect of an ugly split prevent you from packing your bags. Delaying only prolongs the agony, especially in the presence of these signs that it's probably over:

➤ Your sex life is dwindling to a standstill.
➤ Your don't feel any closer to achieving your live-in objective.
➤ You are less happy and satisfied than when you first moved in.
➤ You feel less secure about your relationship.
➤ You have begun to question your partner's loyalty.
➤ Your eye has started to wander.
➤ You and your partner have different agendas.

➤ Trust in your partner and your relationship has evaporated.

➤ You don't like coming home if your live-in is there.

➤ You cannot honestly say you would move in with him/her all over again.

If this evidence is stacked up against you it's time to pack the bags! Rarely will you experience a turnaround for the better once these elements are in play.

Eight Good Reasons to Move Out

Look at it this way: You are giving up much more by staying than by leaving, especially if this list of eight reasons applies to your relationship. It's time to get a new address if your live-in relationship is:

1. Preventing you from furthering your own goals

2. Stifling your growth

3. Taking advantage of your financial resources

4. Turning you into someone's caretaker and housekeeper

5. Preventing you as a couple from addressing and resolving important issues

6. Not providing a healthy atmosphere for your children

7. Detrimental to your well-being

8. Prohibiting you from moving on to a better love relationship

Any relationship in which you are put upon emotionally, physically, or financially, as these conditions would indicate, cannot provide you with a nurturing, stimulating, safe, and happy environment.

Love Lingo

Compatibility among lovers is the capacity for two individuals to get along and satisfy one another's needs. Cohabitation and marital compatibility is enhanced by the ability to appease, share, respect, compromise, sacrifice, love, and support.

Dismantling the Home, Hearth, and Relationship

Once you decide it's over, don't act impetuously. Getting out or removing him/her from the premises without undue problems requires serious preparation. Unless you are in a dangerous situation, don't empty the contents of what was once your love nest into a waiting truck and disappear overnight. Take the following steps:

1. *Make a plan.* You may want to refer back to the daily breakup planner provided in Chapter 6, "Get Ready, Get Set, Break Up." However, certain things will not apply to the couple sharing the same space. Important considerations include:

➤ How long you will give yourself to break up

➤ Devising a time line

➤ Who is going to move out

➤ What you can do to avoid inflicting pain and at the same time keep yourself out of jeopardy

Love Lingo

Sociology professor Diane Vaughn says that relationships that unravel over time begin with the **psychological departure** of the partner who wishes to leave. The psychological departure signifies one person's decision to end the relationship and indicates a loss of that person's romantic interest. It is possible for the other person in the relationship to miss the signs of psychological departure because they are not obvious.

Heart to Heart

Family law experts advise against creating your own cohabitation agreement. It is not as simple a document as it seems. Because of the state of legal flux in this area, it takes an expert to weigh what may or may not be considered counter to the current public policy.

2. *Make the necessary provisions.* Taking these few precautions is not only prudent but necessary. Do not count on your partner being generous or solicitous in a live-in breakup.

➤ Separate any joint accounts

➤ Find a place to live

➤ Make a list of what is yours

➤ Try to even financial accounts before you lower the boom

➤ Make sure you have enough money to get by

➤ Attend to any legalities—like taking your name off the lease and contacting a lawyer if you're not sure of all your legal obligations

➤ If you are moving out, have your name taken off the utility and phone accounts

3. *Stop the charade.* Emotionally and sexually begin to sever your ties to your partner and start doing more things alone.

4. *Confront your partner.* Tell him/her you want to separate. Be firm, organized, and up front about what you have done to ready yourself.

Following steps 1 through 4 will put you on solid ground and prepare you as well as possible for any complications or problems that arise as your love nest breaks apart. You may have warmly walked into your adobe together, but on the way it can get pretty steamy.

On Your Own Again

Greet your new life with enthusiasm. True, there are pluses and minuses to living alone. Like everything, you must make the choice whether to dwell on the positives or the negatives. To make this a winning chapter in your life, consider the upside. For the best results, follow the dos and don'ts in the table below. If you try live-in love one more time, proceed with caution.

The Dos and Don'ts of Living Alone Again

The Don'ts	The Dos
Don't give yourself time to get blue.	Revel in your new-found independence and the opportunity to start a new life.
Don't sit at home alone.	
Don't leave out reminders of your life together.	Get out as much as possible; otherwise, your empty house will become problematic.
Don't move into a place that costs more than you can afford just to make yourself feel better.	Redecorate your bedroom. Pack up painful items and give them back to your ex.
	Get a roommate if you can't afford to singularly fund the standard of living two incomes provided for.

If and When You Try Again

You want to move in with someone else? Don't you dare—until you check every one of these items off the list below. If it doesn't prevent a future breakup, at least it will lessen the blow.

- ❑ Discuss personal agendas.
- ❑ Agree on future course of romance.
- ❑ Set up one household account that you contribute to equally. Keep all other money in separate accounts.
- ❑ Draw up a list of items you each brought to the house or that you purchased with your own money.
- ❑ Find a neutral living space, one not previously resided in by spouses or other lovers.
- ❑ Agree on a policy of honesty if and when one wants to move out. Spell out a bargain.
- ❑ Discuss the possibility of a living-together contract.
- ❑ Consult with an attorney regarding your personal need for a contract.
- ❑ Establish household rules.
- ❑ Discuss what role you want to play among each other's family.

See Appendix C, "The Cohabitation Agreement," for items to have your attorney include in your cohabitation agreement. Contact your local Bar Association for qualified legal assistance.

Bits and Pieces

Results of a Penn State study released in 1998 found that men and women who live with a romantic partner express less enthusiasm over marriage, desire fewer children, and do not have hang-ups about divorce.

Whether you have decided to terminate your live-in relationship or give it more time, you should be better equipped to evaluate the days ahead. Pulling the plug on living together is difficult and involves very specific issues not applicable to other relationships. Give serious consideration to what you have learned and how it applies to you. Go back to the beginning of the book and start again if indecision persists.

The Least You Need to Know

➤ Live-in relationships are often the hardest to extract oneself from.

➤ Live-in love calls for added protection.

➤ Breaking up a live-in relationship calls for extra thought, tact, and finesse.

➤ The aftermath of live-in love may bring out the demons in either lover.

The Trial Separation

In This Chapter

➤ What a trial separation can do for you

➤ How to avoid trouble in trial separations

➤ When to hang it up

➤ Pointers for reconciling

It isn't over until the fat lady sings, as they say. The same rings true for relationships. Separations, legal or otherwise, may be your path to reconciliation when your future is in limbo.

However, separations are to be used sparingly. They don't always solve the problem or make the heart grow fonder. They can just as easily give license to unforgivable behavior and compound troublesome issues.

That's why separations require the wisdom of sages. Don't be rash, pass judgment, or propose a separation until you carefully examine the information provided in this chapter. Make certain a separation serves your game plan before you start down this road.

As in all aspects of your relationship, the thoughtful rather than the sudden, impetuous move serves you best.

Bits and Pieces

Up-to-the-minute research has proven that couples who establish a friendship first become better partners and have lasting marriages.

What Can a Trial Separation Accomplish?

You are married or living together, but the relationship has gone sour. Going your separate ways is the solution both of you consider the most prudent at the moment. Neither, however, has the guts to sign the divorce papers or tear up the lease. So what can a preplanned separation possibly do for you?

Blow the Whistle

Safety first! Victims of domestic violence or individuals living with a partner who suffers from substance abuse may need to remove themselves and their children from the household for their physical and mental well-being. If that's the case, don't delay.

According to research, separations either provide a transition into single life or a period of decision making removed from daily pressures. They afford breathing space, distance, and a neutral zone for communication. Within this setting it may be easier for partners to engage in self-examination, re-establish the friendship, and determine if the relationship is worth salvaging.

A good indication that there is still some stuffing in the mattress is, according to one researcher, if your spouse or partner feels like the two of you are still a unit. He or she will likely empathize with your failures and take pleasure in your achievements. If you don't see any display of this attitude, your partner may already have mentally severed the cord.

Before You Separate

There are several things you should be aware of before you separate. Expect to feel:

➤ Confused and ambivalent

➤ Uncomfortable with the loss of your normal partnership role

➤ Embarrassed by the exposure of your relationship problems

Do not let those uneasy feelings deter you from your work at hand. Try to make a preliminary judgment as to whether a separation might improve the quality of your relationship, boost your chances of reconciliation, or merely postpone the inevitable.

One way to come up with an answer is to evaluate whether you and your partner can make permanent, fundamental changes within your relationship. Answering the following questions honestly will give you an indication if you both have what it takes to accomplish that.

Question	Yes	No	Maybe
1. Was there a period in your marriage or live-in relationship that was satisfying and happy for both of you?	❏	❏	❏
2. Do you each have a clear memory of that period?	❏	❏	❏
3. Do either or both of you want to salvage the marriage or live-in relationship?	❏	❏	❏
4. If your partner wounded you emotionally, do you think you have capacity to forgive him/her?	❏	❏	❏
5. Do you feel as if your spouse has changed but you want to get to know him/her again?	❏	❏	❏
6. Do you think a fresh perspective would help solve your problems?	❏	❏	❏
7. Do you need to separate yourself from the situation to make an independent decision?	❏	❏	❏
8. Are you willing to try and jump-start a romantic affair with your partner?	❏	❏	❏
9. Are you both willing to take the blame for the problems in your relationship?	❏	❏	❏
10. Will you be able to make an earnest attempt to renew your commitment to your relationship?	❏	❏	❏
11. Are you ready to work on the relationship?	❏	❏	❏
12. Are you prepared to compromise for the sake of the relationship?	❏	❏	❏
13. Do you have a sufficient level of trust in one another?	❏	❏	❏
14. Are there at least a few hot embers of love still glowing in the dark?	❏	❏	❏

Your score: It shouldn't take a statistical wizard to inform you that 14 "yes" answers give lasting reconciliation the best chance and that just as many "no" answers the most dismal forecast. An optimistic outlook directly correlates with the number of positive answers you were able to come up with. The responsibility for reconciliation rests squarely on you and your partner's shoulders.

The Dos and Don'ts of Separating

Before you separate, there are a few steps you ought to consider that will make the situation less stressful for you, your family, and your partner.

Do:

1. Try to engineer an orderly separation. Remember you once cared for this other person. A sudden departure is disruptive for children and adds to the humiliation and rejection felt by the party who is left.

2. Act responsibly, show concern, and take care of your financial end of the partnership.

3. Be careful if you date during the separation stage not to get romantically hooked up with someone else.

4. Be patient and practical.

5. Set guidelines, limits, and boundaries regarding your interaction with your estranged partner.

6. Agree on the terms of your separation.

Just as important as heeding the dos above is avoiding the don'ts below. Undoubtedly, any of these foolish actions could lead to unnecessary and prolonged problems.

Heart to Heart

Sociology professor and author of *The Good Divorce* (Basic Books, 1995), Constance R. Ahron asserts that merely making the fun moves to improve your relationships doesn't get to the nitty-gritty of your problems. If you can't tell whether or not you are hitting upon the more fundamental aspects of your relationship, seek the guidance of a professional or the candor of a support group.

Don't:

1. Slam the door or fail to look back unless you are absolutely certain this breakup is for real.

2. Walk out and leave your home without seeking legal counsel, especially if children are involved.

3. Alienate friends and his or her family members. If you reconcile, it won't help having made enemies out of your in-laws.

4. Act out in a way you will be sorry for later. Your behavior during this period can come back to haunt you.

5. Give up control over your actions or emotions. You can't afford to lose your good sense at this critical juncture.

Making the decision to embark on a trial separation is important. However, how you go about putting that separation into play is equally significant. Sometimes the best route is to make it legal.

Should You Get a Legal Separation?

It probably isn't a bad idea. A legal separation spells out financial responsibilities and obligations, childcare arrangements, and household agreements. Why take a chance on having your actions misconstrued later? Only a lawyer familiar with the legal system in your area is equipped to provide you with all the protection you need.

Tina sure wishes she had gone that route. A devoted mother and professional with one child, she remained in her emotionally abusive household until she could no longer take it. Distraught and out of control, she packed her bags and sought refuge at her girlfriend's. Her husband did not see this as a trial separation or a period in which to work out their problems. He got himself a sharp lawyer and won temporary residential custody of their son.

If Tina had called the domestic violence hot line in her locale or contacted a lawyer, she thinks she would have been advised to handle things differently. Now she is embroiled in a bitter custody battle with little hope of winning. In the Ohio city where Tina lives, the courts rarely, if ever, reverse the determination of temporary residential custodial parent. How to find legal representation is explained in Appendix A, "Resources."

Bits and Pieces

Family law experts acknowledge that when joint custody was introduced, it was a revolutionary concept that sought to equalize parental rights. However, shared legal responsibility does not necessarily mean equal custodial rights. Some professionals believe that the battle to gain the upper hand as the residential parent is more about adult anger and rage than what is best for the child.

Splitting and Getting Back Together Again

It can be done. I have interviewed legal separationand watched couples who have been successful at it. Among these couples, three common situations prompted trial separations: the affair, major changes in personal direction, and a mid-life crises. Here are some tips on how to handle each of these stumbling blocks.

> ### Bits and Pieces
>
> Psychiatrist and author Peter Kramer says it may be wise to determine whether you have tried to make the relationship work before you decide to leave for good.

The Affair

A case in point. Saul and Sally are typical of a number of longtime married couples who find themselves in trouble. Sally was busy with her career, raising the kids, and playing hostess for Saul's business. She didn't know he was feeling the pinch of poor economic times or the loss of a major lucrative construction contract. Saul's ego plummeted. Sally did not notice. Along came sexy Samantha. She made Saul feel like a million bucks and thus the affair began.

When Sally found out, Saul agreed to move into his own abode for awhile. Before Sally could even address the issue, she had to get her head together and pick up the pieces of her heart. Fortunately she didn't speak out of turn, held her head high, and sought the assistance of her clergyman. What he helped her see was that she still wanted to make this marriage work. By this time, Saul was repentant and wanted to come home.

Blow the Whistle

Tend his ego! There is ample evidence that men whose egos are not nurtured or massaged are more likely to succumb to an extramarital affair.

Prudent tips. Sally opened the door, but not wide enough for him to come back immediately. She suggested they get an objective counselor and see each other for dinner outside the house where they could talk. When she did allow him to move back into the family home and her bed, it was with the assurance that Samantha was a thing of the past never to surface again.

Sally was willing to forgive, but said she would never forget. Although Sally kept this episode tucked in her memory bank, she did not let it interfere with mending her relationship. She didn't punish Saul with snide jabs or by withholding sex.

Chapter 24, "When to Forgive or Forget," will deal with cheating hearts—when to forgive, forget, or turn 'em loose.

Changes in Personal Direction

A case in point. Melinda married Murray when she was just out of college and became pregnant right away. Murray's career flourished, the family made two moves, and Melinda's resentment grew. "What happened to my private life, goals, and aspirations?" she asked herself 15 years after walking down the aisle.

She was having an identity crisis, blamed it on the fact that the family took their lead from Murray's career, and projected her anger onto her partner.

At first Murray was dumbfounded and confused. Melinda wanted the right to her own life. She thought things could be better on her own. Murray afforded her the opportunity to test it out. He rented a house down the street so he could be near the kids and share responsibilities. Melinda went back to school for her masters degree. She and Murray agreed they could each date if they wished, and Melinda entered the dating arena.

Prudent tips. Murray played Melinda's hand well. He knew she could throw the trump card but didn't quit playing his bid. Once he swallowed his own anger, hurt, and pride, he did whatever he could to help Melinda. He urged her to take some of their savings to pay her tuition, insisted keeping the kids during exam week, and never questioned her about the men he saw pick her up at the house.

Melinda began to see Murray in a new light and finally got a handle on the source of her own frustrations. When she walked into a restaurant with some female companions and saw Murray with another woman, she panicked. The game was over. Her identity crisis had abated. She wanted Murray back.

He was wise to take his time, even though all the while he was packing his bags and getting ready to park his car in his old garage for keeps.

Heart to Heart

Dr. Gilda Carle, author of *Don't Bet on the Prince* (Golden Books Publishing Company, 1998), reported that out of 1,104 women polled, what they wanted more than money or fabulous sex was more free time to themselves. Carle believes that women who deny themselves this may require "time out" of a relationship to figure it out. Are you one of them? It is a good question to pose before you blame someone else for your unhappiness.

Mid-Life Bleepers

A case in point. Ralph was in his early 50s. He had one set of kids between the ages of 20 and 24, another set in the primary grades. He was feeling trapped in his second marriage although he exchanged vows in earnest and with much love. But the confines of this younger family were getting to him at a time of life he thought he would be free to reap the rewards of his hard labors. The quick passage of time began to ruffle his feathers.

Roberta was a first-time mom and had no intention of missing school plays for a night at the theater in New York, nor was she willing to leave the kids behind on the frequent trips Ralph wanted to take. When Ralph took off seeking new adventures, Roberta was not surprised. She didn't panic, call in a team of divorce lawyers, or give Ralph her blessing to sow any leftover wild oats.

Prudent tips. Roberta was not foolhardy. Toward Ralph, she was understanding, supportive, and firm. There were lines not to be crossed that would create irreconcilable differences if they were to work things out as she hoped they would. She recognized that the situation called for a level head, compromise on both sides, and some restructuring of the family.

She patiently awaited Ralph to come to his senses, arranged for sexy sleepovers, and sought an objective counselor to look for deeper seeds of discontent while negotiating a settlement. Roberta put into black and white the way she planned to divide her time into parcels for herself, the children, Ralph, and the family unit. A pie-shaped graph illustrating before and after the separation was a clear-cut way to demonstrate how far she was willing to go.

It took time, but Ralph found his way home, and Roberta was there to greet him at the door.

The story isn't over yet. If you decide to reconcile successfully, there is a set of commandments to learn and obey.

Heart to Heart

Some couples report enjoying the newness of being together after a separation. What they are experiencing is the infatuation stage and all those sexy turn-ons that start love's wheel spinning. The side benefit of all these goodies is that once you are romantically fulfilled and sexually satisfied, the Mr. or Mrs. is generally more receptive to talk and more willing to make some necessary compromises.

Reconciliation Commandments

Reconciliation is more difficult than you may have imagined. It takes determination, forgiveness, and handling ambivalent emotions. You must be able to call upon each of these traits to effectively live up to the commandments that are essential if you take on the task of reconciling.

1. You will commit to the process.
2. You won't punish one another for past wrongs.
3. You won't dwell on the pain of the separation.
4. You will love, respect, and care for each other.
5. You will display an improved attitude toward the health of your relationship.
6. You will actively take responsibility for the well-being of your relationship.
7. You will get the wheel of love spinning by returning now and then to the ecstasy of the infatuation phase.

8. You will take pride in your history together.

9. You will accept the same agenda.

10. You won't promise to make things better just to get your mate to move back in with you.

The trial separation is your chance to bail out and save a relationship. It is one step you can take before untying the knot, walking out the door, or cutting the rope. If you decide to give it a try, do it for the right reasons, employ logic, and maintain a cool head. Remember this is merely a trial. The jury is still out, and a decision will have to finally be made.

The Least You Need to Know

➤ A trial separation is not necessarily the end of your relationship.

➤ If you embark on a separation, use the time wisely to dispel any and all doubts.

➤ A trial separation leads to reconciliation when both partners are willing to address and solve problems, accommodate the other mate's needs, and to love without a grudge.

Chapter 15

Divorce: The Definitive Breakup

In This Chapter

➤ Who gets divorced and why

➤ The after-blows of divorce

➤ How to ensure a good settlement

➤ Marriage odds after divorce

You have tried everything. You failed to resolve conflicts or to effectively communicate, and your marital expectations failed to materialize. The breakup seems inevitable; divorce is the next step.

Most likely the female partner in the marriage will file for the divorce. Two-thirds of the 1.2 million divorces annually are sought by women. This does not mean that they are the only dissatisfied partners, just the mate who is most likely to see divorce as the only solution.

In fact, in a bold argument, Constance R. Ahrons, Ph.D., author of *The Good Divorce* (Basic Books, 1995), pronounces divorce as a normal occurrence. Consequently there are prescriptions for how to get the best possible divorce and how to fare well through it. This chapter will get you started in that direction.

What Happened to Your Marital Expectations?

It is true that happily married couples see each other's faults through rose-colored glasses and display the friendship, respect, and love so essential to good relationships. They also, however, are masters at maintaining a realistic set of expectations toward their marriage and their mate. If the expectations you applied to your marriage sound like the list below, you may quickly discover why you are reading this chapter so intently. There is no room for that idyllic naiveté in the world of matrimony.

Here are some unrealistic marital expectations:

➤ Each day will be happy and filled with love and bliss.

➤ Your spouse will devote his or her attention completely to you.

➤ You will love your partner unconditionally each and every day.

➤ Your mate will ensure your emotional well-being.

➤ Your husband or wife is your soul mate and thus will be able to anticipate your needs.

➤ Your sex life will remain constant and passionate.

➤ Children will not hinder your private relationship.

➤ You will resolve all conflicts without anger or a fight.

➤ You will always be turned on by your mate.

➤ You will never stray for a day from liking that other person.

➤ You will never fantasize about another male or female.

➤ You will never be lonely.

➤ All your hopes and dreams will come true.

➤ No problem will seem insurmountable with your mate.

The statements above are unrealistic expectations of what a marriage relationship is all about. If you tie your happiness to expectations that are unreasonable to achieve, you are shrouding your marriage outlook in doom. Other predictors of unhappy endings are provided for you in the next section.

Bits and Pieces

An Ohio State University study showed that marital discord among newlyweds and older couples tended to release stress hormones that reduced the functioning of their immune system.

Divorce Predictors

Demographic and statistical analysis found that divorce rates are highest among people who:

➤ Marry at an early age

➤ Have less formal education

➤ Fall into lower socioeconomic demographics

➤ Are of different religious backgrounds

➤ Have divorced parents

➤ Live in the western United States

➤ Are Protestants as opposed to Catholics and Jews

➤ Are living through prosperous times

Do not panic. Predictions don't always come true, particularly if you work hard to ensure a good marriage and are able to steer clear of complications that frequently lead to divorce.

Blow the Whistle

The biggest strains on marriages today are changing gender roles and problems incurred in the division of labor.

Common Causes of Divorce

Number One: The extramarital affair supposedly presents the most frequent reason given for divorce. Of course, one must try to understand the underlying reasons for the infidelity. It could be an ego problem that gets massaged elsewhere or a simple lack of sex and romance.

Two through Seven: Sterility or spousal cruelty are the next two in line, followed by a partner's bad temper, jealousy, laziness, or lack of financial support. Poor self-esteem is always problematic to relationships. Without it, you don't have the courage to keep each other in line or secure your own happiness.

Eight through Ten: Don't discount the blow to marital harmony of stress related to job, family illness, and money matters. If the happiest couples report that they are satisfied with their mate's financial input, one might infer the opposite is true of those who flounder putting bread on the table—be it the man or woman.

Eleven: A fresh look at divorce has also indicated that, in the United States at least, our exaggerated sense of personal independence and right to individual satisfaction has affected our williness to stay in the marriages that don't provide enough goodies.

Bits and Pieces

Japanese marriage experts believe that the low divorce rate in their country reflects the lack of personal independence so important in American culture. The inability to function independently, they suggest, may be why almost 40 percent of the women divorced in Japan return to their parents' home.

Who Is Most Likely to Have an Extramarital Affair?

Extramarital affairs are the number one culprits named in divorce, but why do certain spouses take a lover and others don't? Each of us encounter daily opportunities to begin a flirtation or an affair. Values, ethics, and spousal commitment are only part of the answer. There are numerous times during a marriage that men and women are particularly vulnerable.

Researchers who have analyzed this phenomenon from a physiological perspective found increased risk among women in their 30s. Women are concerned with their sexual satisfaction at this time. Their husbands, however, are devoted to getting ahead in their careers and are more likely to neglect their spouses.

Bits and Pieces

Women are more prone to fall in love with an extramarital lover than men are.

The tug and pull of children and hectic schedules further impinge on private time and add to the marital disenchantment partners of all ages experience. In fact, one of the hardest times for a married couple is after the birth of their first child. Marital satisfaction drops, increases slightly when kids reach adolescence, but does not move significantly upward until the kids leave. During any period in which marital satisfaction lags behind, there is the danger of extramarital intrigues.

It is interesting that some sex therapists have recently reported that women with young children find daytime more erotically appealing than men. And why not! By bedtime they are overcome with fatigue.

The 40s display less biological and sexual differences between the sexes. And by the 50s, hormone levels in men and women appear more similar. Their desire for sexual satisfaction is more even now than at any other time.

It is prudent to be on guard during various chronological stages of one's marriage when men and women are more likely to fall prey to extramarital affairs. However, the truth of the matter is, who eventually winds up in bed with someone other than their spouse also reflects a deficiency in marital sex, respect, ego-tending, love, or trust.

For more information on "the affair," see Chapter 14, "The Trial Separation," and the discussion on a couple's separation due to an extramarital affair. Chapter 25, "Re-Entering the Dating Arena," will deal with when to forgive and forget.

What Men Should Expect After the Divorce

If you are contemplating divorce or have already settled on that course of action, you may want to know what to expect. The outcome may be different than what you had in mind.

➤ An average drop in their standard of living by 10 percent

➤ A more difficult post-divorce period than they thought

➤ A realization that even their bad marriage provided them with more of the social support, status, and traditional roles they prefer than single life does

➤ A lack of control over the divorce process and dissatisfaction with the terms of the legal settlement

➤ For men in their 20s, a long-term, strained relationship with their children

➤ Greater confusion pertaining to the problems surrounding breaking up than the actual conflicts in their marriage relationship

➤ A three-times higher likelihood of experiencing clinical depression than their ex-wife

➤ Embarrassment about being dumped, loss of self-esteem, and residual deep-seated anger

➤ Two and a half years to regain a sense of order in their lives

➤ An increased risk of dying from a stress-related illness

Blow the Whistle

Turn off that football game! Wives want husbands to hang out with them. A woman can handle her increased participation in the economic well-being of her family and even expect less financially from a spouse, but she expects him to devote time to companionship.

Awareness is key to handling the breakup of a marriage. Make no mistake about it. You will be up against any number of the factors above. However, knowing what to expect will enable you to go through the aftermath with less wear and tear.

What Women Should Expect After the Divorce

Men are not the only ones to confront a number of negative factors concluding a divorce. Like them, women will do a better job getting through the period of transition if they are well informed about what to expect. Here's what's likely to happen:

➤ An average drop in their standard of living of 27 percent

➤ Easier parenting and more leisure time

➤ A more difficult post-divorce period than they thought

➤ Disappointment at the reality of the freedom they initially envisioned

➤ Not to be pals with their ex

➤ Difficulty with their identity and the loss of their roles as wives

➤ If they were the spouse to leave the marriage, an easier post-divorce period than the pre-divorce period in which they sorted out problems

➤ Discomfort re-entering the dating scene

➤ A spouse who will remarry before her

➤ The woman her ex marries to be younger than she

Accurate expectations alone do not determine how smoothly the period after your divorce goes. Consequently, you may need to rely on some practical pointers that will keep you from ruffling each other's feathers.

Bits and Pieces

Don't look for much help from the law if a suitor wooed away your mate. Most of the "alienation of affection laws" went out with cattle rustling. But before you chuck the idea entirely, see if your state still upholds the antique law. A North Carolina woman sued the gal who stole her hubby and won a judgment for damages of a million dollars.

Practical Pointers

Retaliation, power struggles, and anger won't serve you well in the divorce process. Although you will feel anxious and wish you could proceed swiftly, it is in your best interest to move forward slowly, purposefully, and orderly. Prepare for your divorce wisely; select legal representation cautiously; and investigate alternative routes to dissolution.

Preparing for Divorce

Before you announce your intentions, there are steps you should take to protect yourself. Unfortunately, divorce often brings out the worst in spouses. Therefore, it is important that reason, not emotion, rule how you proceed.

1. Interview lawyers who specialize in family law and divorce. The laws are constantly changing. You need someone who keeps up to date on the legalities.

2. Hire a lawyer and establish his or her legal fees.

3. Build a financial reserve and create your own checking account.

4. Do not move out of your home unless safety is a factor.

5. Collect pertinent evidence that will assist your case: relevant financial material, a list of grievances, pertinent legal documents, etc.

6. Safeguard your possessions.

7. Cancel joint accounts, including credit cards.

Carefully Select Your Legal Representative

Your choice of a legal representative is critical. Domestic court judges will verify that point! You don't want to regret your decision later or lament that someone else could have done a better job for you. Enter round one of your divorce with confidence, armed by the best attorney available to you. Here are some tips on choosing someone to represent you:

1. Take time to get to know your lawyer. It is important that you not only feel comfortable with the pay scale but with him or her as an individual.

2. Inquire whether this individual will see your case through or if you will be handled by a number of people in the firm. Decide for yourself if this is okay with you.

3. Ask your attorney to outline the process for you. Then make sure he or she follows through.

4. Be specific about what you anticipate will be a fair divorce and what kind of child custody you are seeking. Make sure the lawyer agrees with you or can explain what is good or bad about the deal you are seeking.

5. To save yourself wear, tear, time, and money, ask your attorney whether settling outside of court is feasible.

6. Be sure to check out your lawyer's reputation. Consult your local Bar Association and other prominent community leaders and legal experts you may know.

7. Be leery of the lawyer who promises you an easy ride or that you will get everything you want.

8. Don't be afraid to ask how many divorce cases he or she handles annually. You want experienced and expert legal counsel.

9. Never let your spouse chose an attorney for you.

10. Do not use an attorney who offers to represent both of you. It is advisable for each party to have their own legal counsel who can act in their own best interest.

Consider Mediation

Mediation is a relatively new concept in the divorce process. It took hold in the 1980s and '90s. Mediation offers the opportunity to identify issues to jointly work out the terms of one's divorce cooperatively under the supervision of a trained mediator. If successful, mediation can eliminate exorbitant legal fees and avoid ugly impasses.

To engage in meaningful mediation, however, one must be flexible, want to engage in mediation, and bring a willingness to compromise to the bargaining table.

Mediation is not as effective if one mate tries to manipulate the other into a position. Mediation requires a concerted, honest effort to arrive at a settlement that works equally well for both parties. It is particularly valuable in determining details regarding children's living arrangements, parenting plans, and child support.

Heart to Heart

Approximately one-third of the divorced couples in a study defined their relationship with their ex-spouse as cooperative, particularly with respect to caring for their children. Theirs is an enviable position you should strive to attain.

Margaret Miller, mediation program coordinator for the Franklin County Domestic Relations and Juvenile Court in Ohio, said that mediators can help organize the structure of the family on the other side of divorce. How families function in this next phase must be tailor-made, she stressed. In order to protect the well-being of the children, arriving at a workable relationship is imperative. Studies show that kids do better when a more affable settlement is made and when two parents remain involved in their lives.

In some states mediation is the first step required in the divorce process, and court-appointed mediators are provided. If mediation is not mandated by law in your area, it is up to you to find your own competent, trained mediator. In that case, should you wish to try mediation, contact your county court of Domestic Relations and ask for a list of accredited mediators.

Earmarks of a Good Divorce

Under any circumstances divorce is difficult. However, you may gain satisfaction in your settlement if it:

➤ Enables your family to maintain a sense of unity

➤ Minimizes the negative impact on children

➤ Allows you to move forward with the least amount of pain and anguish

According to Constance R. Ahrons, Ph.D., author of *The Good Divorce*, these are the hallmarks of a quality settlement. Perhaps more difficult to qualify in concrete terms are the ways to deal with the emotions that accompany a divorce.

How to Handle the Emotional Overload of Divorce

Be prepared for a surge of emotions that need to be reckoned with following your divorce. No doubt how you go about handling this emotional overload is dependent upon your basic personality. Nonetheless, here are some suggestions that apply equally to everyone:

➤ Talk to someone and express your pain.

➤ Don't force yourself back into the social scene. When you are ready, you'll know it.

➤ Give yourself time to grieve and cry.

➤ Anticipate the difficulty of holidays, birthdays, and anniversaries spent alone. Plan something that will make the day easier for you.

➤ Don't allow yourself to wallow in "what-ifs."

➤ Look for new interests, and do whatever it takes to make you feel good about yourself.

➤ Don't get hooked on chemical means to ease your pain.

➤ Although it makes you feel desirable, be careful how many beds you climb in and out of during the immediate post-divorce period.

More information is provided in Part 5, "Surviving the Breakup."

Getting Remarried

With all this talk of divorce, don't come to the inaccurate conclusion that marriage is on the way out. It is hardly an institution on the verge of extinction, although there are numerous acceptable and competing forms of family today. The preceding pages are sprinkled throughout with the positives of marriage.

Furthermore, most men and women who divorce do remarry. In fact, 40 percent of all marriages in the United States have one partner who has previously been married.

If you really want to be optimistic, keep in mind that within the first year of a divorce 50 percent of the men and 33 percent of the women will remarry. Within the next three years, the figures jump to 83 percent for men and 75 percent for women.

Heart to Heart

When you do remarry, follow the example of the happiest couples I found for my book *Marriage Secrets* (Brich Law Press, 1993). Their priorities go like this: 1) spouse, 2) children, 3) job.

The Least You Need to Know

➤ There is life after divorce.

➤ Your best play is good legal counsel.

➤ You have the right to an equitable agreement.

Part 4
The Breakup

You are posed for the breakup and ready to begin the walk-through in Part 4. The path is all laid out in front of you. The road signs are in place. The hurdles are designated. The dangerous curves marked. Follow the road carefully.

This is a journey you must take on your own. To successfully reach the end of the trail, be thoughtful how you initiate your breakup, be prudent when you choose your goals, and be kind when you select your tactics. Your final roadblock will be the challenge of closure. After you achieve closure, you can say with certainty that your breakup is complete.

Chapter 16

Initiating the Breakup

In This Chapter

➤ Learn how to deliver bad news

➤ What love and sex styles have to do with how you breakup

➤ Pointers to calm the raging waters

You are ready to take responsibility for the course of your love life. You want to call it quits, initiate a breakup, and move on. Be a conscientious and truthful ex; it will ease those inescapable pangs of guilt. And a damage-controlled breakup with carefully weighed words will inflict the least amount of pain.

Your Readiness Checklist

Make sure you are at your peak of readiness. Check off each and every one of the critical items in the list below. Do not begin to initiate your breakup until you have completed this preparation.

❏ At the very least, read Chapters 1 to 11.

❏ Have your objective mindset in place.

❏ Answer the four basic questions asked in Chapter 1.

❏ Subdue your libido.

❏ Complete the love map comparison in Chapter 3.

❏ Make a good list of reasons to break up.

❏ Dispel all doubt.

❏ Visibly hang your breakup banner and complete a daily planner. (See the sample in Chapter 6.)

❏ Put your confidante on the alert.

❏ Remove his or her picture from your nightstand.

The Threefold Breakup

Once you have satisfactorily completed your breakup readiness checklist, you may proceed. It will serve you well in the end if you keep in mind a trio of mechanics:

1. Accommodate what you have to do and say.

2. Get the message across clearly.

3. Cause the least amount of residual pain to yourself.

These fundamentals should guide every action you take. It will deliberate forethought and careful planning on your part to see this through and pull off a breakup that is to your advantage.

An Exercise to Boost Your Nerve

Athletes use imaging to assist them in executing their best shot, play, or strategy. Imaging combines a positive mindset with a visual mental image. For instance, golfers step up to the ball to tee off. They meticulously determine where it is they want the ball to land and visualize the perfect flight of the ball. Then mentally they set off the next shot that will land them squarely on the green. Imaging makes them focus on their efforts, evaluate their plays, and reinforces the potential for success.

Romantic Imaging

Breakup imaging takes you through the sequence that will result in severing your relationship. Visualize yourself approaching your romantic partner in a decisive, controlled, and purposeful manner. See yourself maintaining decorum while you explain your feelings. Anticipate your partner's positive and negative responses along with yours. If you don't like the picture you are getting, try to re-image the scene until you find a scenario with the most positive results. Landing the proper words is the crucial technique here.

Heart to Heart

A breakup that won't plague your conscience later should enlist the support of a warm heart. The reputation of a cold-hearted lover could have negative repercussions later on and affect the way future love interests look at you.

You may find that you aren't quite in your best form and that you have not perfected your technique yet. That's okay. There is plenty of help in the pages ahead. Nonetheless, finish your imaging session. You should repeat it, however, until you have enough information to draw a complete and satisfying picture. That's what the athletes do.

In the meantime, imagine positive results. Feel the relief. See yourself smiling and walking away from the encounter free and happy. You may want to go as far as picturing a serendipitous meeting with your next love.

You should emerge from this exercise calm and confident.

The Flight of Your Words

Keep in mind that your words may land like heavy punches on someone's heart. That doesn't give you license to cop out. On the contrary, use the information social scientists have validated about the flight of your words until you appropriately refine your image. Remember:

➤ Your emotions facilitate or inhibit certain topics of discussion.

➤ What you say can cause pain to someone else.

➤ How a message is received and assessed by that person longingly looking into your eyes across the table is crucial.

➤ If your message is in conflict with their goals, they are likely to be hurt more.

➤ Because romantic relationships are voluntary connections (unlike family relationships), the hurtfulness of a message may be intensified.

➤ Inherent in romantic involvement is physical passion and/or passionate love. In light of this, hurtful remarks may arouse two extreme responses—either a passionate, intense response or a stunned, inactive one.

➤ The impact of hurtful messages in ongoing or waning romantic relationships is greater than in other relationships.

➤ Awareness of the pain a negative message can cause a romantic partner may prevent you from verbalizing it.

Carry this information with you. Be cognizant of the impact of your words. However, do not skirt the real issues because what you have to say may cause pain. Rather, choose your words wisely.

Heart to Heart

It is important to remember that men and women speak to and hear one another differently. Remember to translate your message into the proper gender.

A Critical Breakup Tip

It has been proven that individuals find uncertainty uncomfortable and have a need to alleviate or reduce it. Interestingly, however, there is evidence that if an individual thinks the undisclosed information may be negative, he or she is likely to prefer uncertainty.

The same holds true in romantic relationships. Consequently, the man or woman you are trying to break up with may not want to hear your message and may avoid doing just that. This makes it all the more imperative that your message is clearly delivered without delay.

Breakup Pointers That Facilitate the Deed

Before you get bogged down in planning, there are some pointers you need to take into consideration. Don't make your breakup more cumbersome than it needs to be. At the same time, do not shortchange a love interest that warrants a breakup explanation. Consider these points as you chart your course of action:

1. Not all breakups should be treated equally. Some require more thought and compassion. Exactly what it is you owe this other person depends on several very practical considerations.

2. Design your efforts around:

   ➤ How long you have been going out

   ➤ Your expressed level of prior commitment

   ➤ Inferences given regarding an ongoing and lasting relationships

   ➤ Promises made concerning future, shared events

   ➤ Whether this individual is a jerk or a really nice guy or gal

3. A breakup after only a few dates requires little or no explanation if you terminate your interest early on. It is always nice to say something definite, however, that won't make anyone wonder if they should expect a call. "I'm glad we had the opportunity to meet," is a pleasant enough closing.

Bits and Pieces

Supposedly there is a notable divergence between whom one has a romantic attraction to and whom one ends up marrying. Initially, we are all likely to fall in love or lust with the most physically appealing person. In reality, however, unless we measure up in equal appeal, it's not going anywhere. Findings show that we marry someone who is closer to our own level of attractiveness.

Obviously the longer you have been involved and monopolized that person's time or attention mandates more thoughtful consideration. Your soon-to-be ex has a right to know what went wrong, when you changed your mind, why you decided you weren't right for each other, and why you are reneging on promises. The kind, caring, and sincere person you have been dating and taking to bed deserves your utmost attention.

Mounting a Breakup Campaign That Heads Off Trouble

A good way to head off trouble is to get a handle on who you are dealing with. If you are right on target, you should be able to plan your breakup in a way that minimizes distasteful consequences by reducing the other person's anguish.

There are several ways to predetermine how intense your disappointed would-be lover's reaction will be to your breakup news. The first is to establish whether or not you are dealing with a lover who poses special problems. Furthermore, if you ascertain an individual's love and sex styles, you might have a better idea how much trouble you are in for.

Lovers Who Pose Problematic Breakups

Take time to review the categories of lovers designated in this section. Try to match up your love interest with one of them or recognize qualities from each that apply to him or her. Doing so will give your a better idea of what to expect and how to handle that individual in order to ward off trouble.

➤ *Unrequited lovers.* They already developed a strong attachment to you and hoped to gain your love and affection. They are going to feel rejected, disappointed, and defeated no matter what you say or do.

Bits and Pieces

Roy F. Baumeister and Sara R. Wotman, authors of *Breaking Hearts* (Guilford Press, 1992), explain that loving in vain is akin to suffering a defeat. On the other side of the coin, being the target of someone's unrequited love is similar to experiencing a victory.

➤ *Needy lovers.* These men and women will feel that arrow through their heart. They have personality deficiencies that have been nourished by your presence.

➤ *Sensitive lovers.* These folks will feel a certain amount of rejection. If you don't want to see them cry, try to delicately impart your unpleasant message.

➤ *Aggressive lovers.* They won't shed a tear in front of you, but they could have a show of anger. Depending on how desirous they are of keeping your affection, they could try to talk you back into the relationship. If they aren't all that interested, they will use their energies in finding other love.

Love Styles Impart Important Clues

Love styles are studied by many in the field of sociology, psychology, and romance. However, most professionals refer to the love styles identified by sociology professor John Alan Lee of Toronto University. It is worth the challenge to figure out where your partner fits into Lee's scheme of things, whether you are beginning or ending a relationship. While you are at it, put an I.D. tag on yourself.

➤ *Eros.* This is a mixture of passion, lust, and love. The erotic lover is instantly aroused by a person who displays the set of physical qualities that repeatedly attracts him or her. Unless another love style adds to Eros, the intense physical attraction may subside.

➤ *Storge.* This type of love style takes time to develop. It grows out of affection and commitment. However, storge love is not particularly romantic. On the contrary, storgic lovers are not looking for love and view it matter-of-factly.

➤ *Ludus.* If you are breaking up with a ludic lover, you probably already know it. They are promiscuous and noncommittal. They have multiple partners and no ideal mate in mind. You could say they collect love experiences. They fall in love often and indiscriminately.

➤ *Mania.* Obsessive, preoccupied, possessive, jealous, and in need of love are qualities that describe the manic partner. Manics seek constant reassurance of love and are afraid of not being loved in equal measure. The manic lover, Lee says, is generally incapable of playing it cool with prospective lovers and may pursue an individual unwisely.

➤ *Pragma.* The hallmark of a pragmatic lover is that he or she is looking for Mr. or Mrs. Right. For him or her, that means the individual who can be a compatible partner will be capable of sharing interests and will meet their sociological criteria. Pragma is a combination of elements found in ludus and storge.

➤ *Agape.* Lee thinks this is the least common love style visible in adult relationships. It is characterized by a selfless, altruistic lover who views the act of loving as a selfless duty.

Heart to Heart

No love style is right or wrong. Just different. Finding someone compatible with your love style may be the secret to your further happiness.

If one were to apply common sense in evaluating these love styles, it shouldn't be hard to predict where trouble lies. The most difficult to the easiest lover to part with should fall in order something like this:

1. Mania
2. Agape
3. Eros
4. Pragma
5. Storge
6. Ludus

Clarifying Sex Styles

In the event you are having difficulty determining your partner's love style, his or her sexual responses may help you.

Following Lee's lead, subsequent evidence has been gathered by those who have attempted to connect love styles with sex styles. They have come up with two distinct styles of sex types they call *partner engagement* and *sexual trance scripts.*

➤ *Partner engagement scripts* are based on a loving relationship in which sex is an expression of the love between the two individuals. There is plenty of romance, whisperings of sweet nothings, intimate talk, cuddling, kissing, and affection. The object is to enhance the closeness and connection that accompanies intercourse.

➤ *Sexual trance scripts* are more pleasure-based. Lovers who engage primarily in this kind of sex wish to feel detached from other aspects of their lives. Mood setting, sexual stimulation, and deliberate sex talk enhance the encounter.

Blow the Whistle

Jump out of that hot bed! If you are involved with a ludic lover, chances are he or she views having intercourse with you as a sexual conquest and not much more. Satisfaction is more ego-centered in his corner.

Love Lingo

The meaning of the word **commitment** depends upon gender. For instance, there are researchers who claim that women view commitment in terms of caring and loyalty. On the other hand, some relationship experts assert that men think they are demonstrating commitment when they cease to act on their sexual impulses with someone other than their love interest.

Here's how the acts add up:

➤ Where there is a greater degree of emotional, loving involvement with a sex partner, the sex is likely to incorporate more elements of partner engagement. *These partners won't want to give you up easily.*

➤ Where there is the least amount of emotional, loving involvement, there should be more elements of sexual trance. *These guys and gals won't have a problem giving you back your bed and hopping in with someone else.*

To complicate matters there is, however, a gender difference one should take into account. It is assumed that despite love styles, women in general prefer partner engagement sexual experiences because they demonstrate intimacy and bonding. There is supposition that men favor sexual trance scripts because they focus on intense sexual sensations.

Fingerprint Your Partner

Now is the time to use what you have learned and fingerprint the man or woman you plan to break up with. Filling in the following blanks will ensure more accurate and conclusive prints.

1. Assign your partner a love style.

   _____

2. List three pieces of evidence that you are on the right track.

   _____

   _____

   _____

3. Determine your partner's sex style.

   _____

4. List several characteristics that validate your conclusion.

   _____

   _____

   _____

5. In light of the answers above, jot down expected complications that might follow your negative message.

   _____

   _____

   _____

Understanding the style of love and detachment your partner exhibits should help you to select your immediate course of action as well as the goals you may wish to achieve by your breakup. The next chapter will guide you in determining how to establish realistic goals.

The Least You Need to Know

➤ Your message must be carefully constructed.

➤ A long-term, loyal lover deserves the benefit of your kind-hearted consideration and a thoughtful breakup.

➤ The way in which a person loves determines, to a large extent, how they will respond to your breaking up.

Chapter 17

Establishing a Set of Goals

Your motor is racing to break up. Keep it in neutral for a few more chapters. To make your optimum move, you must establish a set of goals that will attempt to meet your needs. Before you state your goals in black and white, pay attention to what constitutes a good or bad goal. Then consider the popular ones spelled out for you here. This exercise is all about fulfilling your self-interest in a prudent manner!

Criteria of Positive Goals

If your goal doesn't have the potential to meet these criteria, chuck it. You are heading down the wrong road. Breakup goals should:

➤ Make you feel better after the split

➤ Reduce your pain

➤ Be something that you can achieve

➤ Be carefully considered

➤ Be realistic in light of your relationship history

➤ Prevent you from becoming vulnerable and committing acts of revenge

➤ Keep you in control of your destiny

➤ Serve your purpose and secure your end results

Signs of Foolish Breakup Goals

Be careful! Breakup goals are tricky. Don't be cute, overly ambitious, or silly when making up your list. Steer clear of breakup goals that:

➤ Could backfire

➤ Serve no purpose

➤ Make you feel good for the moment but pose future harm

➤ Compromise your emotional well-being

➤ Cannot possibly be achieved

➤ Are hastily adopted

Love Lingo

Webster's defines a **goal** as a place one must reach in a game to gain a point or the object of one's ambition and desire. A **breakup goal** is that you wish to accomplish or end up with after you go your separate ways.

Blow the Whistle

Stop that language! Experts claim that saying, "Let's be friends," in the course of a breakup causes too much confusion. Men use it more than women as a euphemism for, "It is over. I am no longer interested." Women interpret it as anything but a definitive split. It raises expectations that men rarely meet.

The Post-Friendship Goal

The phrase, "let's be friends," is frequently a generic breakup clause. It may in some instances reflect a genuine goal of one party. However, whether or not friendship is a realistic option for people who have been lovers remains to be seen. After all, to transform a romantic relationship into a friendship is no easy task. It requires:

➤ The ability to look at each other differently

➤ The potential to eradicate sexual, love, and romantic ties by both parties

➤ The absence of a plot to draw one back into the romantic part of the relationship

➤ The capability of two post-lovers to remain emotionally intimate in a platonic way

➤ The desire to spend time with one another minus the romantic attachment

Gender Differences Get in the Way of Friendship

First and foremost, just because you aren't enemies doesn't mean you are friends! Friendship has specific characteristics. For women, friendship means a certain degree of emotional intimacy, a sharing of secrets and ideas. Male friendships, however, are more action-oriented and geared toward doing things together.

A majority of men have difficulty making the transition from a male-style to a female-style friendship. If a friendship arises after a breakup, it tends to be more participatory than full of advice, emotional sharing, and support. But when a guy or gal meets a new romantic partner, how much time are they willing to devote to a friend of the opposite sex? More often than not, it isn't much.

Bits and Pieces

Most committed partners and spouses say their mate is their best friend.

Requirements for Friendship

In special cases, there is the potential for a genuine, meaningful friendship. What it usually takes to develop is:

➤ Time for the romantic relationship to completely die

➤ Neither partner harboring ill feelings about the breakup

➤ He or she not assuming the role of a jilted lover

➤ Preexisting conditions that already have the foundation of a good friendship in place

➤ Both parties arriving at the decision to part at the same time

➤ A true and consistent concern about the other person's well-being

➤ The introduction of separate love interests

➤ The understanding and permission of new romantic partners

A Case of True Friendship

True friendship is not always an immediate outcome.

It took Tina and Tom several years to get to that point. In college they formed a satisfying, loving relationship that incorporated all the elements of a supportive friendship.

Once outside the ivory towers, however, Tina began to view Tom differently. She began to pull away from him romantically but did not want to forsake their friendship. She had a genuine interest in him, his well-being, and his future.

161

Tom said it was an all-or-nothing deal. For a while they went back and forth, doing the breakup/back-together routine over the phone. They practically lived at different ends of the world for a two-year period. There were even periods when each demanded a noncontact agreement. But when they were in touch, their letters and phone calls still reflected a mutual support and caring.

Once they landed in the same city three years out of college, they were pals who could talk about their new love relationships, meet for lunch, or call when trouble landed at their doorstep. Although they don't spend a great deal of time together, both agree they are there for each other the way friends ought to be.

If the requirements for a friendship are there but your beau doesn't become your buddy right away, hang in there. There are cases where it takes time for the dust to settle and emotions to cool down. Tom and Tina are a perfect example.

Revenge: To Seek or Not to Seek, That Is the Question

Your partner has acted like a jerk, used you, hurt your feelings, caused you pain, and treated you unfairly. Rightfully, you want to make this the final round of a disastrous love affair. You can't help but feel vindictive. You fantasize about a punishment commensurate with his or her deeds and list retaliation as your number one breakup goal. Before you get too excited over the prospect of revenge, take the quiz below and see if your course of action is justified.

Is Revenge Warranted?

To answer that question, put a lid on your anger and take the following quiz.

A Mandatory Quiz:

1. Is there a just punishment?
2. Can you retaliate and maintain your good name?
3. Would revenge satisfy what ails you?
4. Is devising a scheme worth the effort?
5. Would he or she be sensitive to or suffer from your retaliation?
6. Is there a lesson this person could learn from your act of revenge?

If you have responded with a level head, then chances are your answers reverberate a resounding case against taking revenge. Furthermore, acts of revenge are rarely in your best interest and, therefore, do not make sound breakup goals. The discussion in Chapter 20, "The Emotional Aftermath of Breaking Up," offers more suitable ways of handling the ill-will generated when one love interest bids the other adieu.

Bits and Pieces

The name Casanova has become synonymous with sex, love, and trickery. The eighteenth century Venetian born Giacomo Girolamo Casanova traveled about Europe making his sexual conquests under the distinguished title of the Chevalier de Seingalt. His reputation was built on approximately 132 sexual encounters—a modest accounting by some men's records today. It has been suggested that travel and communication difficulties of the period prevented him from laying claim to hundreds of additional conquests.

Walk Away and Take Your Pride with You

In any set of circumstances walking away with your pride intact is a goal worthy of your consideration and determination. However, in one particular situation it becomes particularly poignant. If you are positive that your relationship is heading for a breakup or that your partner is trying to get rid of you in one of those inconspicuous ways described in Chapter 8, "Gender Differences," go for the preemptive strike that puts you squarely in control.

To accomplish this you must be the one to:

➤ Initiate the discussion about your relationship.

➤ Confront your love interest with what you feel are his or her intentions.

➤ Read all the signs and signals.

➤ Break up first.

Maintain Control Over Your Destiny

No doubt a breakup can be devastating, particularly if it is with a serious lover whom you thought would be an integral part of your future. However, rather than allow anyone to assume control over your destiny because of a broken heart, think about maintaining control as one of your goals.

Blow the Whistle

Banish the double standard! Start applying the same standards and equal judgments to men and women regarding their number of sexual partners. Over 90 percent of men and women polled believe that a double standard regarding men and women's sexual activity prevails today. This fact contributes to women's loss of self-esteem and anger.

163

It works both ways. Peter nearly flunked out of medical school when Penelope gave him up for her old boyfriend whom she married shortly thereafter. Fran, devastated by Fred dumping her, had to take a year off law school to get her head together.

Blow the Whistle

Now listen here! Something is wrong if your love life is taking you away from your professional goals. For instance, Sandra gave up the opportunity to attend Harvard Law School because unemployed Sam refused to move to Boston with her. A year later Sandra and Sam ended their live-in relationship, but Sandra had already lost her scholarship to this premier school.

If you get dumped, it isn't the end of the world unless you tell yourself it is. Whether you find yourself in a satisfying relationship or one that ends abruptly, stay on course. Remember you are an independent human being. Don't let anyone but you alter the course of your destiny.

Don't Suffer Injurious Losses

We're not talking possessions here, although do plan your breakup so you aren't stripped of those either. What we are getting at are those social and professional gains you've made that may be related to the guy or gal you no longer wish to be romantically involved with. You want to break up in a way that the friends or business associates you've made or the contracts you've landed aren't rescinded when you are no longer his or her love mate. Chapter 18, "Using Wise Tactics," will assist you in the critical tactics that will turn your goal into a reality.

Bits and Pieces

Sexual relationships in the workplace abound, according to the most comprehensive report on sexuality since the *Kinsey Report*, *The Janus Report on Sexual Behavior* (John Wiley and Sons, 1994). Here is how the figures on sex in the workplace stack up by regions of the United States: 36 percent in the Northeast, 24 percent in the South, 22 percent in the Midwest, and 38 percent of respondents in the West have had a sexual liaison in the workplace.

A Complete, Definitive, Absolute End

You may call it quits, tell your friends you've parted, or begun dating new love interests, and that's great. But these outward signs of a breakup don't signify the definitive end of a relationship that should be your goal when you determine it's over.

What's needed to prepare for meeting the goal of a complete, definitive, and absolute end to your relationship is:

➤ A determined mindset

➤ Total resolve

➤ Certainty

➤ A rosier vision of the future

Unworthy Goals

If any of the following goals appear on your preliminary list, strike them now. They fall squarely into the negative stockpile of worthless goals that need to be torched.

➤ *Hand holding.* You want to break up in a way that enables you to maintain your ex's support in the same loving manner during an upcoming crises or rope them into taking you to your best friend's wedding. This goes beyond friendship and is predicated upon leading someone on. Therefore, you act less than truthful and lower the boom only half-way until your needs are met.

➤ *Place holding.* Go back and do your homework. Place holding implies breaking up but keeping someone dangling with other fish in the water. That's unfair. There is nothing wrong with wanting to date others, but it calls for honesty when breaking up. You can't have it both ways. Breaking up entails the risk of permanent loss. Be prepared to incur that consequence at your expense, not your partner's.

➤ *Ruining a life and reputation.* That's too severe in most ordinary cases. Everyone makes mistakes, and in an indirect way you may have contributed to your lover's wrong-doing. There could have been times you closed your eyes to the truth or didn't keep them open wide enough.

Your Personal Set of Goals

Select from the items discussed in this chapter and consider others that apply to your personal breakup. Evaluate them in light of the criteria proposed to you. Then compose your personal set of goals. Take them into the next chapter when you select your breakup weapon.

1. _____

2. _____

3. _____

4. _____

5. _____

6. _____

7. _____

8. _____

9. _____

10. _____

The Least You Need to Know

➤ Before you determine how you will break off a relationship, it is imperative that you focus on a set of personal goals.

➤ Unless you are careful in the process of breaking up, it is possible to cause harm to yourself.

➤ You need to keep your ill feelings toward your ex-lover in check.

Chapter 18

Using Wise Tactics

In This Chapter

➤ Lines to breakup by

➤ The 10-step breakup

➤ Selecting your breakup weapon

➤ The surprise attack

Okay, it is time to make some important selections in your arsenal of breakup tools. You already have all of the reasons why you need to choose carefully. Your goals should help evaluate your options and determine your preferences. Don't pick arbitrarily or carelessly. Go for the optimal package.

Gentle Breakup Lines

You are ready to embark on a breakup with someone you care about but no longer have those romantic feelings for. It is recommended that you use gentle breakup lines. To qualify as "gentle," statements should show regret, reflect how bad you feel, say something positive, and avoid finger pointing.

Study these examples:

> "I feel uncomfortable having to say this, but the respect and concern I have for you dictates that I must be honest."

> "Please understand that I am sincere when I say I don't want to hurt you. There is so much that is right about us as a couple, but I don't think we have what it takes to be together for a lifetime. I don't want either of us to make a mistake we will be sorry about later."

"I wish we could keep dating; however, I think it would prevent each of us from moving in the right direction. We have such a great time together, but romantically it just doesn't feel right. I have given our relationship a lot of thought because you are such a special person."

"You have been so generous and supportive. I am really lucky to have spent so much time with you. Even though it is hard for me to give all of this up, I think I need to date others. I hope I am not making a mistake. A man/woman like you doesn't come around often. It's just that I don't think we have that chemistry we both need."

"We were so turned on to each other that I think we got into this relationship too quickly. The problem is, outside of sex I don't think we are on the same track. I wish that weren't the case, but I have thought about it enough to know that this is true. I hope you see it the same way. I wouldn't want to end this on a sour note."

"I know this sounds like one of those trite breakup lines, but it is true. I don't know any other way to say it. I just came out of a long relationship when I met you. I was really attracted to you for a number of reasons. Yet I admit that I am the kind of person who needs a boyfriend/girlfriend. So I started feeling and saying things too quickly without giving myself time to think about what I was doing. I really have to apologize for putting you in a difficult spot. I am flattered that you returned my affection, and I feel like a real jerk, especially that I might be hurting you in some way."

"It's no one's fault that our relationship isn't going any further. I am glad that we gave it a shot and got to know each other. You introduced me to many new things, and I feel I learned a lot from you. I really hope you found the time you spent with me worthwhile, too. You probably see things wrong about us as a couple, too. If not now, I hope you will later."

Heart to Heart

Write a script and practice delivering your lines with resolve. Use the imaging exercise. Imagine yourself giving this address in front of your love target. Don't stop until you repeatedly get the picture you want, feel comfortable with it, and know you can translate it into a reality.

Get the jest of what constitutes a gentle breakup line? Good. Now incorporate these wise tactics into your own breakup message. You should find some measure of comfort in rendering an unpleasant, awkward measure in a gentle manner and in knowing that you have softened the blow of an unwelcome message.

Prudent Breakup Rules

Obey these breakup rules to get away unscathed:

1. Maintain control and stay focused.
2. Act mature.
3. Be gentle, considerate, and kind.
4. Go for honesty.
5. Do not be drawn into an argument.
6. Stay calm, cool, and collected.
7. Speak clearly. Avoid double talk.
8. Stay out of the hazardous defensive zone.
9. Avoid playing games.
10. Treat your partner the way you wish to be treated.
11. Don't leave things unsaid.
12. End things in a civil and adult manner.

Bits and Pieces

A significant number of men and women in a study reported deliberately being unfaithful in order to cause a breakup. It is, however, not an advisable or wise breakup tactic to use.

Choose Your Breakup Weapon

Base your breakup mode on the breakup pointers discussed in Chapter 16, "Initiating the Breakup," and your goals established in Chapter 17, "Establishing a Set of Goals." You may wish to choose from the arsenal in this section, combine elements of several weapons, or concoct your very own device. Whatever you do, observe the match between these breakup techniques with lovers, relationships, and goals. That's an order!

Blow the Whistle

Dump the fiction! Don't focus on a fictitious problem to get out of the relationship. Notorious ones used often are differences of religion or background.

169

The Heart to Heart

Learning the truth can be liberating though painful. But in the end it preserves your integrity and demonstrates respect. The Heart to Heart is an honest, verbal, no-bull breakup. It is conducted in a private, quiet atmosphere where no one will be embarrassed by a show of emotion. It should be done solemnly, tenderly, sensitively, and clearly.

Relationship Factor. This demonstration of caring is a must for the partner with whom you have had a meaningful relationship. If you really care about someone, nothing less will do. It may seem difficult at the moment, but your love interest will feel less manipulated and put upon when he or she looks back in an objective frame of mind.

Goals Served. Post-friendship, proof of your integrity and honesty, display of respect for your love interest, control over your destiny.

The Long-Distance Directive

Distance dictates a dissolution of the relationship without being face to face. Normally one thinks of the "Dear John" letter when breaking up long-distance, but there are better choices. And that doesn't mean e-mail. We're talking about the phone here. If you've been in a relationship with someone, they deserve the courtesy of a personal, honest, spoken breakup. Also, just because he or she can't see your facial expressions or the new girlfriend or boyfriend by your side doesn't mean you have a license to lie. Granted, it is easier to be more evasive via long-distance. However, the Long-Distance Directive can be carried out over the phone, but it won't create the intimacy of a face-to-face breakup.

Relationship Factor. The traditional Long-Distance Directive is okay for a relationship of a limited duration and intensity. However, a more serious, intimate love relationship deserves a better show of consideration if at all possible. If your conscience is in peak form, let it dictate whether you should spend the time and money and expend your courage on a face-to-face breakup.

Goals Served. Taking the easy way out, possibly post-friendship, hopefully proof of honesty and integrity, control over your destiny.

The Last Hurrah

You have a ski trip planned together; the tickets have been purchased, the hotel is paid for, and snow conditions are perfect. Or tickets for the concert you are dying to attend are in his or her pocket. You opt to go knowing full well this is the last hurrah. That's fine and dandy as long as you both are on the same page.

Relationship Factor. The Last Hurrah would be too painful for a serious love relationship or an engaged couple about to call off the wedding. However, for something more sexy and casual, the Last Hurrah is a fun way to part. It can even be upbeat if man and woman are in agreement that each should go their separate ways.

Goals Served. Post-friendship possibility, no injurious losses.

The Public Maneuver

It doesn't have to be shouted across a room or a busy street. However, the Public Maneuver is anything but private. Notification of a breakup could be given in front of friends, family, or coworkers. This breakup style often involves the notification that reparations or repayment of loans are due. It could also serve as public notice that one party is expected to vacate a shared residence.

Relationship Factor. A love affair that has turned sour with nasty consequences is served by this breakup method. Obviously there is hardly a degree of trust, respect, or concern left in the relationship.

Goals Served. Prevention of injurious losses and/or abuse. Provides protection and a definite and absolute end. Exposes others to potential danger of ex-partner's less-desirable characteristics.

The Business Prototype

The Business Prototype is a very proper, unemotional, businesslike discussion that is handled maturely and explicitly face to face. Although parties may have been intimate sexually and emotionally, the demise of the relationship calls for careful, logical planning. Terms of the breakup and potential problems are arbitrated practically and fairly. The object is to ward off future damage to either party and keep emotions in check.

Relationship Factor. Intensity and duration of the relationship is not the key here. The business and professional space that the couple shares is.

Goals Served. Prevention of personal or professional harm and harmony in the workplace. Other goals served include potential for post-friendship, maintenance of pride and integrity, and control over one's destiny.

Blow the Whistle

Stop bargaining behind closed doors! Disaster strikes those who don't employ the above-the-board Business Prototype. Look what happened to Bill Clinton and Monica Lewinsky.

Love Lingo

Gross deception in a romantic context is anything close to being lied to in order to get you into bed; having half-empty, noncommitted "I love you" repeatedly sent your way; or the discovery that you and an ex-boyfriend/girlfriend are competing for the number one spot.

The Surprise Attack

This is the least expected breakup. It comes out of the blue, generally after discovery of a case of infidelity and gross deception. It is swift, certain, short, and to the point. If it is accompanied with a poisoned arrow, there is no opportunity for the partner getting dumped to rebut. Grievances are laid out and the door locked tight.

171

Relationship Factor. In order for one person to feel angry, hurt, or put upon enough to mount a surprise attack, the relationship had to be more than a casual partnership. Generally the Surprise Attack severs a relationship that held some promise for the future, was already at a level of commitment, and had reached a level of trust.

Goals Served. Definitive and absolute end, a preemptive strike, a great deal of pride, and control over one's destiny.

Blow the Whistle

Put a lid on the rage! Rage and fantasies of revenge may be a natural outcome of bitter breakups, but they can land you in trouble. A New York psychotherapist reported several capers of her female clients. They ranged from shredding their male partner's clothing, crashing a car, attempted murder, and murder.

Heart to Heart

Expect to feel lousy, and expect your partner to feel the same if love was sincerely exchanged. Some family therapists have conjectured that only death of a loved one surpasses the emotional pain of ending a serious relationship.

Breakup Styles That Don't Serve Any Positive Goals

There are enough positive breakup styles and maneuvers that one should not have to resort to negative tactics. They accomplish little, cloud the issue, confuse your partner, and delay the inevitable. Stay away from:

➤ Hemming and hawing

➤ Deceptive maneuvers

➤ The set-up, turn-about two-step (see Chapter 8)

➤ Cheating

➤ Purposeful lying

➤ Covert plots

Any of these tactics will divert an effort to break up with integrity, honesty, and respect. They seem like the simple and quick way out; however, in the long run they are apt to cause you more guilt and anxiety.

Select Your Breakup Artillery

It is time to select and record your breakup artillery among the weapons that have been described: the Heart to Heart, the Long-Distance Directive, the Last Hurrah, the Public Maneuver, the Business Prototype, or the Surprise Attack. Secondly, note any modifications you may wish to make. For instance, you might select an overall Business Prototype but in the solitude and privacy inherent in the Heart to Heart.

1. The weapon: _____

2. Modifications: _____

Finally, why not go for the ideal breakup? If you put a lot into the relationship, do the same for the final act. It only takes 10 steps:

1. Set the scene.
2. Slowly introduce the idea of breaking up.
3. Accept and express part of the blame.
4. Offer an honest explanation.
5. Point out the mutual pitfalls of the relationship.
6. Express genuine concern for his or her feelings.
7. Describe what you have gained from the relationship.
8. Recall the good times.
9. Give an explicit picture of the future.
10. Offer a friendly farewell.

Your Dance Card

This is where you need to come up with how you will go about taking the 10 steps described in the "Select Your Breakup Artillery" section, above. It does no good to know what these valuable 10 steps are if you don't use them. Laying out your steps succinctly will encourage you to implement each and every one of them when you handle your breakup.

Fill in the details:

1. _____

2. _____

3. _____

4. _____

5. _____

6. _____
   _____
   _____

7. _____
   _____
   _____

8. _____
   _____
   _____

9. _____
   _____
   _____

10. _____
    _____
    _____

The Least You Need to Know

➤ How you breakup should take into account the nature of the relationship.

➤ Lying will not serve positive breakup goals.

➤ Planning the details of your breakup will make this task easier to carry out and inflict less emotional trauma on both parties.

Chapter 19

The Steps Toward Closure

> ### In This Chapter
>
> ➤ How to close the door on a past love relationship
>
> ➤ What prevents the door from shutting tight
>
> ➤ How to lock that door and throw away the key

You either got dumped or did the dumping, but you can't get that person out of your mind. You are wavering between happy memories of yesterday and the make-believe images of tomorrow. The fact is, you're stuck! You may not even feel the pain of the breakup yet. Certainly in this state you aren't capable of formulating a plan for recovery or moving on.

The hoop you have to jump through is right in front of you. It's called *closure*.

What Is Closure Anyway?

In the *literal sense*, closure means to complete something, to come to the end, to close the door. In terms of your relationship, it signifies that it's over. There is no more need to debate, agonize, or question. It's through!

Once you accept that your relationship has reached the end of the road, you are able to get on with the *psychological components* of closure—namely the analysis of past events and the reconciliation of them intellectually and emotionally within yourself.

Bits and Pieces

Those who gain the most from closure don't fight it. They accept the end of their relationship, are able to separate past from present, and refuse to allow themselves to backslide. Furthermore, they use the insights gained through closure to prevent themselves from making the same mistakes in the future. Women in particular voice a need for closure and a desire to engage in these kinds of mental exercises.

Who Needs It?

The answer is simple: everyone!

University of North Carolina researcher Ann L. Weber discovered that her college students found a breakup without an explanation from the dumper the most difficult kind of split to endure. That includes breakups due to cheating or going back to a former lover. She claims bad news is often more acceptable than no news.

Why? In her book, *The Dark Side of Love* (Laurence Erlbaum Associates, 1998), Weber explains: "Humans need input, information, explanations, sometimes so desperately that we settle for rumor or fantasy in the absence of empirical data."

Love Lingo

In research terminology the phenomenon of two lovers who continue to demonstrate a mutual need for each other after they have ended their long-term romantic relationship is termed **persistence of attachment**. Continuing to hold onto one another prevents the complete dissolution of a relationship and closure.

Why Closure Is Hard to Come By

For most couples a clean break is rarely instantaneous. Studies reveal several factors that complicate the process and make a jump through the "C Hoop" a tight squeeze.

➤ Closure requires a man/woman come to a conclusion about why the relationship ended. That isn't always easy to do. A lack of explanation, mixed messages, an unwillingness to accept the truth, and a refusal to acknowledge that it's over get in the way.

➤ There are a multitude of factors, internal and external, that influence our romantic perceptions: attraction, memories, desire, libido, wishes. The tug and pull of these influences are foolers that interfere with an objective mindset and make it hard to let go of something you wanted.

➤ Love may end, but the need for love remains. Consequently, it is hard to give up that person associated with the fulfillment of those needs.

➤ There is the tendency to believe that the support, comfort, and good feelings felt within this relationship can only be obtained from this particular partner.

➤ Our minds play tricks on us and make us see signs that aren't there. We may have gone so far as to imagine more of a romantic connection or relationship than existed. Therefore, it would be impossible to decipher why someone broke up with you because they never shared your vision of the relationship in the first place. This happens more often than you think.

➤ Although two people may stop loving each other, they can have a problem dissolving the attachment they formed. They persist in keeping contact and emit weak sparks of romantic interest that quickly lose their glow.

➤ We are hesitant to admit that we can't rekindle the lights of desire in the other person.

Love Lingo

In case you need the technical term given for the situation when one partner tries to keep the door open and the fires lit while the other is trying to close the door and douse the flames, it is called **one-sided subsidence**.

Lou's Desperate Attempt to Head Off Closure

Sometimes when men and women refuse to give up on a relationship or a romantic interest, they do foolish things in the name of love. Take Lou for example. He thought if he disavowed Linda's breakup notice, camped outside her dorm room door, and kept popping up everywhere she was, she would change her mind.

Lou's plan was not only silly and immature, but it demonstrated how hard someone will push from the other side trying to keep the door open. Lou had a case of what researchers William R. Cupach and Brian H. Spitzberg call *ORI*, or *obsessive relational intrusion*. It strikes all ages. A severe case of ORI might be considered a stalker. Lou was well on his way to becoming one.

Is Your Ex Showing Obsessive Behavior? Are You?

If Jill is intruding on Jack's space after a breakup by engaging in repeated acts of menacing and annoying behaviors, she is exhibiting unhealthy, excessive behavior. The behaviors noted in *The Dark Side of Close Relationships* (Brian H. Spitzberg and William R. Cupach, eds., Lawrence Erlbaum Associates, 1998), listed below, go beyond a normal persistence to try to win back love and affection.

➤ Calling to argue

➤ Hanging up when the phone is answered

➤ Spying from a distance

➤ Checking up on you through your friends

➤ Repeatedly driving by your house

➤ Doing important favors without being asked

➤ Surprise visits at work

➤ Leaving notes on car windshields

➤ Calling to check up on your whereabouts

➤ Making up lies about you and the extent of your intimacy and spreading rumors

➤ Continually begging for one more chance

➤ Sending gifts and cards

➤ Threatening physical harm or damaging your property

➤ Following you

Testing Your Degree of Closure

Now that you understand how difficult it is to achieve closure but how necessary it is before you can move on, make sure you aren't the culprit with the foot in the door. A "yes" answer to any of these questions is a sure sign you are going to have a sore toe:

Ask Yourself	Yes	No
1. Am I waiting for him or her to call?	❏	❏
2. Did I buy a portable phone in case he or she does call?	❏	❏
3. Do I race to my answering machine or e-mail when I walk in my door hoping my ex-love interest left me a message?	❏	❏
4. Do I find myself talking about him or her with friends?	❏	❏
5. Am I romanticizing him or her or the relationship?	❏	❏
6. Have I been going to places where I think I will bump into my old flame?	❏	❏
7. Do I sit and think about the good times we had?	❏	❏
8. Do I still wish he or she were here?	❏	❏
9. Am I comparing each new love interest to him or her?	❏	❏
10. Do I hang out with my ex-lover's friends to still feel a part of him or her?	❏	❏

Give Yourself an "A" for Effort

Don't be too hard on yourself. You now have an awareness of closure and should begin making the effort to jump through that hoop. If, however, you seem to get tripped up and fall flat on your face, that too is understandable. No one is in control of a song, a place, or even a smell that causes a sudden flash of memory or yearning. As long as you are making the attempt at closure, using your mind instead of your heart, and not giving into these pangs of desire, you deserve an "A" for effort.

Heart to Heart

A good sign that you have reached closure is when you can hear a song you and your honey used to dance to and experience a neutral flow of emotion. That means no regret, no tears, no rapid heart beat, and no outbursts of anger.

What you may continue to feel for a very long time is that craving for companionship, fun, affection, and intimacy that most relationships provide even in the infatuation stage. Don't, however, confuse these natural desires with a longing for your ex-pal. Leave him or her out of the picture in order to make closure conclusive.

How Long Should It Take to Gain Closure?

No one can pin this process to the precise hour hand on a clock or the finite days on a calendar. The realizations and insights that enable you to gain control of your heart and mind take a different amount of time to surface in each individual.

Heart to Heart

Find a role model for your breakup. Seek out someone who has achieved the peace of mind closure brings and then moved on to a happier future. Learn from a healthy example.

One woman in her mid-20s admitted she never experienced closure until another man came into the picture and captured her heart and attention. But that's not closure, that's diversion dependent on outside forces. Closure should rely more on the self, not on others.

There is conjecture by some relationship experts that it can take up to two years to reach closure. This seems unnecessarily long and excessive. How many of us have two years to waste trying to shut the door on a nonmarital relationship? I'd say relatively few!

It seems more reasonable to expect that becoming accustomed to the separation will take several months and possibly several more after that to stop feeling sad and nostalgic. Then add a moderate amount of time onto that to think clearly and find reasons why you should stop wishing he or she were still your love interest.

179

At the outset of a breakup ask yourself how much time you are willing to wallow in self-pity, drown in a pool of longing, and suffer the pangs of heartbreak. One young law student took a year off of school to complete the process. Hopefully she won't regret those 12 months later. Certainly it shouldn't take any longer than that.

A Classic, Time-Consuming Case of Putting Off Closure

Liza dated Lou for a year and a half. He was her first post-college beau. She associated her newfound success with his presence in her life. It all seemed like one big, happy package—a good job, the serious prospect of marriage, and love ever after. When the attraction fizzled and Lou started showing his not-so-nice other side, Liza was reluctant to let go. To help herself make the necessary split, she moved to another city. But after putting distance between them, she stopped short of closure.

Heart to Heart

Here is what to expect. A survey of 200 individuals revealed that the distress from the breakup of a love relationship other than marriage and engagement is directly related to three factors: 1) the length of the relationship, 2) the closeness established between the two partners, and 3) the perceived chances of finding another relationship partner.

She continued to allow him to call, although each contact opened old wounds and prevented her from cooling the embers of love. Her fantasy was to pick up the phone one day and hear him apologize for all his wrong-doings and plead for another chance. She has waited nearly two years hoping he would say, "I love you. I want you back." Recently she installed caller I.D. and has refused to pick up the phone when he calls. But that's not closure either.

Closure would be Liza telling Lou, "Please don't call me ever again." Without that statement, closure in Liza's case will be put on hold. Evidently she isn't ready to let go of the past or shed that tiny ray of hope.

Doorstops

Use some imagery. There are a series of doorstops that need to be pushed out of the way one at a time. Hesitating will only lengthen the time you allotted for gaining closure and increase the weight of the burden. Think of each heavy doorstop as an aspect of your relationship that admittedly you will miss but which must be shoved aside.

1. The physical presence of your love interest
2. The activities you shared
3. The sexual intimacy you engaged in
4. The interdependency you created
5. The hopes and dreams you formulated

6. The satisfaction of needs you attributed to this person

7. The fulfillment found in his or her participation in your life

8. The love you gave and received

The disappointment, anger, rejection, depression, and fear you may be faced with after you remove these doorstops will be dealt with in the following chapters. They will assist you in surviving the breakup and achieving the closure necessary to find a new, exciting, and more appropriate partner.

The Golden Rules of Closure

Once you get close to shutting that door, follow through by using these rules of closure:

1. Stow the idea of a trial separation.

2. Don't be sweet-talked or tempted by memory back into the relationship.

3. Do not, I repeat, do not consider sexual farewells. It is problematic to make a warm bed.

4. Shut your ears to promises you know won't be kept.

5. Stay focused on the future you deserve and desire.

If you have successfully followed the advice and exercises in this chapter you are well on your way to achieving closure. However, you still have to confront the emotional aftermath of your breakup head on in order to close that door and subsequently be ready to re-enter into the dating arena unhampered by reminders of the past.

Don't think for one moment that closure is merely one of those buzz words of the '90s. It is an absolute necessity in the breakup process.

The Least You Need to Know

➤ Without reaching romantic closure, don't expect to be going anywhere soon.

➤ Real closure takes a conscious effort.

➤ Don't dilly dally over closing the door on your failed romance. Accept the reality and move on as quickly as you can.

➤ Closure signifies your relationship has gone through the entire cycle of physical and emotional phases, attraction through detachment.

Part 5
Surviving the Breakup

You will survive your breakup. That's guaranteed even though you can hardly believe it now. However, you should want more than merely getting through the pain of unrequited love, the guilt of initiating a split, or the disappointment over love lost.

You should want to proceed with dignity. There are helpful hints on how to do precisely that. Once you gain some control over your emotions and put a bandage on the open wounds, you will be ready to transform yourself from victim to victor.

With this improved perspective and mindset in place, you will be prepared to assess whether there is any reason to forgive and forget your lover's past transgressions or enter the dating scene looking for a fresh, new experience. Cautionary notes and serious considerations will put you on the right track for assuring more success in your next bout with love.

Chapter 20

The Emotional Aftermath of Breaking Up

In This Chapter

➤ Releasing your anger

➤ First-aid for unrequited lovers

➤ Throwing rejection aside

➤ Stomping out rejection, depression, and fear

You broke up and it hurts! You don't think anyone else could possibly understand how miserable you are. There are emotions running rampant that you don't want to admit even to yourself, let alone to others. However, the pain, anger, disappointment, fear, and rejection you are feeling is probably normal. What you don't want is to let a single one of these negatives get out of control. If you understand what is happening inside yourself, there is a better chance of tempering the pain and eventually rising above it.

After all, who wants to wallow in self-pity? Not you!

Angry? You Bet!

Anger is a natural reactive emotion. An unkind word, disappointment, or dissolution of a love relationship can unleash your anger. Here's how it works. You feel angry when:

➤ Your personal needs are not fulfilled.

➤ You perceive of real or imagined injury to yourself.

➤ A situation is extremely unacceptable, disturbing, or damaging to you.

➤ You experience frustration.

➤ Your state of pleasure is interrupted.

The Eruption of Romantic Anger

All of the factors mentioned above contribute to the anger you feel over lost love. Add the following for a complete list of causes:

➤ A lack of closure

➤ The inability to reunite with your loved one

➤ The lack of opportunity to communicate with your estranged partner

➤ Failure to convince your partner to keep on loving you

➤ Discovery of false perceptions and intentions

➤ Not fully comprehending why love failed

Blow the Whistle

Watch what you say! Lashing out in anger and spouting hurtful statements can do irreparable harm to your relationship. In fact, spouses who deal calmly with anger and guard their statements report a more positive level of marital satisfaction.

Is Your Anger Showing?

We all develop a way of reacting to anger that becomes a habit. What is your mode of action?

Reaction	Yes	No
1. Do you explode in a loud fury?	❏	❏
2. Do you lash out at others?	❏	❏
3. Do you stomp away with exaggerated, fast body movements?	❏	❏
4. Do you pout?	❏	❏
5. Do you fume inside?	❏	❏
6. Do you tense your muscles, wear a grimace, and pose in a rigid stance?	❏	❏

Is your anger excessive? It very well could be if you display rage, fury, and wrath. But as we all know, sometimes it is difficult to control our anger. According to Chicago educator, author, and psychotherapist Kenneth S. Isaacs, it's because anger is a part of our animal nature that encourages us to harm others as a means of protecting ourselves.

Consequently, in the dissolution of love relationships, men and women verbally lash out at each other, say things they don't mean, and regret those statements later.

Bits and Pieces

Studies prove that women frequently express anger toward the gal who took their place rather than at the man who left them. They prefer not to acknowledge the faults of their lover and pin the rap on the "other" woman instead.

Here's a simple exercise to reduce anger:

1. Talk it out with someone.
2. Expend energy. Jog, play a sport, spar with a punching bag.
3. Do a time out. Count to 10, take a walk around the block, sit quietly by yourself.
4. Talk to yourself.
5. Focus on a productive way to work through it.
6. For excessive, uncontrollable anger, seek help immediately!

It isn't wise to let your anger simmer, boil, and overflow. It will undoubtedly get in the way of making prudent, rational decisions pertaining to your love relationships and be counterproductive in handling any breakups. If you have established that you make a habit of displaying excessive anger, make a concerted effort to practice using the exercise above to get it under control.

Bits and Pieces

Even Venus, goddess of love and amorous delights, experienced the pain of unrequited love, according to Shakespeare's poetic version of her tale. She may have conquered Mars, made him a prisoner, and taught him to love, but she never got anything from Adonis but a flower.

The Pain of Unrequited Love

Mutual love and affection bring happiness. The opposite is true when love is not reciprocated. Unrequited love begets agony, misery, and unhappiness. Unfortunately, that may be what you are feeling!

According to well-documented research, women suffer more from broken hearts, the demise of a relationship, and unrequited love than men. Furthermore, females are more likely to feel exploited or mistreated and, consequently, experience greater harm from breakups than do their male counterparts. Men, on the other hand, believe they have been used for emotional support or an ego boost when women abruptly withdraw their romantic interest. This isn't nearly as shattering.

Documented Injuries from Unrequited Love

A range of injuries may result from unrequited love. Ask yourself if you are suffering from those that have already been documented in others:

1. A loss of self-esteem
2. Personal thoughts of worthlessness and inadequacy
3. Eruption of self-doubt
4. Diminished confidence
5. Erosion of trust
6. Feeling vulnerable
7. The onset of depression
8. The rise in tension
9. A sense of grief
10. Leaning toward self-pity
11. Heavy doses of rejection
12. Inward movement and erection of barriers

Once you have assessed your injuries, you can use the first-aid tips that follow to tend to your immediate wounds.

First-Aid Tips and Antidotes for Romantic Injuries

The following first-aid tips are designed to relieve your suffering and assist the healing process. Each one is a potent dose of medicine.

1. Acknowledge the pain.
2. Unload your discomfort and unhappiness.
3. Don't dwell on the question, "What's wrong with me?"

4. Ask what's wrong with the other guy and why he or she didn't appreciate you.

5. Hang out with people who give you praise and who do wonders for your flailing self-esteem.

6. Complete tasks or concentrate on work that improves your confidence and eliminates self-doubt.

7. Go out with a guy or gal who is excited by what they see in you.

8. Discover new ways to fulfill your need for love and belonging.

9. Don't allow yourself to sit home and pout.

10. Seek the company of others.

A bushel of additional suggestions for quick fixes follows in Chapter 21, "Quick Fixes."

It is difficult to recover from a serious illness without identifying the symptoms and making an accurate diagnosis. The same holds true for one suffering from romantic heartache, disappointment, and rejection. It is imperative to grasp how you have been wounded by love and to understand the ways in which you are manifesting that injury. Self-knowledge will speed your recovery and help determine where you need to apply the bandages or when you need to get a transfusion of self-confidence and self-respect.

Love Lingo

A quick definition of **self-esteem** is belief and pride in oneself. Your level of self-esteem is gauged by how much you like and respect yourself. A low level of self-esteem can land you in the dumps.

A New Take on Rejection

Sensitivity to rejection is another one of those annoying, inevitable, but natural conditions of being human. And with it comes that miserable sensation of humiliation and loss of acceptance. If you can rapidly move beyond the emotional side of rejection, however, to the intellectual sector of your brain, there is a chance to look at it objectively.

Let's say that Robby broke up with Robin. Immediately Robin wondered what was wrong with her that she couldn't hold onto Robby. She felt dejected, unhappy, and unattractive. When she stopped to analyze the situation, she realized that Robby was more perceptive breaking up with her than she first understood. After all, she was smarter than Robby, had more ambition than Robby, and was more physically active than Robby. They simply weren't compatible. There wasn't a thing wrong with her. It wasn't a good match. That's all.

It never occurred to Robin, however, that the initial sting of rejection she experienced stemmed all the way back to something in her past. Elayne Savage, Ph.D., author of

Don't Take it Personally (New Harbinger Publications, 1997), suggests we stockpile notions of rejection from childhood through adulthood. This repository of rejection influences how we feel when someone fails to invite us to a party or doesn't ask for a second date.

For instance, Robin's dad walked out on the family when she was seven. At the time, Robin heard her mother tell friends that something must be wrong with her if her husband didn't love her anymore. Robin picked up on this response and incorporated it into her own belief system. Consequently, whenever she encountered male rejection, she thought it was due to her own inadequacy.

Chapter 11, "Unintentional Precipitators of Breakups," touches on this subject as well, and a rejection-sensitivity quiz can be found in Appendix B, "Are You Primed for Rejection? Quiz."

Beating Rejection

According to rejection expert Elayne Savage, Ph.D., you can beat the rap if:

1. You don't take rejection personally until you figure out whether your feelings are warranted or rooted in the past.

2. You develop an ability to empathize and figure out where the other person is coming from.

3. You step outside the situation to gather a better understanding of what happened and reduce the flood of emotions.

4. You don't allow someone's personal rejection to invalidate who you are or intrude on your self-image.

5. You share your feelings of rejection.

6. You acknowledge the rejection, admit it hurts, then move on.

7. You don't let the fear of rejection prevent you from acting.

Bits and Pieces

Random questioning of women in their 20s and 30s about past snubs revealed that rejection from unrequited love was the offense that was referred to with greatest frequency.

With your new take on rejection and seven good suggestions on how to get over it, you are ready to wade out of the murky waters of self-doubt. It may take some practice to get in step, but it is well worth the effort. Once you refuse to take rejection personally, you will gain self-determination, confidence, and empowerment. What could be better than emerging from the harsh reality of a breakup buoyed by these three attributes?

Toppled by Romantic Depression

Feeling tense, tired, stressed out, worried, angry, blue, and dejected?

Well then, you have the symptoms associated with depression. However, there is no need to panic or book an appointment for immediate, intensive, and exhaustive psychotherapy sessions. Mild depression is common among individuals between the ages of 25 to 40 and certainly an appropriate response when love dies. Nearly everyone experiences a touch of the blues weekly. The primary cause of men's woes is money; for women, it's relationships.

Climbing Out of the Dumps

You may be able to get out of the dumps by yourself. Individuals are used to unconsciously changing their moods everyday and finding suitable diversions. When you are feeling blue, you may choose to see a funny movie, plan a trip to some place sunny and warm, or treat yourself to carbs or chocolate (if you're a gal) or red meat and protein (if you're a guy).

Most likely you have established your own way of climbing out of the dumps. Through trial, error, and repetition, you have discovered what evokes the best results for you and boosts those positive feelings. Because you are conditioned to this response, you automatically revert to this behavior when you feel down. For some it is a glass of wine, socializing, watching TV, running several miles, or calling a good friend.

If you haven't found your magic bean yet, keep trying. The important thing is that you manage these emotions in a positive way that leads to action, says psychologist Ellen McGrath, author of *The Complete Idiot's Guide to Beating the Blues* (Alpha Books, 1998) and *When Feeling Bad Is Good* (Henry Holt and Company, 1992).

Blow the Whistle

Watch out ladies! Studies show that women are two times more likely to suffer from depression than men. However, there is evidence on the other side of the coin that women are more efficient about dealing with and changing their negative moods.

Out-of-Hand Depression

Signs that your depression has gone beyond a normal, mild range and requires professional assistance include:

1. The inability to sleep
2. A serious lack of energy

3. A perpetual state of agitation

4. Continual fatigue

5. A serious drop in self-esteem

6. The inability to experience pleasure

In the event you are experiencing any of these serious side effects from romantic depression and are unable to lift off the shroud of doom and gloom, you should consider seeking professional help.

Up Against Fear and Worry

You are standing in a restaurant dumbfounded. Frieda or Fred just broke up with you. Whether you admit it or not, fear and worry creep into your system right alongside the pain and disappointment. You ask yourself, "Will I ever meet someone to love and marry me?"

And, so say experts in the field, the more you worry, the more you think you have to worry about. If you are skilled at worrying, undoubtedly you will find some angle of the breakup to worry over, imagine the worst possible scenario, fixate on the dark side of things, and focus on what is wrong even if everything is A-OK.

The perpetual worrier exaggerates. For instance, he or she will worry over never finding a love mate, rather than simple worries like where to meet a new love interest or who is going to be their date to that black-tie affair for work next week.

Blow the Whistle

Worrying isn't good for you. It causes stress and anxiety and affects your general health. It can become a problem that interferes with your everyday functioning and prevents the body from healing. Too much worry can even kill you.

Defining Worry

Think about it. Worry is an outgrowth of fear. You take a simple fear and add emotion, a piece of memory, a portion of anticipation, a dose of imagination, and, *voilà*, you are given something more to worry about that makes you feel vulnerable and powerless.

Worry signifies a lack of trust and troublesome uncertainty in the future. Unfortunately, the sympathy of others only reinforces the notion that something is awry and that there is a need to worry.

Ways to Curb Your Romantic Worries

No one can escape worrying altogether. Everyone does it. German scientists even discovered a "worry gene" in 1997. However, psychologists maintain that the gene is secondary in determining how much you worry and what you worry about. Your environment and how you learn to approach situations and solve problems is of primary importance. You can exhibit control over your worries and should not allow them to cause you undue stress or anxiety. Here are some ways in which you can curb those romantic worries that surface:

1. The best remedy is exercise. And while you are at it, do it at a gym where you will meet someone desirable to go running with.

2. Meditation and prayer is relaxing and curbs worry. Besides, nearly every church or synagogue has a singles group.

3. Keep going out and meeting new and interesting people. They will affirm that there are plenty of eligible men and women out there for you.

4. Brad Schmidt, associate professor of psychology at Ohio State University, thinks the best way to curb worrying is to identify precisely what it is you are worried about and then honestly evaluate whether or not the worry is reasonable and realistic. More often than not you will probably conclude that your worry is not justified by the circumstances.

Bits and Pieces

Perpetual worrying affects your overall level of comfort, happiness, and peace of mind. Furthermore, it impedes physical healing and diminishes the effectiveness of one's immune system.

Worrying is only one of the emotions that rain down in the aftermath of a breakup. However, like the accompanying anger, pain, depression, and rejection, there are ways to lessen the impact of fear and worry. The process to understand and control this emotional aftermath was introduced in this chapter. Discussions in the following chapters will offer further assistance.

The Least You Need to Know

➤ Your anger over lost love is justifiable.

➤ Shared, mutual love brings pleasure and happiness. Unrequited love is full of pain.

➤ You can overcome the negative emotions that bombard your system immediately following a breakup.

➤ Rejection is sometimes perceived incorrectly.

➤ If you understand the nature of fear and worry, you might eliminate some unfounded worries.

You're free!

Chapter 21

Quick Fixes

In This Chapter

➤ How to admire yourself in the wake of loss

➤ What to do about sexual desires

➤ Ways to make yourself happy

➤ Feel-good practices

You need readily available and quick fixes to get over those post-breakup humps and bumps that bombard you when the door closes on love. Quick fixes serve as your first line of defense and get you up on your feet again. Walking back onto the playing field comes a little bit later.

Sexual Substitutes

Let's face it. Life without sexual gratification is a bummer. Physically, you require it. The closeness and the affection an intimate partner offers is a bonus but not an absolute must. Reaching an orgasm only takes one. Consequently, when asked what her post-breakup sexual substitutes were, a woman in her 20s blurted out without hesitation, "Masturbation and chocolate!"

Strip away the embarrassment! Stop hiding the fact. Masturbation is widely practiced by men and women with and without regular sexual partners. Sex educator Betty Dodson, Ph.D., dubbed the mother of masturbation and the author of *Sex for One* (Crown Publishing, 1996), advocates spending 30 minutes to an hour making love to yourself. Masturbation, she contends, is a good way to relax, to explore your body, to enhance partner sex, to practice safe sex, to reach orgasm, and to release semen buildup in men.

Bit and Pieces

Ladies, try chocolate kisses as a delicious substitute for male affection. According to Deborah Waterhouse, a noted dietitian for women and author of several books, a few chocolate kisses a day can elevate your sagging mood. It seems chocolate affects your estrogen level (as well as your level of serotonin, the chemical that's associated with depression; that's why so many of us feel better after eating chocolate).

Masturbation Is Out of the Closet

The American Medical Association announced that masturbation is normal sexual behavior, and prohibition of masturbation was removed from the *Boy Scouts Manual* decades ago. A Miami University student in 1995 founded an official masturbation society on campus. For those in the dark, a string of masturbation clinics popped up around the United States to teach the fine art of climaxing independently.

Love Lingo

Masturbation is self-manipulation for sexual pleasure with or without the presence of a partner. That entails stimulating the clitoris in women and the penis in males to achieve an orgasm.

A Pocket of Resistance

Admittedly, masturbation still gets a bad rap in some circles. Religious admonitions and parental embarrassment of children's public displays often prevail. Furthermore, it is widely believed that U.S. Surgeon General Joycelyn Elders primarily lost her prestigious post because she suggested masturbation ought to be included in sex education in schools.

Bits and Pieces

Women who use vibrators are identified as white, college educated, in their 30s. They own one or two vibrators and use them alone or with a partner to satisfy themselves sexually.

Who's Doing It?

There are numerous studies that disclose exactly who is engaging in masturbation and how often. The information below demonstrates the prevalence of masturbation as a regular sexual practice.

Studies reveal that:

➤ Masturbation is common among adults of both genders.

➤ Nearly 60 percent of women and 90 percent of males have masturbated at some time.

➤ Fifty-five percent of men surveyed said they masturbate on a regular basis.

➤ Thirty-eight percent of women surveyed said they masturbate on a regular basis.

➤ Fifty percent of career women are likely to masturbate while only 21 percent of female homemakers do.

➤ Eighty percent of men with graduate degrees masturbated within the past 12 months.

➤ Fifteen percent of *Playboy Magazine*'s readers masturbate.

➤ Significant numbers of divorced women report they use masturbation as an acceptable alternative to couple sex.

Heart to Heart

Ladies: If you are masturbating with greater frequency than most women, it isn't because you are love-starved. Women with higher testosterone levels masturbate more often than women with lower levels of the hormone. You can always get your hormone levels tested if you wish.

How Often Are They Doing It?

Numerous studies reveal precisely which men and women are masturbating at least once a week. Furthermore, these results clearly show that men engage in masturbation more often than women in each comparable category.

Here's who's doing it at least once a week:

➤ Forty-eight percent of never-married men

➤ Twenty-eight percent of never-married women

➤ Sixty-eight percent of divorced men

➤ Thirty-seven percent of divorced women

➤ Forty-four percent of married men

➤ Sixteen percent of married women

The sheer numbers of men and women who masturbate weekly confirm that it is a widespread and satisfying sexual practice. This is particularly true among men and women who are not involved in a marriage relationship. The numbers are higher yet for those individuals who have been married and are now divorced.

Despite the numbers of men and women who masturbate, most individuals find sex with a partner more pleasurable than flying solo. Those who advocate masturbation as a means of self-discovery usually recommend this information then be used to achieve sexual satisfaction with a partner. While masturbation is a normal and gratifying sexual substitute and variation, it should not be viewed as a healthy and total replacement for partner sex.

A feel-good substitute for partner sex is not the only way to get a physical or emotional high in the wake of a breakup. There are plenty of other quick fixes to choose from.

Positive Breakup Ideas

Keep these thoughts in the back of your mind and come up with some of your own. There are some plus factors in your breakup. Just look for them! Recite them out loud. They will prepare you to get in the mood for the quick fixes that will follow later in the chapter.

➤ I am happy to have my freedom.

➤ I can benefit by the space.

➤ I can do whatever I want, when I want.

➤ I will have more money and time for myself.

➤ I don't have to be concerned about pleasing anyone else.

➤ I am too cool to waste my energy pining away for this guy or gal.

➤ I will be better off without this person.

➤ I will find a more satisfying love relationship and a better companion in the future.

➤ I can meet this challenge.

➤ I am too good to put up with someone not treating me in a special way or loving me with all their heart.

➤ I will be a better person because of this breakup.

One of the most productive breakup ideas to adopt and put into play is the notion that adversity can be a positive thing. Challenge yourself to use the adversity caused by heartache to propel you into action. You just might prove that adversity can be a personal plus.

Now is the time to concentrate on you. Stop focusing on what was or what could have been. All of that is beyond fixing now. Go for fixes that satisfy you personally. Enjoy the time you have to yourself.

A Tad of Narcissism Goes a Long Way

Concentrate on yourself physically and mentally. Nurture yourself and no one else!

➤ Focus on your goals and aspirations.

➤ A good mental exercise that *exorcises* uncomfortable, private thoughts is to keep a journal. It may be instructive to you or one of your friends later on, too.

➤ Post-breakups are a good time to admire yourself and dwell on your own perfection. Make a list of your good points.

➤ If you don't like the results, get to work. Reduce the negatives and add to the positives. Try body building, join a gym, get a new hairdo, go on a diet, try a more fulfilling job, or stimulate your intellect.

> **Blow the Whistle**
>
> Don't be overly critical of yourself! Ladies, when you look in the mirror, be positive. There is a dangerous mindset out there. Nearly 95 percent of all women find something they don't like about their body packaging. That attitude won't do you any good.

Adversity Can Be a Plus

Make adversity work for you. It has for countless others. If you allow it to, adversity will make you a stronger, more competent and confident person.

1. The first thing you must do is stop judging this momentary adversity in your love life as a calamity of monstrous proportion, an earth-shattering disaster, proof of your own bad luck, or an insurmountable defeat.

2. Engage your adaptive powers. All humans have them! These powers enable us to meet challenges, change our environment, and overcome obstacles. Taking advantage of your adaptive powers puts you in control.

3. If you are stuck with a case of narrow, pessimistic post-breakup vision, adjust your sights to encompass broad, optimistic horizons.

4. Focus on new possibilities and possibilities in love, work, and play.

5. Once your motor is up and running, the best modes of action to overcome adversity, according to experts in the field, are to build on your natural talents and contribute to others.

Adversity Control

Don't simply turn the page! Do not delay a moment longer! Stop right here and design a plan. You cannot control your adversity until you fill in the blanks. List four of your natural talents:

1. _____
2. _____
3. _____
4. _____

Designate which talent you will focus on first:

_____

Write down ways in which you intend to foster this growth:

1. _____
2. _____
3. _____
4. _____

Set a deadline date to begin:

1. Day: _____
2. Time: _____

Pick two ways in which you can help someone else:

1. _____
2. _____

Make yourself follow through. Select a starting date:

1. Day: _____
2. Time: _____

Added Benefits of Adversity Control

There is even more to be gained from adversity when you rise above it. Here is what experts say could be in store when you use adversity to your benefit, gear up your motors, and step into a bright new world solo:

➤ Gets you out of the house

➤ Provides possibilities for meeting stimulating, new people

➤ Assists in your personal growth

➤ Helps promote individual harmony and happiness

If you make the adjustment and begin to view romantic adversity as a plus, all kinds of rewards await you. Don't say you won't buy it until you try it!

A Mixed Bag of Quick Fixes

Want some fixes that will make you feel good but that you can perform out in the open? Try some of these:

1. Join a jogging club. Exercise releases tension, and the social factor is an added benefit.
2. Go shopping. Buy something that makes you feel fabulous. Put it on, go out, and count all the admiringly glances.
3. Try something novel, and explore new terrain. Take cooking classes, learn how to scuba dive, or sign up for a crash course in any stimulating subject.
4. Treat yourself to a spa day.
5. Take in a rash of funny movies.
6. Jump into some volunteer work. An act of philanthropic kindness benefits you and others.
7. Hang out with the guys or gals.
8. Do things that make you laugh. When you hear the sound of your own laughter, you know things can't be as bad as they seem.
9. Go to a concert, art museum, the zoo—anything you have missed out on for a while.
10. Take a weekend holiday with a friend. Don't go alone.
11. Surround yourself with happiness; steer clear of depressing subjects, movies, books, or people.
12. Throw a party.
13. Redo your home environment. Buy new sheets, and add fresh flowers.
14. Remove heart-tugging reminders of your love interest.
15. Look for adventure!
16. Make a list of your ex-lover's flaws. Make sure it's a long one. Post it on your fridge door.

Whatever you do, don't just sit around and mope after you break up. If one quick fix doesn't get the job done, try another one!

Assert Your Independence

It is advisable to reserve this fix for a second line of defense primarily because it requires time alone, and that isn't the very best posture immediately following a romantic disappointment. Nonetheless, exercising self-reliance and realizing that you can do anything you want by yourself provides an invaluable asset in all avenues of life.

Social psychologists tell us that the independent or "self-contained individual" is healthier and more growth-oriented than the dependent man or woman. For our romantic purposes it is important to note that the dependent personality forms limited interpersonal relationships and love partnerships based on need.

Blow the Whistle

Stow the macho image and quit grumbling, guys! Face up to your heartbreak and grab a quick fix. Most men hide their post-breakup hurt and don't complain about their wounded hearts. This only adds to their stress and depression. Admit the pain, share it with a confidante, and try to let go of it.

Love Lingo

A. H. Maslow, noted social psychologist, called love based on an individual's attempt to fulfill unmet personal needs within the perimeters of an intimate relationship **deficiency love**. Obviously this is not a positive state of love.

Exercise Your Independence

Once you feel more comfortable being alone and don't find yourself slipping into depression or the doldrums without your ex-partner's company, work on your independent side. It is worthwhile to prove to yourself that you can do things without the constant companionship of your old love interest. Furthermore, doing things alone empowers you to succeed on your own and makes you less dependent on others. After all, it may be a while until you discover a romantic partner with whom you wish to share your time. In the meantime, prove you can do it on your own:

➤ Take in a movie solo.

➤ Drive to someplace new and explore the environs alone.

➤ Go to a party stag.

➤ Make decisions singularly.

➤ Try a short trip on your own.

➤ Figure out what you are hesitant to do without a pal and try it yourself.

Additional handling of independence in the realm of love follows in Chapter 23, "Blossom from Victim to Victor."

You have come a long way. If you have been dumped and tried the fixes in this chapter, you're on the road to recovery. If you were the one to do the dumping and needed a boost, hopefully you found it in this chapter. However, don't jump the gun and think you have fully faced the aftermath of your breakup. The next phase is the cool down.

The Least You Need to Know

➤ Masturbation is a normal part of human sexuality.

➤ You are more equipped to meet your own sexual, emotional, and social needs in the wake of a breakup than you think.

➤ If you are willing to try, you can help yourself with quick fixes while the deeper healing takes place.

➤ Adversity in love is not the end of the world.

➤ There is absolutely, unequivocally no substitute for self-reliance.

Chapter 22

The Cool Down

In This Chapter

➤ Making love discoveries to last a lifetime

➤ Your three-tier learning chart

➤ Where did trust go?

➤ Romantic axioms to love by

The facts are nonmarital breakups do not receive the sympathy or support marital breakups do. Therefore, plan to recuperate largely on your own. This task falls squarely on your shoulders once friendly solicitations from the immediate aftermath disappear.

But that's okay. You'll do just fine. The cool down provides an excellent opportunity for you to further necessary introspection, fix what ails you, and at the same time prepare to eventually re-enter the dating scene. It is a time after the smoke settles when you begin to see things clearly and learn critical lessons.

A Loss of Trust, the Downside

About this time you notice yourself saying things like:

> "I'll never believe what a guy tells me again!"

> "They all lie."

> "You can't take anybody at their word."

> "Who knows if he or she really means it when they tell you they love you."

> "He just wanted to get me into bed. He didn't mean all the things he said and the promises he made."

> "She was only interested in me because she was desperate. Once she found out I had my own financial problems, she deserted me."

Each of these statements represent the natural skepticism, lack of trust, and self-doubt that follows a disappointing love relationship. You aren't alone if you have quietly uttered anything that resembles these statements. What you don't want to do is allow these beliefs to linger too long or permanently color your future romantic outlook. Make this a passing phase, one which you will eventually find yourself ready and able to leave behind.

In the meantime, consider the upside incurred from your momentary loss of trust.

Heart to Heart

California psychotherapist Nathaniel Branden wrote in *The Psychology of Love* (Yale University Press, 1988) that courage is a requirement of finding romantic love. That includes the courage to trust. Opting for safety instead of the courage to risk pain results in a failure to love.

A Loss of Trust, the Upside

It is normal to experience doubt, even a loss of trust. Although this is a negative lesson, it has an upside. It is prudent in matters of the heart to be *cautiously optimistic*.

Helpful thoughts you might want to keep in mind yet *not get carried away and apply to an unproductive extreme* include:

➤ A new love interest must prove that he or she is worthy of your trust.

➤ Do not trust indiscriminately.

➤ Do not assume a love interest is trustworthy until you see definite, concrete signs.

➤ Look for signs of character.

Early Indications of Trustworthiness

Mark this page for future reference. Once you are ready to start meeting new romantic partners, you can take this quick quiz to see whether or not you should extend your trust to him or her. We aren't talking blind or complete trust. That is built over time.

A Quickie Quiz to Determine the First Layer of Trustworthiness

Does He or She...	Yes	No
1. Call when they say they will?	❑	❑
2. Honor plans made together?	❑	❑
3. Give a reasonable explanation when plans for awry?	❑	❑
4. Represent themselves accurately (job, family status, education, availability)?	❑	❑
5. Appear to tell the truth to others?	❑	❑

If you can answer "yes" with certainty for each question, your new partner has passed the first level of surveillance.

Bits and Pieces

A lesson, right or wrong, that many people say they learned in the aftermath of a failed romance is how hard it is to find someone to love. However, that opinion is not always well founded but motivated by one's immediate state of disappointment.

A Springboard for Growth

Poets, writers, and social scientists agree that the loss of love not only offers individuals a unique opportunity to learn more about themselves but provides lessons in romance as well. There is much to gain from one's romantic errors—a clearer image of what is required in an intimate partner and how one can improve one's own romantic identity.

To make the most of the cool-down period, partake in a three-tier lesson plan that evaluates how you performed in the relationship, where your partner's deficiencies lay, and where the relationship went wrong.

The Three-Tier Learning Chart

Start with a personal exam. How wisely did you participate in your past relationship?

I. Self-Examination

Test your level of performance. How much or how little did you display of each of these qualities?

Rate yourself on a scale of one to six. One means you displayed very little of a particular quality. Six, on the other hand, means you exhibited a great deal of it. Once you have concluded all three parts of this learning chart, we will discuss the implications of your scores.

Quality Evaluation	1 = A Little, 6 = A Lot
1. Gullible	_____
2. Unassertive	_____
3. Weak	_____
4. Needy	_____
5. Feelings of unworthiness	_____
6. Low self-esteem	_____
7. Acceptance of poor treatment	_____
8. Failure to express needs	_____
9. Unable to demonstrate love	_____
10. Incapable of showing trust	_____
11. Jealous	_____
12. Sexually uncooperative	_____
13. Selfish	_____
14. Demanding	_____
15. Controlling	_____
Total	_____

II. Partner Examination

Test your partner's level of performance. How much or how little did they display of each of these qualities?

Quality Evaluation	1 = A Little, 6 = A Lot
1. Gullible	_____
2. Unassertive	_____
3. Weak	_____
4. Needy	_____
5. Feelings of unworthiness	_____
6. Low self-esteem	_____
7. Acceptance of poor treatment	_____
8. Failure to express needs	_____
9. Unable to demonstrate love	_____
10. Incapable of showing trust	_____
11. Jealous	_____
12. Sexually uncooperative	_____
13. Selfish	_____
14. Demanding	_____
15. Controlling	_____
Total	_____

III. Relationship Examination

Test the strength and health of your past relationship. How would you characterize your relationship?

Quality	1 = A Little, 6 = A Lot
1. Inconsistent with personal love map	_____
2. A lack of situational reality	_____
3. Full of deception and lies	_____
4. Uneven exposure to personal feelings	_____
5. Inadequate sexual intimacy	_____
6. Eruption of hurt feelings	_____
7. Differences of values and attitudes	_____
8. Uninterested in each other's lives	_____
9. Hurtmates instead of helpmates	_____
10. Multiple priorities in front of the relationship	_____
11. Unhappy in each other's presence	_____
12. Took each other for granted	_____
13. Open to cheating	_____
14. Unequal partners	_____
15. An absence of encouragement for personal success and achievement	_____
Total	_____

Interpreting the Results

In case you didn't notice, you were testing negative factors. So don't get excited if you turned up with high scores. The lower the numbers the better, but higher numbers indicate you were right to get out of the relationship.

In my book, anything more than a high of 20 on the self exam or the partner exam means you both need to work on yourselves and your ability to partake in a love relationship.

A low score for one partner and a high score for the other means the latter was too dominant and

Heart to Heart

A worthwhile question to ask yourself is, "Are you disappointed in the loss of love and the idea of having a love mate, or do you genuinely mourn the loss of your loved one?" It's time to come clean with yourself.

Heart to Heart

Men are more black and white when it comes to breaking up. When asked how he handles the end of a relationship, a 28-year-old male professional admitted to me, "Get another one." Ladies, you may find comfort in knowing that while he thinks you are interchangeable and expendable, painful memories do linger—especially in the supermarket when he sees a product his last love interest particularly enjoyed.

the former too passive to make a relationship together work out with any semblance of compatibility. Whichever you are, either tone down your act or gear up your confidence. It takes a healthy individual to nurture a good and lasting relationship.

Some things just aren't meant to be. If you lasted a long time in a relationship that scored a round of high numbers, you were fooling yourself. There is just as little room for chalking up the points on the relationship exam. None of these 15 characteristics should have been present with any degree of frequency. You were obviously hanging on for the wrong reasons. But that's okay; now that you are a well-informed would-be lover, you can try again and be more discriminating the next time around!

A Lesson Plan for the Future

Formulate your future course of action by asking and answering the following questions:

1. Does your love map need alterations? Perhaps it is unrealistic, not serving your needs well, or missing the point about what qualities make a good partner.

   Adjustments to be made:

   _____

   _____

2. What behavior did you exhibit in your last relationship that worked against you?

   Adjustments to be made:

   _____

   _____

3. What did you tolerate in your partner that you shouldn't have?

   Adjustments to be made:

   _____

   _____

4. What were the major flaws in your interpersonal relationship? What would contribute to a more fruitful outcome?

   Adjustments to be made:

   _____

   _____

Romantic Axioms

Keep the following thoughts in mind. You may want to memorize them. These wise axioms are born out of experience and research. They will enlighten your further quest for love.

1. Everyone is rejected at least once by a romantic love interest.
2. If you are rejected by a love interest, he or she isn't the right partner for you.
3. Love is fulfilling, but it can also be self-serving. Love satisfies one's need to be cared for, to achieve physical closeness, and to express sexuality.
4. Only mutual love is completely satisfying.
5. As humans we have the need to love, connect, communicate, and receive affection.
6. Convert neediness for love into readiness for love.
7. True love is when one responds to the other's needs, whether it benefits the giver or not.
8. Human needs are eternal; love often is not.
9. Self-defense is a strange bedfellow when it comes to matters of the heart, but in the long run it serves you well.
10. Love lasts longer than lust, but it is not as combustible.
11. The strength of a relationship is directly correlated to how rewarding it is to both participants.
12. If you want the truth, be prepared to accept it.
13. We are attracted to others who treat us as if we are special.
14. We attract others whom we treat as special.

The Least You Need to Know

➤ Before you can love one more time, you must work to regain a basic degree of trust.

➤ If you examine your past relationship, you can learn by your mistakes and ensure a better future.

➤ Learning a lesson is not good enough. You have to put it into practice to improve your love outlook.

➤ Love is sweetest when it complements your entire life.

Chapter 23

Blossom from Victim to Victor

Get ready to take charge of your attitudes. No more wallowing in self-pity over this breakup. If you dumped or were dumped, get on with life and love. Understandably, this command is more difficult for the rejected party to obey but all the more essential. However, if you have been following along conscientiously, making the mental move from victim to victor is only pages away.

Perception Is Key

Throughout our discussion of the full course of relationships from attraction to breaking up, there have been continual references to perception. It should be obvious by now that how you, your partner, and outsiders perceive one another and your relationship has tremendous room for variation. Some researches go so far as to assert that how the interpersonal relationship is perceived by each partner is more important than the actual reality.

Some individuals perceive events in a way that enables them to cope better for the moment. Those who don't may distort events in a negative direction that causes a loss of control, a demise of positive moods, and an increase of stress. That's where the victim mentality comes into play.

The Victim Mentality

The individual with the romantic victim mentality displays an overabundant number of self-defeating behaviors. Check off how many of these qualities you have on the following list when it comes to love:

Self-Defeating Behaviors	Have	Don't Have
1. Fear of future relationships	❏	❏
2. Fear of planning future events	❏	❏
3. Loss of self-esteem	❏	❏
4. Loss of trust	❏	❏
5. Dependency	❏	❏
6. Fear of inadequate relationship skills	❏	❏
7. Inability to make healthy decisions	❏	❏
8. Loss of ego	❏	❏
9. Feels used, ill-treated, and lead on	❏	❏
10. Helpless	❏	❏

Any check marks in the "Have" column are reason to pause. Each behavior is representative of someone who views themselves as a victim of love or a love partner. The more "Have"s you total, the harder you will have to work to evolve from victim to victor. Yet, if you fail to acknowledge a twinge of at least one of these behaviors following a breakup and all your marks fall into the "Don't Have" column, you are either in denial or are not being completely honest with yourself. Face up to the loss, how it made you feel, and what you can do about it. The options offered throughout this guide are plentiful.

Love Lingo

Empty love is defined by Yale University professor Robert J. Sternberg as love that encompasses a commitment but not passion or intimacy.

A Woman's Thing

Women are more prone to see themselves as victims of love than men are. They berate themselves for giving too much in a bad relationship and failing to get enough back. In the extreme, this scares women enough to avoid romantic possibilities, erect emotional walls, and impede self-disclosure—an essential ingredient for love to take hold.

Bits and Pieces

Did you know that you can be feeling lonely in two distinctly different ways after a breakup? There is the loneliness attributed to the isolation you incur after separation from a loved one and the loneliness you feel from losing your partnership status or place in a particular social circle.

Love's Essential Ingredient

Don't moan or groan. Yes, it is time for the proverbial, required topic in all romantic discussions—self-esteem. Whether you view this as a beginner or refresher course, pay close attention to every word of this important message. Your level of self-esteem could sabotage a relationship in one of two ways:

1. You could have so much self-esteem that you expect and demand too much from someone else in a relationship and deem their needs, interests, or goals as less important than your own. Too much self-esteem can make you overly confident and inflexible to other points of view.

2. You could have too little self-esteem and accept any partner who will offer you rewards, possibly mistreat you, or fail to recognize your needs.

Just the Right Measure of Self-Esteem

We have already noted that too much or too little self-esteem can be lethal to a romantic relationship. What then, is the right amount? I offer you two views—mine and that of psychotherapist Nathaniel Branden. They are not mutually exclusive. Rather, they compliment one another and create a healthy picture of what just the right level of self-esteem should provide for you. Strive for this level.

My choice: Enough self-esteem to:

➤ Ensure maintenance of your own identity

➤ Maintain respect for your partner's identity

Heart to Heart

Ladies, you are at the disadvantage here. Even feminist Gloria Steinem lost sight of herself in love and admits that she became who her male partners wanted her to be rather than who she really was. Once you get a clear picture of that woman staring at you in the mirror, be true to her image.

➤ Monitor your relationship

➤ Keep a good relationship on track

➤ Value yourself

➤ Demand respect, consideration, love, comfort, and support

Psychotherapist Nathaniel Branden defines a healthy level of self-esteem as that which enables an individual to feel:

➤ Competent

➤ Lovable

➤ Deserving of happiness, love, admiration, and respect

Bloom into Affirmation

Every breakup lowers your self-esteem to a degree and for a measure of time. Negative thoughts about yourself are normal and natural. Make sure, however, that they are fleeting. Here are some tips on how to shatter your self-doubt and reaffirm your identity and self-worth:

➤ Look for proof of your competence, whether that be in sports, work, family relationships, hobbies, school, or friendships. If that requires a change in your job or field of study, so be it. Competence in one endeavor promotes overall self-esteem.

➤ Take time to get to know who you are and not through the eyes of others. Self-discovery can be exciting, stimulating, and challenging. Without knowing who you are, you may impair your individual power, fail to use your abilities, and never nurture a healthy level of self-esteem.

➤ Learn to love and value yourself. If you do, you get a bonus. Self-actualization theorists who promote this idea say it is impossible to love someone else until you love yourself first.

➤ Develop appreciation for your body—intimate body parts, odors, and all. Unless you achieve this, you may find yourself sexually dysfunctional and see your self-esteem remain in the depths of despair.

➤ Work on becoming autonomous. Autonomous individuals are independent and self-directed. They govern themselves and move their will into action. They are self-sufficient and responsible for themselves.

Bits and Pieces

There is the assumption among some researchers that the rise in premarital sex that oc-curred after the sexual revolution reflected, in part, women's desire for sexual autonomy or control over their own sexuality.

Prune When Necessary

Don't get carried away and let your self-esteem become overgrown. It is a defense mechanism that might get in your way. Overcompensating for a real lack of self-esteem or a temporary lapse of it in the wake of a breakup can make you come off cocky and turn potential love interests away.

Cut back the self-esteem that grows out of control. Sure signs you need to prune are convincing yourself:

➤ You are always right.

➤ No one is good enough for you.

➤ You can't find anyone worthy of bestowing your love upon.

➤ No one can appreciate just how wonderful you truly are.

➤ Only you have the secret of how to love.

Once you have attained the level of self-esteem that will enable you to insist upon and function in a healthy, equitable relationship, you will automatically begin to shed your victim mentality. Other signs that you are on your way to becoming a victor will be described for you.

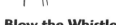

Blow the Whistle

Don't get carried away with your autonomy! Barbara Dafoe White-head alleges in her book, *The Divorce Culture* (Knopf, 1997), that the individual and individual freedom are so highly prized in American society that they actually support, idealize, and inadvertently encourage divorce. Be careful before you assume that you would be happier going it alone, and don't forget all the needs men and women meet when they couple.

Budding Signs of a Victor

The individual who eventually emerges from love's disappointment fully intact is a victor. He or she has developed a healthy potential for love. Therefore, he or she:

➤ Trusts their own expectations of success

➤ Maintains a realistic perspective

➤ Has ample self-esteem and confidence

➤ Demonstrates an understanding of love's strengths and weaknesses

➤ Uses cautious optimism when approaching a new love interest

➤ Asks for the truth and is able to accept it

➤ Extends trust to others in a wise and prudent manner

➤ Realizes they learned something valuable from their lost love relationship

A Victor's Truths

Victors, not victims, carry these truths with them. So should you. Repeat these truths to yourself until you commit them to memory:

1. I will not allow one person's crushing blow to break my spirit, diminish my self-esteem, or damage the essence of my being.

2. I will not delude myself into accepting a bad relationship.

3. I know I can do better and am ready to seek greater happiness.

4. I am unwilling to put up with untruths.

5. I am not desperate to find a mate.

6. I value myself and will make healthy decisions that foster my well-being.

7. I am aware of the good and bad consequences that may evolve out of a new love relationship and am prepared to take that chance.

8. I am going to be smarter and act more cautiously in the dawn of my next love relationship.

9. I am not going to allow my passions to put me in harm's way.

10. I am going to take my next relationship slowly.

Bits and Pieces

It is worthwhile to keep in mind that love and relationships bear cultural differences. In many countries, including the United States, where the individual is the center of all things, the emotional attachment to a partner is of primary importance. In societies that do not place as much importance on the individual, such as China, dependence upon one another rather than heartfelt love is the glue that binds.

The Last Step: Turn Off the Grief

You've come a long way. Be careful not to undo your hard work. All of the steps taken thus far should have helped to expel every ounce of grief. Yet, there is that human tendency to continue to recycle grief over and over again.

Make sure that once you have dealt with the loss of love—whether the grief is attached to an individual, a fantasy, or a romantic ideal—you do not revisit the scene. Visualize this endeavor as a walk down a one-way street. Once you reach the end of the block and look back, there is a big DO NOT ENTER sign staring you in the face.

There is no joining the crowd of victors until grief is entirely out of your system. If you have not yet resolved your grief, you may continue to feel a yearning for and an irrational desire to reattach to your lost love object. Employ a strong effort of mind over matter here in order that you may proceed to a happy ending.

It may take longer than reading this chapter to transform yourself from victim to victor. Do not hesitate to linger, review, or reread. Keep working at it until you feel like a victor and not a victim.

The Happy Ending, a Victor's Tale

Pauline and Paul had a six-month fling. Paul spouted refrains of love right off the bat, and Pauline took them for fact. Never mind that he put himself first, kept her guessing about their weekend plans, was too undependable to rely upon, and hardly measured up to her love map.

Pauline talked herself into thinking that love would turn Paul's faults around and that the fun, companionship, and mad attraction she had for him was enough. She didn't see herself slipping out of control or her self-esteem sinking while he kept her off-balance and her life in turmoil.

When Pauline finally stopped deluding herself that Paul might be the one and quit putting up with his shenanigans, she tossed him a quick and absolute farewell. At first she felt the pain of lost love, then the disappointment of a failed relationship, a tinge of regret, and finally remorse. She swore off men for a while, poured herself into her work, and affirmed that she deserved more.

Several months later she decided to date again, but this time she vowed no one was getting the better of her. She wasn't waiting for three strikes before calling the next guy out; she wasn't putting anyone before her career; and she wasn't going to accept anything less than reality. Despite her improved attitude, however, it wasn't until she met Pete that she could honestly admit to herself and others she was glad she had experienced the anguish of love with Paul.

If she hadn't, she feared she might never have realized just how special Pete was. He is a man of his word, goes out of his way to make things happen to be with her, and is just as much fun as Paul ever could be. The difference is Pete doesn't have to tell her he cares about her; it's obvious in his actions.

Still, Pauline is taking her time to get to know the real Pete. There is nothing make-believe about this chapter of love.

The Least You Need to Know

➤ In the wake of a breakup, women are particularly vulnerable to self-defeating behaviors.

➤ It is impossible to have a healthy love relationship without each partner owning the right amount of self-esteem.

➤ Self-esteem protects each partner and enhances love.

➤ Before you begin to date again, give up being the victim. Assume the identity of a prudent and wise victor.

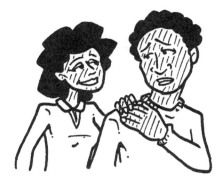

When to Forgive or Forget

After all is said and done, there will be those moments of doubt before closure not only closes but locks that door. You hear about married and unmarried couples breaking up…then getting back together again…then breaking up one more time. If either partner had taken time to rationally pinpoint reasons to forgive or forget, they could have saved themselves another bucket full of heartache and misery.

A Case for and Against Misunderstanding

Before you entertain the idea of forgiving, let's talk about whether or not a case could be made for misunderstanding. Don't jump to any quick conclusions or pick up the phone just yet!

Your understanding of a love interest and his or her behavior is highly subjective. The nature of your love, outlook, bias, familiarity, personal motivations, and perceptions color your interpretation of events that are seemingly ambiguous to you.

Bits and Pieces

"Love is not about power. Romance is a means to the end of self-completion, but love is an end in itself...If we love someone, we want them to continue being the essence of themselves. If so, then we can't own, absorb, or change them. We can only help them to become what they already are."

—Gloria Steinem

However, the more you know someone, the less likely it is that you are guilty of a simple case of misunderstanding. Alan L. Sillars of the University of Montana found that "innocent misunderstandings"—in which there are no personal motivations behind them—normally result from a lack of information between couples who don't know each other well.

So if your ex was a long-term lover, be leery when he or she pleads you got it all wrong. Don't take kindly to the notion that a serious infraction or an unforgivable act was simply a case of misunderstanding!

Blow the Whistle

Get help! There are at least 1,000 shelters across the country for victims of domestic violence and a hot line in nearly every city. Appendix A, "Resources," tells you how and where to get the help you need.

Unforgivables

If you need it spelled out for you, unforgivable acts are ones that:

➤ Intentionally attempt to control you

➤ Harm you physically, mentally, or emotionally

➤ Diminish your stature or self-esteem

➤ Purposefully encourage unhealthy dependence

➤ Demean you in any conceivable way

A discussion of these behaviors and when and how they are acted out will leave no doubt when you are up against a love interest or partner that should not be forgiven.

Abusive Behavior Among Married and Dating Couples

Domestic violence falls squarely into the category of unforgivable! It is not limited in scope to married couples or socioeconomic groups. You can be involved in a dating or cohabitation arrangement and be the victim of physical, emotional, or sexual abuse. The punches do not have to land a black eye and broken arm to count. Oftentimes the harm perpetrated is invisible to the naked eye. Nonetheless, emotional battering is just as serious an offense.

Sometimes the abuse starts with an emotional jab or insult, then escalates into a slap, and culminates in a severe beating. Despite the severity, the end result is always the same. The victim is diminished in statue and fearful of the abuser. Indecision, lack of confidence, financial hardships, fear, and love cause women in violent situations to leave their abuser on the average of seven times before they make a final split.

Abusers are out to win control over you. They do this by:

➤ Playing mind games

➤ Making all decisions

➤ Causing you to feel guilty, inadequate, and undesirable

➤ Inflicting bodily or emotional harm

➤ Separating and isolating you from family and friends

➤ Taking charge of your daily life

➤ Preventing you from working

➤ Handling all money matters

➤ Threatening violence, suicide, or murder

➤ Showing weapons

➤ Talking you into doing things you normally would not consider

➤ Determining where you go and who you see

➤ Blaming you for eruptions of their anger

➤ Claiming acts of abuse never happened

Bits and Pieces

Four thousand women die from battering each year. Four million are beaten annually. One-third of all married women report at least one incidence of domestic abuse. More than $5,000,000,000 in health-care costs can be attributed to domestic violence annually.

Abuse in Dating Relationships

There has been some research done just on abuse in dating relationships. Still, all of the information pertaining to domestic violence applies here, too. If you skipped that section, go back and read it. Even if it doesn't apply to you, chances are you will have the opportunity to help someone else. Whether you are aware of it or not, each of us regularly encounters situations of abuse among family, friends, roommates, acquaintances, or coworkers.

In dating relationships, anything done by your partner to reduce your status is considered abuse. Coercion plays a big part in that and is reportedly done through slamming doors, insults, swearing, or forceful language.

Average reports of physical violence in dating relationships range from 20 to 50 percent. Both men and women suffer this form of dating violence; however, women are more likely victims. Thirty-one percent of women and 15 percent of men suffer major trauma. Reports of sustained injuries are 18 percent for women and 10 percent for men.

Sexual Abuse, Absolutely Unforgivable

The statistics are staggering! A national study revealed that 15 percent of college students had suffered rape. Some estimate that one in four women will be raped. Most women who are raped know the rapist. Among college students, 50 to 80 percent of the women knew the offender; he was either a date, an acquaintance, or a steady beau.

Force does not necessarily have to be exhibited in order for sex to be considered abusive. Sex that engenders sexual humiliation or denigration and is performed out of fear or emotional coercion is every bit as abusive as rape, note Neil Jacobson, Ph.D., and John Gottman, Ph.D., authors of *When Men Batter Women* (Simon & Schuster, 1998).

Bits and Pieces

Nearly one-third of men and women between the ages of 17 and 30 surveyed over a two-week period admitted they consented to having sex with their committed partner when they didn't want to. The reason they did was to avoid tension, promote intimacy, and satisfy their partner's needs. The majority of these individuals claimed their behavior yielded positive outcomes. As long as their sexual activity does not become abusive, their motives and actions do not appear to be unhealthy.

A Case of Twenty-Something Cohabitation Abuse

Molly was 26 when she moved in with Michael and walked into a dangerous three-year nightmare. Raised in a protected, upper-middle class, suburban home, she ignored her family's advice and fell prey to Michael's charm and looks. She could hardly believe that he was interested in her. "I would have gone to any lengths to make sure we were together," she admitted.

Moving in together was her game plan for keeping him under wraps and away from other women. Supporting him was her way of making him dependent. However, the tables turned quickly.

"Michael worked on my self-esteem," Molly revealed. He told her enough times she was crazy and unappealing and ignored her sexual advances that she began to question her own sanity and doubted anyone else would want her. Every time she made the attempt to throw him out, Michael would change her mind by making love to her and giving her the attention she needed.

One night he began yelling, screaming, and hitting. He socked Molly repeatedly and knocked out several of her teeth. She was bruised all over and had to be taken to the hospital. When he threatened to kill her, she called her parents and got a restraining order. Later she found out that she was the sixth woman to file a domestic violence complaint on him.

"I still can't believe I allowed this to happen," Molly said six years later.

Sexual Coercion, No Forgivable Matter

Ladies, sex that has been coerced in any way violates your personal boundaries—mind, body, and heart. It is not to be tolerated.

Gentlemen, sex that has that been initiated by a woman who thinks she can suck you into a relationship you won't feel right leaving is not worth the second helping.

Persuasion, pressure, persistence, and deception are measures of entrapment used to coerce a person into sex. Techniques include untrue confessions of love, false promises of engagement and marriage, and other lies. Additional techniques involve making the unwilling party feel guilty or inadequate.

Coercive sex is premeditated primarily by men who press for intercourse early on in a dating relationship. Alcohol plays a big part in this type of sexual encounter.

Getting and Staying Out of an Abusive Relationship

If you have encountered any forms of the emotional, verbal, physical, or sexual abuse described in this chapter but have had difficulty getting out and staying away, pay close attention to the advice that follows. No one should have to subject themselves to another individual who compromises their physical, mental, or emotional well-being. That's not what love is all about.

225

At the same time, I will acknowledge that it is difficult to extricate oneself from an abusive relationship. That is why the most prudent thing you could do the first time you are abused in any way is to leave that guy or gal behind. Abuse is notorious for escalating. It is not a behavior or problem that resolves itself. If you are unsure whether or not your love interest or partner has performed in an abusive manner, call the National Domestic Violence Hot Line at (800) 799-7322, consult a local expert, and refer back to the way abusers seek to gain control described earlier.

Blow the Whistle

Call for help! Never hesitate to call your local police department or 911 if you are in immediate danger. Do not let them leave you in a dangerous position. Insist they help you vacate the house, arrest your abuser, or take you to a shelter.

Heart to Heart

Women normally leave an abusive relationship seven times before they leave for good. Frequently their re-entry into the relationship involves a honeymoon period characterized by pleas for forgiveness, promises of better treatment, and acts of kindness. Unfortunately, most battered women laugh at the honeymoon phase. They are all too aware that it quickly dissipates and is replaced by the typical patterns of abuse they previously endured.

If you are stuck in an abusive relationship and can't get out, you are not alone. There is a consensus of opinion among those who work with victims of domestic violence that women who are battered are inhibited to leave because of:

➤ Fear of death, injury, or separation from their children

➤ Emotional and financial dependence

➤ Shame and embarrassment

➤ Uncertainty

➤ Low self-esteem

➤ Hope and wishful thinking

➤ Love

➤ No where to go

➤ Belief that they caused the abusive behavior in some way

Women who have found themselves in this predicament admitted that they had to face the harsh facts of reality before they were motivated to leave. They had to acknowledge and accept that their relationship was not going to improve, that their abuser was not going to change, and that it was time to give up that fantasy. Once they adopted the conviction they were going to leave, most set about making a plan. Others have left under immediate threat of bodily harm.

Interestingly, researchers have found that women who leave impulsively incur less success staying away than do those victims who carefully plan their exit. Your plan should include:

➤ A family member that will provide shelter, protection, and understanding

➤ A shelter for battered women if you need to go into hiding

➤ An agency that can assist you to find work and permanent housing

➤ Someone who can validate that your feelings and actions are justified

➤ Ways in which you can build your self-esteem, become employed, and remain independent

Bits and Pieces

A study of approximately 200 men and women of college age revealed that men became more upset by their female dating partner's sexual infidelity with another male than with a female. Women, on the other hand, were more jealous when their male dating partners had a sexual encounter with another male than with a female other than themselves.

Infidelity, a Serious Infraction

There are some individuals, both professionals and novices, who claim that it is unreasonable to think you could make a lifetime commitment of love to one person, let alone remain sexually faithful. They use the argument that the notion of monogamy, fidelity, and lifelong love belonged to an era of lesser life expectancy. But then that throws out all we have learned about love—namely, that love grows and intensifies over time.

A fundamental element of true love is trust. As long as infidelity is considered as breaking that trust, infidelity will remain a serious infraction within your married or dating love relationship.

Bits and Pieces

A study of 190 cultures found that only 10 of those shared the Western Judeo–Christian values and traditions that denounced extramarital sex. Despite the prohibition against infidelity in our society, approximately 65 percent of men admit having at least one extramarital affair by age 40. There is evidence that as many as 34 percent of women have had sex outside of marriage as well.

Is Infidelity Forgivable?

Although infidelity is widely practiced privately under the covers, there is little public tolerance for it. Only about 35 percent of marriages within the general public survive extramarital affairs. Women are more likely to forgive their husbands than husbands are to forgive their wives. Women who stay are those females who perceive themselves as having more control over their lives and who don't accept the victim mentality. Generally they have a higher level of self-esteem and a better sense of self.

Infidelity the first time around is easier for women to forgive than repeated subsequent transgressions.

Forgive Yes, Forget No!

The women who forgive but prudently don't forget are wives whose spouses' infidelity was:

➤ Not overly exposed and did not cause them a great deal of public embarrassment or humiliation

➤ More of a sexual nature and did not involve love or emotional attachment

➤ Caused, they feel in part, by unrecognized and unsatisfied sexual needs on their behalf

Other women are motivated to give their cheating spouses another chance because of:

➤ A long marital history

➤ Religion

➤ Love

➤ Financial considerations

➤ A promise to remain faithful

➤ The desire to raise their kids together

Does Forgiveness Last?

Forgiveness can and does last, especially in those cases where the guilty partner is truly repentant and feels the pain caused to family members. In long-term marriages where some degree of love, trust, mutual respect, and passion remains, the odds are pretty good for a permanent reconciliation.

Forgiveness is short-lived when men put the blame for their philandering on their wives and often engage in further betrayals. This results in a complete and irreparable loss of trust. At this stage, women frequently become angry with themselves for staying in the first place and leave immediately.

Questionable Reasons to Stay

There are those women who will stay in a relationship no matter how they are treated. It isn't my position to place a value judgment on their reasons for staying or how they rate their priorities in life. Nonetheless, anyone who stays for questionable motives ought to make sure the trade-off is a plus in their favor. Too often these women are suffering in silence.

Questionable motives include:

➤ Protection of financial and social status

➤ Martyrdom

➤ Punishment by evening the playing field through their own affairs or costly shopping sprees

Men Are Unlikely to Forgive

The idea of a woman having sex with someone else drives a man crazy. It attacks the very core of the male ego. Sixty percent of men in a survey said that sexual infidelity was more disturbing than emotional betrayal. Unfortunately, the two often go hand in hand for women. Sexual infidelity by women is most often born out of marital dissatisfaction and combines sex and an emotional attachment to another person. Men are even less able to handle the surprising discovery that they are not the biological father of their supposed child. Approximately 13 percent of all children have incorrectly identified biological fathers.

How to Forgive and Forget Infidelity

If you do decide to try and forgive a partner's infidelity, you will need to work at it. Emotionally it can be a struggle, but one that can be overcome. Living examples of happy couples who have done it are all around you. Here is a prescription of forgiving and forgetting:

1. Determine each and every cause of a partner's cheating ways.
2. Deal candidly with all the causes of the indiscretion.
3. Work on marital dissatisfaction together.
4. Don't put your head in the sand.
5. Go slowly.
6. Expect trust to build over time.
7. Try to put aside the pain.
8. Do not punish a partner by withholding sex or love.
9. Reaffirm the love you hold for each other.
10. Work hard to eliminate anger.

11. Focus on the future life you want together.

12. Appreciate the family and history you share.

13. Root out any seeds of jealousy.

If you are having difficulty following this prescription and are unable to forgive or forget, you may have a case of unresolved jealousy.

The Jealousy Factor

Jealousy is frequently a reflection of an individual's sudden or sustained lack of self-esteem, unworthiness, inadequacy, incompleteness, and insecurity. Romantic jealousy is associated with the fear of losing the exclusive attention of a love interest. Therefore, some say romantic jealousy is based on some degree of possessiveness.

The Jane who exhibits romantic jealousy will look over her shoulder for the woman who is prettier, smarter, or more successful than she and who she thinks might be able to steal her playmate away. The jealous Joe will do the same thing. When Joe and Jane become jealous, their happiness melts into anger, fear, brooding, sickness, worries, and sadness. They feel a loss of control, uncertainty, and betrayal that can spark dangerous emotions, aggressive behavior, argumentative communication, belligerent actions, and revengeful acts of retaliation. Hardly the stuff that forgiving and forgetting are made of.

Unresolved jealousy shatters any hope of trust, adds suspicion, and stands in the way of normal problem solving. In the extreme, jealousy is the major cause of murder among marriage partners.

Heart to Heart

Seventy-four percent of single women in Shere Hite's study left relationships that made them unhappy. You would be wise to follow their lead.

A Forgive or Forget Quiz

To further help you determine whether or not you would be wiser to forgive or wiser yet to forget, take the following test. It will help measure the overall climate of your relationship and whether or not there is sufficient substance to merit risking forgiveness.

Answer each of the following questions honestly!

Question	Yes	No
1. Did you have a higher level of self-esteem before your relationship?	❏	❏
2. Were you more capable of making independent decisions before you met your last lover?	❏	❏

Question	Yes	No
3. Were you frequently forgiving your love interest for his or her unacceptable behavior?	❏	❏
4. Did you often make excuses to family and friends for your partner's actions?	❏	❏
5. Did family or friends tell you this was an unhealthy relationship for you?	❏	❏
6. Were you constantly agitated by him or her?	❏	❏
7. Did you find it difficult to trust this person?	❏	❏
8. Did you feel as if you had lost control over your life?	❏	❏
9. Did you frequently partake in sex or sex acts when you did not want to?	❏	❏
10. Do you feel happier most of the time without this person in your life?	❏	❏
11. Did your partner tell you what to do or prevent you from doing what you wanted?	❏	❏
12. Did your partner discourage you from seeing family and friends?	❏	❏
13. Was it difficult for you to exert your independence in this relationship?	❏	❏
14. Did your partner make a habit of lying to you?	❏	❏
15. Did your partner cheat on you?	❏	❏
16. Did your partner makes promises to straighten up his or her act and not carry through with them?	❏	❏
17. Did your partner have a substance abuse problem and refuse to get help?	❏	❏
18. Did your partner take advantage of your financial resources?	❏	❏
19. Was your love interest constantly critical of you?	❏	❏
20. Did your love interest frequently insult you?	❏	❏

Forgive Him/Her Scale:

If you have tallied 20 or more "yes" answers, forgiveness should be out of the question. Your partner's behavior and the general health of your relationship reveals that you are lucky to have split. Five "yes" answers indicates that forgiveness should be given some serious but skeptical consideration. For the individual who didn't have a single "yes" answer, you need to remember why you broke up in the first place, evaluate how serious of an infraction occurred, and whether or not you care enough to make the relationship work. There is nothing in your quiz results to indicate an unforgivable action.

The Danger of Forgetting

Twenty-something Howard was the first man Helen, a then 18-year-old dark-haired Spanish beauty, had sex with. He was also the first man to dump her.

"Howard said I was too young and that he wanted to date other women after we slept together. I hated him. We had a lot of friends in common, so I had to see him everywhere. I was so upset when I saw him because we had had sex. Several years later I saw him, and he apologized and invited me back to his place to talk."

It wasn't very far into their conversation that Helen realized he was trying the same old thing. It made her feel terrible all over again but at least this time she didn't give in to sex.

Emotions rise and fall during the aftermath of a breakup. We have been careful to explore the many ups and downs throughout the previous chapters. It is particularly important when your mind wavers and you question your original decision to call it quits that you have a guide available for when to forgive and when to forget. When in doubt, open this book to this chapter for objective guidance.

The Least You Need to Know

➤ Never allow a love interest to control or abuse you in any way.

➤ There is help if you are a victim of abuse.

➤ Forgiveness should be handled just as judiciously as if you were breaking up all over again.

➤ Sexual coercion should not be tolerated.

➤ Use rational thinking when deciding whether or not to forgive an act of infidelity. Wait until the emotions settle before saying "yea" or "nay."

Re-Entering the Dating Arena

You have gone through an intense and extensive breakup training course. Before you step back into the dating scene, let's see how well you have learned your lessons and how well prepared you are to avoid the same mistakes. To get the most benefit out of this chapter, do not rush through the following examinations. If you score poorly on a set of questions, go back and spend time on the issues under analysis.

We are talking about the future success of your love life here, the potential to meet those inevitable breakups head on, and the ability to land on your feet.

Your Dating IQ

What does intelligence have to do with the cycle of attraction, love, and breaking up? Plenty!

Your intelligence is a mark of your ability to understand events, learn from experiences, respond quickly, successfully meet the challenge of new situations, reason, and solve problems.

Interpret this in lover's terms. Your romantic intelligence is a mark of your ability to understand a love interest's intentions, learn from previous romantic attachments, size up a potential new relationship quickly, know whether or not this is a good relationship for you, make yourself move on if necessary, and make any adjustments that will enhance your prospects for lasting love.

An IQ test measures that degree of intelligence. A romantic IQ test has been devised to indicate your level of intelligence when it comes to matters of breaking up.

A Romantic Breaking Up IQ Test

Get ready to test your intelligence quotient when it comes to romantic breakups. This information isn't innate. It has been given to you in pages throughout this guide. If you get stumped, you could go back and look up the answer. Proceed by responding true or false.

True or False

1. Men and women think differently. _____
2. It is not always easy to determine exactly what the opposite sex is saying. _____
3. Sex is one of the basic human motivators. Logical thinking is not. _____
4. Sex is a complicating factor in early love relationships. _____
5. Love always lasts a long time. _____
6. Lust can be stronger than love. _____
7. Sex is in the minds of men at least three times a day. _____
8. As soon as you feel dissatisfied with a relationship, you should break up immediately. _____
9. One person is always at fault when a relationship breaks up. _____
10. Physical attraction is what gets the ball rolling first. _____
11. Revealing too much or asking too many questions when you first meet can be a turn off. _____
12. Eighty percent of infatuations turn into love. _____
13. Some experts think love could be 90 percent sex. _____
14. Monogamy is a fact of nature. _____
15. Most animals mate for life. _____
16. Mature love is based on companionship and intimacy. _____
17. Lasting love formulates quickly. _____
18. Playful frolicking is not necessary to ensure the duration of love. _____
19. There is no difference between love and infatuation. _____
20. Purely romantic relationships run their course in 18 months to three years. _____
21. Humans are romantically influenced by their biological makeup. _____
22. Boredom is the number one reason couples break up. _____
23. Love addiction is a fallacy. _____
24. Love alone is enough to formulate a sound foundation for a lasting relationship. _____

True or False

25. Men stonewall making a commitment more often than women. _____
26. Men prize their freedom more than women do. _____
27. Absence always makes the heart grow fonder. _____
28. Premarital counseling decreases the chance of divorce. _____
29. There is no risk in occasionally having sex with a prior love interest. _____
30. Breaking up is done in stages. The first stage is a loss of infatuation. _____
31. Men are less likely to use lies to break up than women. _____
32. Men tell women exactly what they want to hear. _____
33. Men find it easy to confront a woman honestly. _____
34. Women are more adept verbally than men. _____
35. The "set up" is a deliberate exit plan used primarily by men. _____
36. Men prefer that a woman do the dumping. _____
37. Breaking up is never empowering. _____
38. There is nearly always some small shred of evidence that a breakup is in the air. _____
39. If a love mate rushes out after sex with a quick good-night, that could be a signal of distress in the relationship. _____
40. Diminished sexual appetite can be caused by something other than waning attraction. _____
41. Male hunters frequently change typecasts and become marriage seekers. _____
42. A woman is never a seductress. _____
43. Lying is part of our everyday lives. _____
44. Men never lie solely for the purpose of having sex with a woman. _____
45. Women plot their lies more carefully than men. _____
46. It is better to tell a lie than hurt someone's feelings when breaking up. _____
47. If you think a love interest will dump you, the probability is he or she will. _____
48. Self-fulfilling prophecies do not relate to matters of the heart. _____
49. Intimacy is the core of a love relationship. _____
50. You should explicitly reveal the details of your sexual history to a new love interest. _____
51. Love is a human need. _____
52. One hundred thousand weddings get canceled each year. _____
53. Cold feet based on a doubting case of love is natural before a marriage. _____
54. Living together before marriage increases the chances of marital success. _____
55. Most states still honor common-law marriages. _____
56. Individuals who live together express greater enthusiasm over the idea of getting married. _____
57. Married couples who separate are wise to obtain separation agreements. _____

continues

continued

True or False

58. It is better to try to work it out before deciding to split for good. _____

59. It takes two healthy people to have a healthy relationship. _____

60. The right person can fulfill all your needs and desires. _____

61. Prosperity influences higher divorce rates. _____

62. Spousal cruelty is the number one cause of divorce. _____

63. It is okay for a couple to use one divorce lawyer to represent both of them. _____

64. Knowing why your partner wants to break it off will make you feel better than not knowing. _____

65. Needy lovers are easy to break up with. _____

66. It is common for men to think of commitment as foregoing sex with other women. _____

67. Being friends with someone you were romantically involved with is a realistic breakup goal. _____

68. The double standard in sex is still in play despite the sexual revolution. _____

69. Breaking up does not require a plan or set of goals. _____

70. All breakup lines are equally hurtful. _____

71. It is unimportant to carefully choose where you break up. _____

72. In order to get completely over a breakup, one has to reconcile past events emotionally and intellectually within oneself. _____

73. Everyone can use closure, but men need it more than women. _____

74. An ex-partner who spies on you, makes surprise visits at your workplace, or keeps calling to check on your whereabouts is doing nothing you should worry about. _____

75. Even if you subconsciously wait for your immediate past lover to phone, you could have achieved closure. _____

76. You should be able to achieve closure within a month of a breakup. _____

77. Anger is unnatural when you break up. _____

78. Physical exercise reduces anger. _____

79. Men suffer more from broken hearts and unrequited love than women. _____

80. Self-doubt is a natural by-product of breaking up. _____

81. There is such a thing as romantic depression. _____

82. A lack of energy, the inability to sleep, and a serious drop in self-esteem are signs your romantic depression is out of hand. _____

83. You should anticipate feeling fearful and worried when you first break up. _____

84. Looking for sympathy is a good way to alleviate your worries. _____

85. Masturbation is a normal sexual substitute following a breakup. _____

86. There are no positive conclusions one can draw from a breakup, only pain. _____

True or False

87. Adversity never makes you a stronger or wiser person. _____

88. Learning to meet your own needs and being able to spend time alone are valuable breakup tools. _____

89. A dent in your sense of trust signifies a severe problem in your post-breakup identity. _____

90. Helping someone else and trying something new that will enhance your growth are positive steps in the post-breakup period. _____

91. Only mutual love is completely satisfying. _____

92. Lust lasts longer than love. _____

93. True love is selfish love. _____

94. Love can be empty without passion and intimacy. _____

95. Your perception of events may impact you more than the real circumstances. _____

96. Being loved is a good substitute for having little self-esteem. _____

97. You can't be too independent in a love relationship. _____

98. Misunderstanding a love interest's intentions or actions usually occurs after you get to know each other well. _____

99. Abusive behavior should never be readily dismissed. _____

100. There is never a good reason to forgive infidelity. _____

Answers to IQ Questions:

1. True	21. True	41. False	61. True	81. True
2. True	22. True	42. False	62. False	82. True
3. True	23. False	43. True	63. False	83. True
4. True	24. False	44. False	64. True	84. False
5. False	25. True	45. True	65. False	85. True
6. True	26. True	46. False	66. True	86. False
7. True	27. False	47. True	67. False	87. False
8. False	28. True	48. False	68. True	88. True
9. False	29. False	49. True	69. False	89. False
10. True	30. True	50. False	70. False	90. True
11. True	31. False	51. True	71. True	91. True
12. False	32. True	52. True	72. True	92. False
13. True	33. False	53. False	73. False	93. False
14. False	34. True	54. False	74. False	94. True
15. False	35. True	55. False	75. False	95. True
16. True	36. True	56. False	76. False	96. False
17. False	37. False	57. True	77. True	97. False
18. False	38. True	58. True	78. True	98. False
19. False	39. True	59. True	79. False	99. True
20. True	40. True	60. False	80. True	100. False

Evaluating Your IQ

It is not unreasonable to expect 100 percent accuracy on this breakup IQ test. The facts are the easy part when it comes to dating, sex, and love. The hardcore test of your IQ comes when you try to put all of this information into action. You can, however, prove to be a genius at relationships and breaking up if you proceed with forethought and carefully observe all the signs and signals around you.

Any score less than 90 requires a makeup test. It isn't safe to resume dating and risk a breakup until you show more proficiency in this area. Go back and reacquaint yourself with the material in the previous chapters in order to improve your score.

Are You Still Vulnerable to Heartbreak?

Make sure you have the issues regarding love, sex, lust, relationships, and breaking up referred to in the quiz above under control. Feel confident you can handle the consequences if applied to a love interest. If you feel comfortable with your level of proficiency, step back into the arena.

The following are absolute necessities to insulate a would-be love from sins and sorrow:

1. You accept that breaking up is a normal risk of dating.
2. You understand that either partner may undergo a change of heart.
3. You can put rejection, real or imagined, into the proper perspective.
4. Your eyes are wide open and your perception sharp.
5. You are willing to thoughtfully explore a potential love mate.
6. You have your needs under control.
7. Your self-esteem is at a reasonable level.
8. You aren't carrying negative traces of past love relationships around with you.
9. You can keep your body heat in check.
10. You have a clear picture of where you are headed.
11. You are confident in your ability to attract the opposite sex.
12. You are strong enough to walk out on a bad relationship.
13. Your love map is a realistic representation of your hopes and dreams and life's realities.
14. You understand the need to be objective and have the ability to be just that.
15. You have taken time to evaluate past love relationships and grasp where things went wrong.
16. There is not a trace of desperation in your pursuit.
17. You have a reasonably complete understanding of the nature of love.

238

18. You are able to use typecasting as a code buster.

19. Your lie detection system is up and running.

20. You are mature enough to break up without seeking revenge or inviting reprisals.

If you do not posses the vast majority of these qualities, qualifications, and abilities, sort out your deficiencies and get to work. Without comprehending and accepting the normal risks of love relationships you are sure to get burned. Failure to develop self-control, objectivity, or patience will surely get you into a dangerous hotbed of romance. There is an extra warning for women over 30 that follows.

A Special Note of Caution for Single Women Over Thirty

Women over 30 are under suspicion and should be particularly careful going back into the scene of uncommitted singles. Men automatically think you have a timer on your biological clock and that you are desperate for a mate. Unfortunately, this places an extra burden on you to demonstrate right off the bat that they have pegged you wrong. It is most definitely sexist and unfair, but the truths in the world are what you have to deal with. To make certain you project the right message, here are a few more things to keep in mind:

1. Display your self-sufficiency.

2. Demonstrate your independence.

3. Do not voice your desire right off the bat to find a suitable marriage partner.

4. Demonstrate that you like your date for his positive qualities, not for his gender.

Heart to Heart

Marriage is not the only option. Here is something to think about, particularly if you are entering the dating scene after the breakup of a marriage that has given you all the kids you want. Don't be foolish and give up companionship, sex, support, fun, and comfort by demanding that a new love interest be a potential lifetime mate.

Dating from a Position of Power

There are too many distractions along with abundant competition in the single world to be a passive dater. Serendipitous meetings do happen sometimes and for the lucky John and Jane lead to love ever after. But if you aren't willing to rely on luck when you head out the door next time, don't leave home without your seat of power. It should lie firmly within yourself.

2

You can feel the pleasure of power in the simplest things you do. There is power in recognizing that you have options in a social setting. For instance, there is the power in being able to say yes or no to a date. There is power in whom you smile at, where you go, what you wear, and how you react when a man or women does or doesn't respond to your overtures. There is even power in leaving a party or staying.

Bits and Pieces

"When you meet someone you never dreamed you'd meet, you're taken by surprise, so you haven't made up any fantasies and you're not let down."

—*Love, Love, Love* by Andy Warhol

Believing in and feeling the steady presence of your seat of power oozes with attractive confidence and helps you partake in activities you might otherwise be reluctant to attempt. The next time you walk into a crowded room solo, feel your seat of power in your posture, your walk, and your voice. Know it is there when you go up to the bar to get a drink, smile at someone across the room, comfortably settle into a seat alone, or begin to flirt.

Bits and Pieces

"The mystery was gone, but the amazement was just starting."

—*Love, Love, Love* by Andy Warhol

Master the Art of Flirtation

Knowing how to flirt will take the edge off of re-entering the dating arena. Flirting is playful and fun. It isn't meant to be serious. Nor should it be offensive. Sex is not the initial object of the game. It's a feel-good exercise that flatters the parties involved. Flirting done artfully should entice the opposite sex, peak interest, and arouse expectations.

A good flirt is like a fly fisherman. He takes his time to gracefully toss out the lure, put it in the water without a big splash, and land it close to the fish he wishes to catch.

Instructions for Flirting

Flirting is carried out by using verbal and physical signals.

➤ A well-practiced flirt uses body language and conversation. Physical signals—a smile, a little eye contact, an innocent touch of the body—gets the juices flowing.

➤ Making conversation that is easy to participate in shows interest in the other person and can jump-start an attraction.

➤ The eyes send the strongest message. From the moment you begin talking to that other person, he or she must win the total focus of your attention.

➤ Artful flirts never let the person they are flirting with think they are being toyed with.

When Not to Flirt

There are inappropriate times to flirt. Cross that line, and your flirting could backfire. Before you start trying to attract a new love interest, know when to and not to turn on the charm.

Heart to Heart

A new place to hook up is a running club. You know you'll get someone fit, and if you're not interested, all you have to do is speed up.

Blow the Whistle

It is not a good idea to send a guy a gift at the office if you aren't in a relationship. It puts him in a position where everyone starts asking questions. If he isn't interested, he won't appreciate your public advance. If you want to send him a card to show you're interested, mail it to his home. Don't put it on his desk at work.

➤ Ladies, don't flirt when a guy is participating in an athletic event. Men take them too seriously. Wait until he wins and then make a big fuss. Don't be the cause of his defeat.

➤ Guys and gals, don't flirt during important business meetings. It makes you both look bad. If you get him or her off track, it could be held against you forever.

➤ No one should flirt at a solemn occasion. It will be perceived as a sign of disrespect.

➤ Guys, don't flirt with your ex-lover when your new love is present. She will think you are a jerk.

➤ Attention all would-be flirts: Don't innocently flirt with married persons in a public setting. You don't know who could be watching or which single man or woman you might turn off.

Deceptive Dating Practices

Here's what a vast amount of research tells you about what you might hear when you re-enter the dating arena. There is a consensus of opinion that most of what comes out of a prospective date's mouth is true and by most standards accurate.

Nonetheless, a 1991 study charted the deceptions men and women most readily used to buoy their identity in a dating situation. They devised their deceptions according to what the opposite sex found most appealing. Of the 112 participants in a 1996 study, 90 percent admitted they told one or more lies to perspective dates. But keep in mind that this same body of research shows that men and women with a higher level of integrity are less likely to be deceptive about themselves.

Here's what to be on the lookout for: Men are more willing to tell a lie to a prospective date than women are. Primarily, men lie in a way that will make them appear more sincere, humble, resourceful, and trusting than in truth they are. Women's deceptions generally have to do with their body and or love attitudes. Forty-seven percent of men and 45 percent of women were found to lie and underestimate the number of their previous sex partners. Lying in this particular instance about one's past sex life could be dangerous and should not be tolerated.

Blow the Whistle

Look and listen for the truth! According to all the experts, lying is an inevitable part of early relationships. A lie that makes a man or woman look better than they are when getting to know a perspective love interest is given without hesitation.

Generally, however, as already mentioned, the lies you might encounter when you first meet someone will be of a less serious nature. If the individual doesn't exhibit an overall pattern of lying, their small untruths are probably forgivable. It's the guys and gals that make a habit of lying, have something to hide, or are insecure about their real identity that you have to watch out for. Because deceptive dating practices are a reality you will have to face, you may want to refer back to Chapter 10, "Is There Room for Honesty?"

Bits and Pieces

Those who have the stats on lying say that most lies are given to benefit the liar. Only one-fourth of the lying that's going on is done to benefit or bolster someone else.

The Least You Need to Know

➤ Make sure that you are ready to enter the dating arena with a wise outlook. Do not lose it in the shuffle or flurry of a busy social life.

➤ Be sure that you have moved beyond a vulnerable past to a seat of power that you carry around daily.

➤ Do not enter the dating scene until you feel confident to handle all the ups and downs.

➤ Be on the lookout for love, but watch for anyone who might deceptively offer it to you.

Chapter 26

Dating on the Rebound

In This Chapter

➤ The singles sex scene

➤ What rebounders look like

➤ Transitional lovers, good or bad?

➤ The hazards of love on the rebound

Romeo was on the rebound when he met Juliet, and you know how that story ended!

You are about to embark on another critical juncture in your love life. Because you are a human with human frailties, you will encounter some dangerous emotions that need tending. Expect these to erupt despite all you have recently learned. The best you can hope for is keeping them under control until you reach a new level of dating comfort.

Awareness is the key to success here. That is why we need to spell out the rebound mindset for you and paint a picture of what you are likely to feel. Those of you who have worked on your self-confidence and self-esteem and have found new avenues of growth and expression will be less likely to succumb to a sexual frenzy, a rebound romance, loneliness, or despair. Nonetheless, there is a powerful pull for all to go in that direction.

A Rebounder's Backdrop: The Singles Scene

More singles are out there today than a decade ago. The single adult population is over 23 million. Why is it bursting at the seams? Men and women are prolonging marriage by as much as five years from past generations, postponing having children, concentrating on having fun, staying in school longer, and worrying about finances. Then there are the boomers and the divorced population that figure into the single picture. Furthermore, women are enjoying more economic and emotional independence that enable them to function well in the single world and stay there longer.

Nonetheless, there is a resurgence in the desire for matrimony and a growth in the status of it that diminished after the sexual revolution. Research plainly reveals that singles want a committed relationship. Love, they believe, offers the greatest fulfillment in life. According to *The Janus Report of Sexual Behavior*, more than 50 percent of never-married singles don't find single life all that satisfying. Loneliness is the biggest problem facing both sexes.

Sex in the Single Lane

Single men and women may be equally romantic, but they exercise more caution in their love life. That caution, however, doesn't necessarily include their sex lives.

➤ Forty-five percent of singles consider themselves sexually active.

➤ Ninety-five percent of men report having sex before marriage.

➤ Eighty-one percent of women report having sex before marriage.

➤ Most singles practice safe sex and carefully discriminate among sexual partners.

➤ A majority of both men and women agree that sex and intimacy are two separate things.

➤ Single women today are more aggressive sexually than in the past.

➤ Single women are faking fewer orgasms today.

➤ Approximately 34 percent of single men lie about their sexual history.

➤ Approximately 10 percent of single women lie about their sexual history.

Bits and Pieces

According to Bernie Zilbergeld, Ph.D., author of *The New Male Sexuality* (Bantam Books, 1984), men report they aren't getting what they generally want out of a sexual relationship. Guess what, ladies? You're more in control than you think.

An Unsettling Undercurrent

Samuel S. Janus, Ph.D., and Cynthia L. Janus, M.D., discovered the "What's Next?" syndrome among a large number of singles they interviewed. Despite a current sense of well-being and happiness and irrespective of a current love interest, unmarried men and women could not help but express anxiety about what was in store for them later. It seems that future planning was inhibited by the absence of a committed partner.

Bits and Pieces

Neil Jacobson, Ph.D., and John Gottman, Ph.D., authors of *When Men Batter Women*, found that in our society, the interim between committed relationships is viewed as a transition period—not a desirable or workable lifestyle in and of itself. This compounds the already difficult adjustment one has to make to loneliness and being without a partner.

Signs of men and women under the influence of a syndrome similar to "What's Next?" that I have interviewed include: constantly looking to the future for gratification, wishing away time, failure to make the most of present opportunities, and pervasive loneliness and dissatisfaction without a current partner. The perpetual anxious look into the next step of the future where love hopefully awaits shortchanges the pleasures of the present.

Granted, finding a romantic partner can be worrisome. However, when "What's or Who's Next?" inhibits sound decision making, pervades the mood of the present, or feeds depression or loneliness, it's time to make some mental adjustments.

The problem is you can easily be operating under this syndrome and be completely unaware of it. Take Carla. She was a graduate student in the last few months of her Ph.D. program and was scouting the job market. Her social life had fizzled, and she felt as if she had exhausted all single men in the area. Rather than expand her social circle outside of the university circle, the normally resourceful young woman sat home alone, focused on her next move and contemplated the crop of men a new city would yield in a few months. In the meantime, she decided to forego meeting people and having some fun.

Carla and others like her would be a lot happier if they stopped obsessing over finding a partner and fixating on what's next on the romantic horizon. The best antidote is:

➤ Live in the present.

➤ Enjoy the moment.

➤ Make decisions that satisfy your independent goals.

➤ Explore new territory and exciting people.

Bits and Pieces

Many single men and women who fear that marriage might not be in the picture refuse to negate the experience of parenting. Thirty-eight percent of single men and 45 percent of single women in *The Janus Report* express interest in having or adopting a child. Women who have done it include entertainment stars Diane Keaton and Rosie O'Donnell.

The Rebound Mindset

Whether you are recovering from your breakup at a fast, medium, or slow speed, there are certain feelings most rebounders have in common:

➤ You need to feel desirable.

➤ You require reassurance that the breakup or divorce wasn't because of your deficiencies.

➤ Whether you leap into another relationship or try to stand back, you fear making a mess of love.

➤ You feel a certain degree of panic that you will never find anyone to love, to love you, or to marry.

➤ You feel a disappointment that the fairy tale ending of having the perfect mate step out of the lonely shadows has not become a reality.

➤ You feel unsure of yourself entering the dating world.

➤ You feel a void and look for a relationship to fill the loneliness and the unhappiness of being alone.

➤ Even if you desire and seek a relationship, you may be internally hesitant and shy.

➤ You are uncomfortable with the changes that your breakup has made in your life.

➤ All of these factors feel more intense if you have been jilted often or have just come out of a long-term relationship.

Heart to Heart

You aren't the only one who is disillusioned about love and marriage, but the moral of the story is don't give up. It has been written that just about the time Barbara Streisand and James Brolin met, they were each ready to give up hope of ever finding love.

What you need to be careful of here is not allowing the rebound mentality to hang around too long or influence romantic decisions before it dissipates entirely. Why? Anyone displaying signs of this rebound mindset are still operating under the cloud of lost love and are affected by its emotional scars. Consequently, a rebounder is normally not operating at their level best and may be incapable of making sound judgments. That's how some rebounders get caught up in hurtful relationships or an unhealthy sexual frenzy.

A Rebounder's Sexual Frenzy

It looks like it's a matter of feast or famine when it comes to a rebounder's sex life. On the average, women report not having sex for a year following their breakup, men 10 months. By then they say they are climbing the walls. In the meantime, masturbation has proven to be a viable option. Single women reported masturbating three times a month, single men six times a month.

The fact is, according to Janus's comprehensive survey, over 85 percent of single men and women felt sex was "deliciously sensuous." No one wants to give up the goodies. However, with 33,000 new cases of sexually transmitted disease reported daily in the '90s, it's a good thing men and women are both shopping for condoms these days. Men may be buying 60 percent of condoms, but women are taking care of the other 40 percent.

Among some rebounders there is a greater sense of urgency to jump right into bed, drown their sorrows in sex, affirm their attractiveness, demonstrate their sexuality, and prove breaking up was not their fault.

The problems of going this route are many. If you are going for a sexual frenzy, chances are you aren't getting to the root of your problems. Nor is sex a very positive way of overcoming loss, trauma, or self-doubt. Nonetheless, it's exactly what some rebounders seek.

Mel and Mindy's sexual frenzy and confessions are not unique. Not by a long shot!

Mindy's True Confession

Mindy is representative of a ton of young to middle-aged, pretty, bright, creative, and financially well-off, love-starved women who are looking for reassurance after a divorce. The first place they seek it is in bed.

Mindy made a habit of visiting a bar where she knew none of her friends went. Night after night, she would get picked up by a younger man and stumble home before dawn. Her escapades lasted for months until her sense of self-preservation took charge. Then she settled into a sex trio and regularly had relations with a couple she met by happenstance.

Mel's True Confession

Thirty-something Mel was broken-hearted when his wife gave him a painful surprise and asked for a divorce. Nonetheless, he admits he felt like a kid in a candy store when it came to sex, although he has slowed down somewhat because of the fear of AIDS.

Blow the Whistle

Stop buying into the worst predictions! Throw out that supposed male shortage with the garbage. Ninety percent of women are married by age 40. The other 10 percent may not be interested.

Married young, adult, single life was like nothing he had ever experienced. He has a vivid memory of what he has dubbed his "first coming out sex partner." She was followed by enough sexual encounters that he refers to himself at that time as a male slut.

"I would wake up in the morning in a woman's bed and not remember how I got there."

Both Mindy and Mel were classic examples of rebounders caught up in a sexual frenzy they thought would ease their pain, affirm their sexuality, and prove their desirability. Unfortunately, once the cloud lifted overhead, they looked back with regret and embarrassment at their frenzied sexual escapades that did little to improve their level of self-worth or promote healing.

If you find yourself waking up in strange beds like Mel and Mindy, stand back and take stock. Rarely will affection and sex void of shared intimacy and mutual caring improve your emotional outlook. Look for affirmation outside the bedroom and get to the root of the problem. This entire guide is designed to help you do just that. If you must, go back to page one and start again.

Love on the Rebound

A survey of men and women in their 20s revealed that most do not rush into love on the rebound. Men waited an average of 15 months to start a new relationship, women 11½ months. In my book, that's a reasonable amount of time to digest all of the material, get yourself physically and emotionally in shape, tone up the self-esteem, and accomplish closure.

Relationships that give rebound love a bad name occur primarily among those who move full speed ahead into the dating arena, can't stand to spend time alone, and haven't either gotten over their previous partner or completed the necessary preparation for re-entry. Men are more likely to fall into this category than women. So what happens is, they get themselves involved:

➤ In a love relationship they aren't ready to fulfill

➤ With someone who takes away the immediate pain

➤ With a guy or gal who can fill the void and emotional vacuum in the short term

➤ With someone whom during sex they fantasize is their lost love

Despite the negatives of love on the rebound, you do need to be cognizant of this note of caution. If you meet someone who seems like a genuine possibility for serious and lasting love relationship while you are still subject to the rebound mentality, don't throw out the opportunity even though it presents itself in an untimely fashion. Work through your feelings slowly, cautiously, and honestly.

A Rebound Nightmare

April's marriage ended after 11 years. She was lonely, devastated, and afraid with her two young children in her big, new, suburban home. Vulnerable to the slightest attention after her husband took off with another woman, she allowed herself to blindly rush into the arms of another man. April met Andy through a friend while she was at home visiting her folks, but no one had a clear I.D. on him. He invited her on a cruise which she said she would take if her children could come along. Shortly she found herself on a private yacht with a guy who acted like a big deal maker.

"I wasn't thinking," April admitted. "I came into a ton of money after my divorce. I spent hundreds of thousands of dollars on travel with Andy. I was having fun. My husband never had time for me."

April and Andy became an exclusive item. She sold her house, moved to her hometown, bought a duplex, and allowed him to move into the vacant side rent free. Before long, she had him move in with her. She rationalized she could rent the other side, but what it really accomplished was curing her loneliness and her worry that he would escape.

"I began to trust him completely," April said. "I wanted to get married but never said anything because I didn't want to scare him off. He ended up betraying me. He called my best friend for a date. He had to know I would find out. I was so mad that I had an affair with his best friend."

April doesn't put all the blame on Andy. "He set me up, but I went along willingly. He still owes me $30,000."

Now that you've read April's story, learn by her example. There is no need to repeat her mistake now that you've been forewarned. She sadly exemplifies the affects of the rebound mindset at its worst.

Handling a Rebounder

Now that you know what rebounders are all about, you might want to keep these tips in mind if you find yourself dating one. Rebounders don't mean to cause harm or mislead you, but their state of mind can cause them to make rash judgments and commitments they can't possibly fulfill.

1. Check out how long the person was on the front porch before he or she started dating. If there was little time between breaking up and starting to date, you may be going out with a speeder. That spells trouble.

2. Take any expressions of love or commitment lightly.

251

3. Wait for solid proof of real interest.

4. Don't get under the covers. It could be for the wrong reasons, and you might be sorry later.

5. Enjoy his or her company, but be on guard.

6. Don't give up the chance to go out with others until you are sure this isn't a quickie rebound romance.

7. Despite their protests that this is not a rebound relationship, stay on guard.

8. Encourage them to allow the relationship to grow slowly.

9. Let time be the best judge of their true emotions and intentions—and we're talking weeks here.

10. Understand the rebounder's frame of mind and immediate needs.

11. If you are sincerely interested in this person, give them time and space.

12. Don't press them into a committed relationship.

Dating a Rebounder

If you find yourself dating a rebounder freshly released from a relationship, be on the alert. However, there isn't any need to back off entirely if you can keep your emotions on a leash and don't pin your hopes too high. You need to protect yourself, but you don't want to miss a real opportunity of getting to know someone who you find attractive and interesting. Remember, dating, love, and relationships are full of risk. On the other hand, if you aren't willing or able to chance disappointment, get out quickly.

If you have misjudged a love interest with whom you have become involved only to find they are a quintessential rebounder in the stall mode, step back, take stock, and review Chapters 3, "Are You Sure You Want to Break Up?" 4, "Still Suffering from Uncertainty?" and 5, "Time, a Double-Edged Sword."

Transitional Lovers

Unfortunately, transitional lovers are great therapy for the person in transition but can be deadly for their partner. Still, these relationships abound.

Transitional relationships are generally short-term affairs that ease a rebounder back into the swing of things. Generally, if pressed to admit it, a rebounder knows when this first post-breakup relationship is nothing more than a transitional happening. These guys and gals are consciously aware that they needed someone to verify their attractiveness, build their ego back up, and get them used to having sex with someone else. In the meantime, they are having fun but in the back of their head know they don't really want this romance to last.

Rita and Randy

Rita went so far as to get engaged to her transitional lover. I call it a faux engagement. She was having a hard time being alone and quickly learned to hate the singles bar scene. Her life was totally upside down. She had been a wife and homemaker for nearly 15 years. She was used to having a man around and liked the idea of a ring on her finger. Randy did not move in, however. Rita didn't want him to, but he was on call.

After spending several hours in an interview with Rita when she couldn't come up with a wedding date, she told me, "I'm never going to marry Randy. I would have to give up my alimony, and what he makes would never cover my lifestyle. He is wonderful to me and has made me feel so desirable again. But he's not the one. I know eventually I'll give back the ring."

Howard and Heidi

Heidi is another married gal who found out her husband had never been faithful. She started dating a friend of hers who she felt completely comfortable with. He fell for her hook, line, and sinker. "I was totally flattered," Heidi revealed. "Being with Howard helped me so much. I had never slept with anyone but my husband. He really got me ready to go out into the world."

All along Heidi knew she would never settle down with Howard. They dated for nearly six months before Heidi starting pulling away. Howard interpreted her retreat as Heidi's decision to find a husband and his determination to remain single. Still, in the quiet of his office, he hinted that he might have given in and married Heidi, the one woman he claims he really loved.

It took Howard ages to recoup after Heidi was out of the picture. It is the one romance of his life that truly left a dagger in his heart.

You have been forewarned of the rebounder's fragile mindset, how to recognize one, and how to deal with being one or dating one. A rebounder is not a perish—they're not totally turned off to dating, but they aren't ready to be a cuddle fish either. Approach this stage in one's romantic progression with caution.

The Least You Need to Know

➤ There are a lot of people out there looking for love. Make sure you are looking for the right reasons.

➤ Rebounding can be dangerous when you least expect it. That first relationship must be watched carefully lest you get carried away.

➤ As a rebounder, you are in a position to wound someone who cares about you deeply. Don't become so absorbed in your own heartache that you cause pain to someone else.

➤ Sex will not and cannot cure what ails you. A rebounder's problems are deeper than that.

Chapter 27

Love Is Around the Corner

In This Chapter

➤ Where love awaits

➤ Romantic starters

➤ Sex tips for your special partner

➤ Dos and don'ts to keep you out of trouble

You are at your very best. Your mind is sharp. Your heart has healed. Your body is toned. You have located your seat of power, and your outlook is confident. You are stimulated and excited by new and challenging endeavors. Your positive aura attracts people to you.

You are ready for love!

So the next question is, "Where do you find it?"

This chapter will give you the up-to-the-minute report on where love begins. To help you along, I'll give you some tips on fanning the flames of romance and sex. True to our theme of being optimistic while remaining cautious, a list of dos and don'ts will keep you on track.

Pick a Love Theory

There are two basic outlooks about finding love. Researchers have given them the titles of "destiny theorists" and "growth theorists." For our purposes ordinary terms will do:

➤ Leaving it to fate

➤ Finding the right mate

Before you decide which approach you wish to take, examine the pros and cons.

Leaving It to Fate

A fatalist believes that his or her love mate has already been selected for him or her in the grand scheme of things. There is little or nothing they can or should do to alter the master plan. Time will unravel the mystery and produce the single partner they are destined to fall in love with.

Pros. This theory enables the would-be lover to relax, sit back in an easy chair, and wait for love to appear on the scene. It prevents one from obsessively looking for love under every nook and cranny and puts the lid on desperation.

Cons. The fatalist may have unrealistic expectations. They usually assume that fate is going to produce a mate, and that it will be a perfect match. The problem is perfection doesn't fit into the scheme of love. People do not fit together like adjacent pieces of a puzzle. Not even destiny can produce that magic! Those who opt for the destiny theory unwisely fail to make opportunities to find love interests and might easily dismiss potential mates who don't readily measure up to their ideal. According to Raymond Knee, a University of Houston psychologist, these fatalists will drop you like a hot potato if they don't think you are the one and only. Furthermore, their outlandish expectations may create dissatisfaction down the road in a committed relationship or marriage.

Finding the Right Mate

Growth theorists are not committed to the idea that there is only one needle in the haystack that is right for them. They are likely to hesitate about readily accepting or rejecting a potential love interest on the spot and give an initial attraction time to grow. They believe that the closeness and compatibility representative of love will take time to develop between two people.

Blow the Whistle

Steer clear of symbiotic love! It isn't healthy. People who form a symbiotic attachment do not feel complete without their partner. They lack individual identities. In the extreme, the dependence may encourage an obsession and fear of separation that leads to mistrust and paranoia.

Pros. Growth theorists are willing to get to know more potential partners and keep their options open. They understand that the enduring components of love, like intimacy and closeness, require time to develop. They are not discouraged by obstacles or challenges but accept them as opportunities to work out difficulties with their love interest that might bring them closer together.

Cons. Although a destiny theorist may be too rash, a growth theorist might be too passive. These individuals are likely to stay in a relationship that has little real potential and wait for time to make everything right. The danger of dating growth theorists is that they may hold on despite their lack of satisfaction. That won't serve anyone in the end.

My Personal Opinion

The way I see it is right down the middle. The romantic notion of fate is a comfort on the darkest days. Yet, the practical concept of growth implies more individual control over one's future when fate isn't producing any results. I like the idea that around *many* corners a love mate might be awaiting your arrival. I think it is prudent to accept that once you bump into each other, time, magic, and nurturing will produce the best and lasting results.

Bits and Pieces

A study by a University of California psychologist did not find impressive results from dating services in helping individuals find mates.

Where Might Your Next Love Be Hiding?

Weddings, small parties, and fix-ups are great ways to meet a potential love interest; however, there is one place that is even better!

If you are willing to take the word of the Bureau of National Affairs, you are more likely to meet your future wife or husband at your place of work rather than at school or in outside social settings. That makes your job environment look pretty important.

Evidently, convenience, long hours, working closely together on common ground, and pumping adrenaline promotes romance. The workplace helps to reduce fantasy and showcases your abilities. It is a good, safe place to get to know someone and size them up before going on the first date. It worked for Bill Gates, billionaire founder of Microsoft. He married coworker Melinda French. Gates admitted to *Playboy Magazine* there may have been some magic involved, but that he is attracted to people who are smart and independent.

Although there are all sorts of admonitions and warnings against office romances, from anthropologist Margaret Mead to corporate heads, a survey of companies found that over 90 percent did not have a policy against dating a coworker. Actually, some companies are inadvertent helpmates in the process by arranging social events and encouraging group activities among coworkers. No wonder office romances are on the rise, as are the number of married couples working in the same office. A whopping 80 percent of employees say they have either been a partner in an office romance or known someone who was.

Blow the Whistle

Be careful who you smile at! According to *Psychology Today*, one-third of office romances are between two people—one of whom *is* already legally attached to a spouse.

Geography and Gender Advantages

You should be forewarned about how a male shortage—even the slightest—influences a single guy's dating mindset! According to Keith Davis, Ph.D., a psychology professor at the University of South Carolina, the most subtle differences in gender ratio reduces a man's incentive to tie himself up with one woman and make a commitment. Consequently, Davis says males who have the numerical advantage don't treat women with as much respect. Just the reverse is true where men tip the scales and women are less abundant. Men behave better trying to battle the competition for a woman's attention.

Rather than pack your bags if you are living in cities that are top heavy with females between the ages of 18 and 24, don't get desperate like research says women often do. If you can't take the pressure, move. Otherwise, enjoy your professional opportunities, the many things your city has to offer, and tell a wiseguy who thinks you are expendable that you are too special to waste your time on him!

And by the way guys, you, too, can be tossed aside. Mind your manners.

Playing the Geography Game

If you are in the market for a new job or just want to make a fresh start after a disastrous love affair, you might consider a city with a singles population that will benefit you.

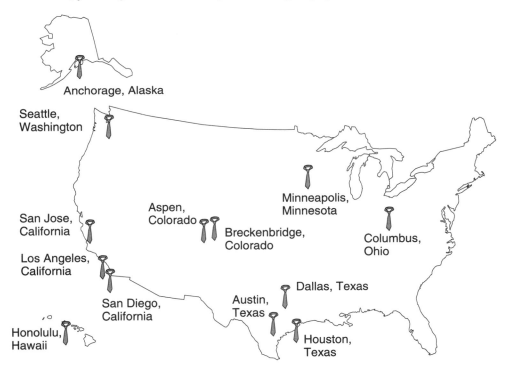

Cities top-heavy with men

Cities with one to 10 men less per 100 women

When looking at these maps be cautious. Don't select a site to live in based simply on the male/female ratio. Use this as one factor among many from which to draw a choice. Professional opportunities, climate, family, and lifestyle preferences are just as critical in selecting a city in which to reside. However, if finding a mate is one of your goals, then it would be foolish, if you were a woman, to move to a locale where single men were few and far between. Further investigation might also be prudent. Some areas are top-heavy with males or females because of military bases or college populations. Nonetheless, the maps provided give you a good indication which city to choose if you were offered equal opportunities in Boston, New York, or Los Angeles.

Romantic Starters

Okay, let's say there is someone in the office who has caught your eye, but you haven't as yet caught his or hers. Try one of these ideas to jump-start the attraction. But before you begin, do yourself a favor. Number one, make sure the other person isn't already irrevocably committed to someone else. Number two, promise to put a halt to the advances if after a reasonable time you don't get any positive feedback.

1. Use good taste to make yourself stand out. If everyone in the office is wearing a blue blazer or a black dress, go for something more colorful. Add flowers to your desk or put out a candy dish.

2. Compliments go a long way. Everyone likes to feel they are special. It shouldn't be too hard to say: "Great tie." "Good job." "Really nice presentation." "Congratulations. I heard you got a promotion." Just don't overdo it. This type of approach takes time.

3. A smile meant just for him or her will invite one in return. If it doesn't, flash it in another direction.

4. Friendship is a good entree. So, if you just happen to have tickets for a concert or event you know your coworker wants to see, invite him or her along. It doesn't have to sound like a date. You had the ticket and knew it was something the person would like. Rather than offer the opportunity to someone else, you thought of him or her first.

5. Office parties are fine, but a smaller group at your place is perfect. Invite a few people over to your house. Before you go to a lot of trouble, make sure he or she is free that night. Prepare something that you know is a favorite dish.

6. Go out of your way to get a handle on his or her interests. Building on common ground makes erecting a friendship more steadfast. Comment on a book or movie you have found out your coworker particularly enjoyed.

Don't Cross the Line of Good Taste into the Land of Harassment

Overzealous attempts to attract someone or win their attention and affection may become annoying and construed as harassment. Compliments can cease to be a welcome message. The way to prevent yourself from crossing the line is to be honest and perceptive when judging a love interest's response to your romantic starters. Read these responses clearly. Do not look for hidden messages or try to read between the lines. If he or she refuses to respond to several overtures, take it as a sure sign they aren't interested.

Blow the Whistle

You better listen up guys! According to Dalma Heyn, author of the *Erotic Silence of the American Wife*, the way to arouse a woman's sexual fervor whether she is in the dumps or having a "fat day" is to be there for her. Listen, ask her what is on her mind, what she's feeling. But you have to be sincere.

Sex Tips for Your One and Only

You can turn on or turn off a love interest in the bedroom. When you find your one and only, you want to light the fireworks. However, don't think that sex will cure all that stands in the way of a good relationship or patch up every disagreement. The consensus of opinion between men and women is that lovemaking is not the best way to make up. Sex shouldn't be your hook either. There's a big difference between reaching a climax and achieving intimacy.

Still it can only help knowing what Jane or Joe likes and doesn't like in sexual matters.

Jane's Sexual Preferences

You aren't going to get anywhere, Joe, if you rip off Jane's clothes and play rough. According to Wendy Dennis, author of *Hot and Bothered* (Bantam Doubleday, 1994), slow, verbally sexy seduction sets the tone. Women like sex that is initiated with tenderness, teasing touches, and kisses. There must be an air of intimacy and a bond of trust. Throwing in a compliment or two couldn't hurt.

If Jane is going to reach an orgasm, her mind has to be clear and focused on sex. Clitoral stimulation should get her to climax within 10 to 30 minutes. Don't try to hurry her along, make her feel guilty about the time, or rely solely on your penis to produce the necessary friction. More than half the women say that alone won't get the job done. According to the *Janus Report*, approximately 70 percent of women prefer to achieve orgasm through intercourse. Around 18 percent prefer orgasm through oral sex and 8 percent through masturbation.

Joe's Sexual Preferences

Jane, your sexual responsiveness is critical. Joe, like most men, gets turned on seeing you writhing with pleasure. If he doesn't, he wonders what's wrong with himself. In fact, it is so significant for men to feel they satisfy women that more than half say women's sexual pleasure is more important than their own. Without achieving orgasm, Joe tends to feel inadequate. However, be careful how you hand out the necessary instructions. Joe likes to think he knows what he's doing. Tell him what feels great or good. Maybe ask him if he has ever tried x, y, or z. He'll catch on and try it.

Whatever you do, never make negative comparisons. If you don't have anything flattering to say about Joe's sexual powers, don't say anything at all.

Men like to vary their sexual practices. To really turn him on, use creativity and change your techniques. Some men like to feel the fresh air and the excitement of the outdoors. More than 80 percent of men prefer to achieve orgasm through intercourse, but I doubt you will find a male who would object to a change of pace. Insisting he lay back, relax, and allow you to make love to him can't be beat now and then, especially if your guy is one of the 10 percent who prefer to climax through oral sex.

When it is all said and done, don't jump up to go to the bathroom. Men hate that. Just stay close and cozy. You can freshen up later.

Jane and Joe Together

Joe and Jane clearly had a thing for each other. Jane wanted to make sure that the first time they slept together was memorable. She decided to try and pick the perfect setting that would completely wow Joe's male sensibilities. Joe, on the other hand, was waiting for the sign to proceed. He knew Jane needed to be smothered with kisses and affectionately seduced into intercourse.

Jane chose a sunny, intimate Saturday afternoon aboard her parents' 28-foot cabin cruiser for this chapter of their love story. Shortly out into the open water where they would drift without anyone or anything around, she unlocked the cabin door, left it open so that the salty fresh air could blow through, and invited Joe inside. She had previously arranged an iced bottle of champagne and fresh flower petals around the cabin. The next move was up to Joe. He read all the signs right and proceeded to delight her with all the aforementioned sex tips.

Although this is fiction, translate into fact when you find your one and only. Before that time don't stray off track.

Heart to Heart

Women have the tendency to go to extremes in trying to please a man. If you are always going out of your way or find yourself changing to accommodate him, you are going too far. Once you cross that line, there are indications that you may start resenting him or her and sabotage the relationship with your extreme pleasing.

The Dos and Don'ts to Keep You on Track

In a few moments you will probably finish reading this guide. You will have handled your breakup in an exemplary fashion and readied yourself for love. If a suitable partner doesn't phone the second you close the book's cover or appear at the next party you attend, don't flounder or falter. To stay on track, carefully adhere to this important list of dos and don'ts.

Don't:

➤ Lose the dream.

➤ Make a new commitment too quickly.

➤ Hop into bed just because it's cold outside.

➤ Confuse need for love.

➤ Call old lovers when you are feeling blue.

➤ Make excessive demands on your love interest for affection or unconditional loving.

➤ Force intimacy—let it grow naturally.

➤ Get discouraged.

Do:

➤ Stop guessing what your romantic partner is thinking: Ask him or her.

➤ Only go so far to please someone you are attracted to. Love is a give and take relationship.

➤ Let your love interest become emotionally invested before you start acting and sounding like you're a couple.

➤ Make honesty and forthrightness a primary goal.

➤ Be true to yourself.

Okay, now it's time to test the waters. Go for re-entry. If anywhere along the way you find yourself in a jam, sliding backward, or uncertain about how to proceed, go back to the sections of this guide you think helped you the most. Treat it like an old friend, waiting to help you when you need it.

The Least You Need to Know

➤ You should understand how your theory of love affects your chances of finding it.

➤ If you previously thought office relationships were taboo, think again. They may be your best bet.

➤ Leave little to chance, especially sexual satisfaction. There is an art to making love.

➤ You can be smart trying to jump-start an attraction, but you don't want to be foolish and keep trying to turn the key when the ignition refuses to turn over.

Resources

Locating a Premarital Counselor or Program

There are several ways to go about finding assistance. However, it is your responsibility to evaluate and select the type of premarital counseling or counselor that best suits your needs and represents your values.

1. If you wish to find a qualified therapist in your area, the American Association of Marriage and Family Therapists has a helpful web site (www.aamft.org) that will provide you with a list of names.

2. Many major universities that have graduate programs in marriage and family therapy run affordable counseling programs. If you reside near a university, check with their Department of Marriage and Family Counseling for information.

3. A number of workshops are also available nationwide and internationally. They may be taught in your city by members of the clergy, health professionals, and lay leaders. The names and contact numbers to inquire about programs in your area are:

   ➤ Premarital Relationship Enhancement Program (PREP), (303) 759-9931

   ➤ Life Innovations, Inc., (651) 635-0511

   ➤ Relationship Enhancement, (800) 432-6454

   ➤ Practical Applications of Intimate Relationship Skills (PAIRS), (888) 724-7748

   ➤ The Association for Couples in Marriage Enrichment, (800) 634-4325 or e-mail at wsacme@aol.com

How to Find Qualified Legal Representation for Divorce, Separation, Child Custody, or Child Support

Agencies in your area to contact:

➤ County, city, or state Bar Association

➤ Your local Legal Aid Society

➤ County Court of Domestic Relations

Help for Victims of Domestic Violence

The National Domestic Violence Hot Line is available 24 hours a day at (800) 799-7233. You can call toll free to receive crisis intervention counseling or information about shelters and agencies in your area.

There is a large network of shelters in the United States as well as local domestic violence hot lines. They should be able to refer you to agencies in your specific area and answer questions about domestic violence.

If you need immediate protection, call your local police department.

Are You Primed for Rejection? Quiz

Check "yes" or "no" for each of the following:

	Yes	No
1. Is there a lack of loyal friends and family members who can offer you support?	❏	❏
2. Do you view snubs and rebuffs as your own fault?	❏	❏
3. Have you refused necessary therapy or counseling?	❏	❏
4. Is it nearly impossible for you to respond with humor when slighted?	❏	❏
5. Do you seek excessive signs of acceptance?	❏	❏
6. Do you have a case of low self-esteem?	❏	❏
7. Do you anticipate being rejected?	❏	❏
8. Do you overreact to disappointments?	❏	❏
9. Do you display unrealistic expectations of others?	❏	❏
10. Are you unable to distance yourself from old feelings of rejection?	❏	❏

Each "yes" answer brings you dangerously close to perceiving rejection that is not there. That is the affliction of an individual who is primed for rejection.

The Cohabitation Agreement

A cohabitation agreement is a formal contract between two parties not covered by matrimonial law. The agreement should be written, preferably by legal counsel, and bear the signature of both parties. In order for the agreement to prove binding in court, it must be entered into freely and with full disclosure. If a discrepancy arises in adjudicating the agreement, the conditions of contractual, not matrimonial, law prevail.

What the agreement should cover:

1. A comprehensive list of each parties' financial responsibility within the cohabitation arrangement such as rent, other living expenses, child support, and joint loans or mortgages.

2. Exact terms of the equitable dissolution of the living together arrangement. Because each couple's financial picture and needs differ, the best cohabitation agreement is a product of negotiation between representative counsel for each participant that takes into account their unique situation. However, the minimum considerations include:

   ➤ Determination of ownership of capital items
   ➤ Determination of distribution and ownership of items and property
   ➤ Responsibility and settlement of debts
   ➤ Monetary value and compensation of services exchanged
   ➤ Arrangements for children and pets
   ➤ Responsibility for legal fees incurred in a split-up
   ➤ Determination of ownership of season tickets
   ➤ Settlement of joint leases

From *Living Together Trap: Everything Women and Men Should Know*, by Rosanne Rosen (New Horizon Press, 1993).

Love Lingo Glossary

Breakup goal   What you wish to accomplish or end up with after breaking off a romantic relationship.

Commitment   To pledge oneself as a romantic partner.

Compassionate love   Love that embodies the feelings of affection, intimacy, and attachment to individuals with whom our lives are intricately woven.

Compatibility   The capacity to get along and satisfy one another's needs.

Compatible partner   Romantic partnership based on similar backgrounds.

Deficiency love   Love sought for the purpose of fulfilling unmet personal needs.

Dehydroephiandrosterone (DHEA)   A hormone from which most other human sex hormones are derived.

Empty love   Love that embodies a commitment but not passion or intimacy.

Gross deception   An exaggerated premeditated lie with purposeful, selfish gain in mind.

Hug   An embrace that provides comfort and affection. It takes four hugs a day to satisfy one's needs.

In love   To be under the spell of romantic love. To burn with desire, need, commitment, and passion.

Infatuation   An early stage of love driven by passion and fantasy. A state void of mutual understanding, caring, and support.

Intimacy   The core of a love relationship, revealing information about oneself, and exchanging personal information.

Jilted   Recklessly tricked and indiscriminately rejected romantically.

Libido   The instinctual drive associated with the need to fulfill sexual desire and seek sexual gratification.

Lie   A statement intended to deceive someone and benefit the liar.

Love   An inexpressible connection that makes you feel complete.

Love map   A term coined by sexologist John Money. It encompasses the qualities one seeks in a love interest.

Love talk   A talk about the state of and the direction of your love relationship.

Loving   To act with love but not passion. To feel a deep connection to and caring for someone.

Masturbation   Self-manipulation for sexual gratification.

Mum effect   The pattern to avoid telling someone you are not romantically interested in them. To remain silent.

One-sided subsidence   The persistence of one partner to try and keep a relationship going when the other partner wants to break up.

Persistence of attachment   Lovers who continue to demonstrate mutual need and hang on to one another despite severing romantic ties.

Phenylethylamine (PEA)   An amphetamine compound in the body. Biological and chemical components that influence love.

Porcupine dilemma   The ambivalence in breaking up between the need to be free and the need to connect.

Pragmatic lover   An individual who consciously seeks a compatible partner based on similarities in background and interests.

Psychological departure   An emotional and mental departure from a relationship.

Seduction   The act of persuading someone to engage in sex.

Self-esteem   Belief and pride in oneself.

Set up   A deliberate and premeditated plan to create a breakup.

Sex   In the formal sense, sex means engaging in intercourse. A more inclusive definition means intimate body contact that is sexually pleasurable.

Spouse equivalent   According to the U.S. Census Bureau, a cohabitational partner.

Index

D